The Complete Tragedies, Volume 2

THE COMPLETE WORKS OF LUCIUS ANNAEUS SENECA

Edited by Elizabeth Asmis, Shadi Bartsch, and Martha C. Nussbaum

Seneca

The Complete Tragedies, Volume 2

Oedipus, Hercules Mad, Hercules on Oeta, Thyestes, Agamemnon

TRANSLATED BY SHADI BARTSCH,
SUSANNA BRAUND, AND
DAVID KONSTAN

EDITED BY SHADI BARTSCH

The University of Chicago Press CHICAGO AND LONDON

The University of Chicago Press, Chicago 60637
The University of Chicago Press, Ltd., London

Published 2017
Paperback edition 2022
Printed in the United States of America

31 30 29 28 27 26 25 24 23 22   1 2 3 4 5

ISBN-13: 978-0-226-01360-2 (cloth)
ISBN-13: 978-0-226-82108-5 (paper)
ISBN-13: 978-0-226-01374-9 (e-book)
DOI: https://doi.org/10.7208/chicago/9780226013749.001.0001

Library of Congress Control Number: 2016030088

♾ This paper meets the requirements of ANSI/NISO Z39.48-1992 (Permanence of Paper).

Contents

Seneca and His World

ELIZABETH ASMIS, SHADI BARTSCH, AND MARTHA C. NUSSBAUM

Seneca once remarked of Socrates that it was his death by hemlock that made him great (*Letter* 13.14). With reason: Socrates' death demonstrated the steadfastness of his philosophical principles and his belief that death offered nothing to fear. When Seneca himself, then, was ordered to commit suicide by Nero in 65 CE, we might well believe Tacitus's account in his *Annals* (15.63) that the Roman Stoic modeled his death on that of Socrates, discoursing calmly about philosophy with his friends as the blood drained out of his veins. In Tacitus's depiction we see, for once, a much-criticized figure living up to the principles he preached.

Seneca's life was mired in political advancement and disappointment, shaped by the effects of exile and return, and compromised by his relationship with the emperor Nero—first his pupil, then his advisee, and finally his murderer. But his many writings say little about his political career and almost nothing about his relationship with Nero except for what can be gleaned from his essay *On Clemency*, leaving us to turn to later sources for information—Tacitus, Suetonius, and Dio Cassius in particular. We know that Seneca was born to a prominent equestrian family in Corduba, Spain, some time between 4 and 1 BCE. He was the second of three sons of Helvia and Lucius Annaeus Seneca (the youngest son, Annaeus Mela, was the father of the poet Lucan). The elder Seneca had spent much of his life in Rome, and Seneca himself was brought to Rome as a young boy. There he was educated in rhetoric and later became a student of the philosopher Sextius. But his entry into political life was delayed, and when he did enter upon the *cursus honorum* late in Tiberius's reign, his ill health (he had asthma and possibly tuberculosis) was a source of difficulty. In any case his career was cut short. He survived Caligula's hostility, which the sources tell us was thanks to his talents in oratory, but was sent into exile on Corsica by Claudius shortly after Caligula's death in 41 CE. The charge, almost certainly false, was adultery with Caligula's younger sister, Julia Livilla. Seneca spent his time in exile in philosophical and natural study and wrote the *Consolations* to Helvia (his mother) and to Polybius (Claudius's freedman secretary), revealing in the latter how desperately he hoped to be recalled to Rome.

When Seneca did return in 49 CE, it was under different auspices. Claudius had recently remarried, to Germanicus's daughter Agrippina, and she urged him to recall Seneca as tutor to her son, the twelve-year-old Nero. Claudius already had a younger son, Britannicus, but it was clear that the wily Agrippina wished to see her own flesh and blood on the throne. When Claudius died five years later, Agrippina was able to maneuver Nero into position as emperor—and Britannicus was dispatched by poison shortly after, in 55 CE.

From 54 until his influence waned at the end of the decade, Seneca acted as Nero's adviser, together with the praetorian prefect Sextus Afranius Burrus. We know he wrote a speech on clemency for Nero to deliver to the Roman senate soon after his accession, and Seneca's own essay *On Clemency* may contain some inkling of his strategy to keep the young emperor from running amok. Seneca's use of the term *rex*, or king, applied to Nero by analogy in this piece, is surprising from a Roman senator, but he seems to have hoped that flattering Nero by pointing to his limitless power and the value of clemency would be one way to keep him from abusing that power. Both Seneca and Burrus also helped with the civil and judicial administration of the empire.

Many historians, ancient and modern, feel that this early part of Nero's reign, moderated by Seneca and Burrus, represented a period of comparative good rule and harmony (the "*quinquennium Neronis*"). The decline started in 59 CE with Nero's murder of Agrippina, after which Seneca wrote the emperor's speech of self-exculpation—perhaps the most famous example of how the philosopher found himself increasingly compromised in his position as Nero's chief counsel. Certainly as a Stoic, Seneca cuts an ambiguous figure next to the others who made their opposition to Nero clear, such as Thrasea Paetus and Helvidius Priscus. His participation in court politics probably led him to believe that he could do more good from where he stood than by abandoning Nero to his own devices—if he even had this choice.

In any case, Seneca's influence over Nero seems to have been considerably etiolated after the death of Burrus in 62. According to Tacitus, Seneca tried to retire from his position twice, in 62 and 64. Although Nero refused him on both occasions, Seneca seems to have largely absented himself from the court after 64. In 65 CE came the Pisonian conspiracy, a plot to kill Nero and replace him with the ringleader, C. Calpurnius Piso. Although Seneca's nephew Lucan was implicated in this assassination attempt, Seneca himself was probably innocent. Nonetheless, Nero seized the opportunity to order his old adviser to kill himself. Seneca cut his own veins, but (so Tacitus tells us) his thinness and advanced age hindered the flow of blood. When a dose of poison also failed to kill him, he finally sat in a hot bath to make the blood flow faster. His wife, Pompeia Paulina, also tried to commit suicide but was saved on orders from Nero.

Because of his ethical writings, Seneca fared well with the early Christians—hence the later forging of a fake correspondence with St. Paul—but already in antiquity he had his fair share of critics, the main charge arising from the apparent contradiction between his Stoic teachings on the unimportance of "externals" and his own amassing of huge wealth. Perhaps for this reason he never gained the respect accorded the "Roman Socrates," the Stoic C. Musonius Rufus, banished by Nero in 65, even though Seneca's writings have had far more influence over the centuries. In Seneca's own lifetime one P. Suillius attacked him on the grounds that, since Nero's rise to power, he had piled up some 300 million sesterces by charging high interest on loans in Italy and the provinces—though Suillius himself was no angel and was banished to the Balearic Islands for being an embezzler and informant. In Seneca's defense, he seems to have engaged in ascetic habits throughout his life and despite his wealth. In fact, his essay *On the Happy Life* (*De vita beata*) takes the position that a philosopher may be rich as long as his wealth is properly gained and spent and his attitude to it is appropriately detached. Where Seneca finally ranks in our estimation may rest on our ability to tolerate the various contradictions posed by the life of this philosopher in politics.

A Short Introduction to Stoicism

Stoicism is one of the world's most influential philosophical movements. Starting from the works and teaching of the three original heads of the Greek Stoic school—Zeno of Citium (335–263 BCE), Cleanthes (331–232 BCE), and Chrysippus (ca. 280–207 BCE)—it became the leading philosophical movement of the ancient Greco-Roman world, shaping the development of thought well into the Christian era. Later Greek Stoics Panaetius (ca. 185–109 BCE) and Posidonius (ca. 135–51 BCE) modified some features of Stoic doctrine. Roman thinkers then took up the cause, and Stoicism became the semiofficial creed of the Roman political and literary world. Cicero (106–43 BCE) does not agree with the Stoics on metaphysical and epistemological matters, but his ethical and political positions lie close to theirs, and even when he does not agree, he makes a concerted effort to report their positions sympathetically. Roman Stoics Seneca, Epictetus (mid-first to early second century CE), Musonius Rufus (ca. 30–ca. 102 CE), and the emperor Marcus Aurelius (121–80 CE, emperor 161–80) produced Stoic works of their own (the last three writing in Greek).

The philosophical achievement of the Greek Stoics, and especially that of Chrysippus, was enormous: the invention of propositional logic, the invention of the philosophy of language, unprecedented achievements in moral psychology, distinction in areas ranging from metaphysics and epistemology to moral and political philosophy. Through an accident of history, however, all the works of all the major Greek Stoics have been lost, and we must recover their thoughts through fragments, reports (particularly the lengthy accounts in Diogenes Laertius's *Lives of the Philosophers*, in Cicero, and in Sextus Empiricus's skeptical writings, since the Stoics are his primary target), and the works of the Roman thinkers—who often are adjusting Stoic doctrines to fit Roman reality and probably contributing creative insights of their own. This also means that we know somewhat less about Stoic logic or physics than about Stoic ethics, since the Romans took a particular interest in the practical domain.

The goal of Stoic philosophy, like that of other philosophical schools of the Hellenistic era, was to give the pupil a flourishing life free from the forms of distress and moral failure that the Stoics thought ubiquitous in their societies. Unlike some of their competitor schools, however, they emphasized the need to study all parts of their threefold system—logic, physics, and ethics—in order to understand the universe and its interconnections. To the extent that a Roman such as Cicero believed he could uphold the moral truths of Stoicism without a confident belief in a rationally ordered universe, he held a heretical position (one shared many centuries later by Immanuel Kant).

Stoic physics held that the universe is a rationally ordered whole, and that everything that happens in it happens for the best of reasons. (It is this position, in its Leibnizian incarnation, that is pilloried in Voltaire's *Candide.*) Rejecting traditional anthropomorphic religion, the Stoics gave the name Zeus to the rational and providential principle animating the universe as a whole, and they could find even in the most trivial or distressing events (such as earthquakes and thunderbolts) signs of the universe's overall good order. This order was also a moral order based on the inherent dignity and worth of the moral capacities of each and every rational being. The Stoics believed that this order was deterministic: everything happens of necessity. But they were also "compatibilists," believing that human free will is compatible with the truth of determinism. They engaged in spirited debates with "incompatibilist" Aristotelians, making lasting contributions to the free will controversy.

Stoic ethics begins from the idea of the boundless worth of the rational capacity in each and every human being. The Roman Stoics understood this capacity to be centrally practical and moral. (Thus, unlike Plato, they did not think that people who had a natural talent for mathematics were better than people who didn't, and they became more and more skeptical that even the study of logic had much practical value.) They held that all human beings are equal in worth by virtue of their possession of the precious capacity to choose and direct their lives, ranking some ends ahead of others. This, they said, was what distinguished human beings from animals: this power of selection and rejection. (Unlike most other ancient schools, they had little concern for the morality of animal treatment, since they thought that only moral capacity entitled a being to respect and good treatment.) Children, they said, come into the world like little animals, with a natural orientation toward self-preservation but no understanding of true worth. Later, however, a remarkable shift will take place, already set up by their possession of innate human nature: they will be able to appreciate the beauty of the capacity for choice and the way in which moral reason has shaped the entire universe. This recognition, they said, should lead people to respect both self and others in an entirely new way. Stoics were serious about (human) equality: they urged the equal education of both slaves and women. Epictetus himself was a former slave.

Stoicism looks thus far like an ethical view with radical political consequences, and so it became during the Enlightenment, when its distinctive emphases were used to argue in favor of equal political rights and more nearly equal economic opportunities. However, the original Stoics maintain a claim of great significance for politics: moral capacity is the only thing that has intrinsic worth. Money, honor, power, bodily health, and even the love of friends, children, and spouse—all these are held to be things that one may reasonably pursue if nothing impedes (they are called "preferred indifferents"), but they have no true intrinsic worth. They should not even be seen as commensurate with moral worth. So when they do not arrive as one wishes, it is wrong to be distressed.

This was the context in which the Stoics introduced their famous doctrine of *apatheia*, freedom from the passions. Defining the major emotions or passions as all involving a high valuation of "external goods," they argue that the good Stoic will not have any of these disturbances of the personality. Realizing that chance events lie beyond our control, the Stoic will find it unnecessary to experience grief, anger, fear, or even hope: all of these are characteristic of a mind that waits in suspense, awestruck by things indifferent. We can have a life that truly involves joy (of the right sort) if we appreciate that the most precious thing of all, and the only truly precious thing, lies within our control at all times.

Stoics do not think that it is at all easy to get rid of the cultural errors that are the basis of the rejected passions: thus a Stoic life is a constant therapeutic process in which mental exercises are devised to wean the mind from its unwise attachments. Their works depict processes of therapy through which the reader may make progress in the direction of Stoic virtue, and they often engage their reader in just such a process. Epictetus and Marcus Aurelius describe processes of repeated meditation; Seneca (in *On Anger*) describes his own nightly self-examination. Seneca's *Letters* show the role that a wiser teacher can play in such a therapeutic process, but Seneca evidently does not think that even he himself is free from erroneous attachments. The "wise man" is in that sense a distant ideal, not a worldly reality, particularly for the Roman Stoics. A large aid in the therapeutic process is the study of the horrible deformities that societies (including one's own) suffer by caring too much about external goods. If one sees the ugly face of power, honor, and even love clearly enough, this may assist one in making the progress toward true virtue. Thus Seneca's *On Anger* is an example of a genre that we know to have been common in Stoicism.

Because of their doctrine of value, the Stoics actually do not propose radical changes in the distribution of worldly goods, as one might suppose equal regard for the dignity of all human beings would require. They think that equal respect does require dignified treatment of each person; thus Seneca urges masters not to beat their slaves or use them as sexual tools. About the institution of slavery, however, there is silence, and worse than silence: Seneca argues that true freedom is internal freedom, so the external sort does not really matter. Musonius, similarly, advocates respectful treatment for women, including access to a Stoic education. But as for changes in the legal arrangements that confined women to a domestic role and gave males power of life and death over them, he too is silent, arguing that women will manifest their Stoic virtue in the domestic context. Some Roman Stoics do appear to have thought that political liberty is a part of dignity and thus died supporting republican institutions, but whether this attention to external conditions was consistent with Stoicism remains unclear. (Certainly Cicero's profound grief over the loss of political freedom was not the attitude of a Stoic, any more than was his agonizing grief over his daughter's death.)

There was also much debate about whether the Stoic norm of *apatheia* encouraged people to detach themselves from bad political events in a way that gave aid and comfort to bad politics. Certainly Stoics were known to counsel retirement from politics (a theme in Seneca's own life as he sought Nero's permission for retirement, unsuccessfully), and they were thought to believe that upheaval is worse than lawless tyranny. Plutarch reports that Brutus (a Platonist) questioned potential coconspirators in the assassination of Julius Caesar by trying to determine whether they accepted that Stoic norm or believed, with him, that lawless tyranny is worse than civil strife; only non-Stoics were selected for the group of assassins. During Nero's reign, however, several prominent Stoics—including Seneca and his nephew, Lucan—joined republican political movements aimed at overthrowing Nero, and lost their lives for their efforts, by politically ordered suicide.

Stoics believed that from the moral point of view, national boundaries are as irrelevant as honor, wealth, gender, and birth. They held that we are, first and foremost, citizens of the universe as a whole. (The term *kosmou polites*, citizen of the universe, was apparently first used by Diogenes the Cynic, but the Stoics took it up and were the real forefathers of modern cosmopolitanism.) What cosmopolitanism meant in practical terms was unclear, for the reasons already given—but Cicero thinks, at any rate (in *On Duties*, a highly Stoic work), that our common human dignity entails some very strict limits on the reasons for going to war and the sort of conduct that is permissible in it. He thus adumbrated the basis of the modern law of war. Cicero denied, however, that our common humanity entailed any duty to distribute material goods beyond our own borders, thus displaying the unfortunate capacity of Stoic doctrine to support the status quo. Cicero's *On Duties* has had such an enormous influence on posterity in this that it is scarcely an exaggeration to blame the Stoics for the fact that we have well worked-out doctrines of international law in the area of war and peace, but no well-established understanding of our material duties to one another.

Stoicism's influence on the development of the entire Western intellectual tradition cannot be underestimated. Christian thought owes it a large debt. Clement of Alexandria is just one example of a Christian thinker steeped in Stoicism; even a thinker such as Augustine, who contests many Stoic theses, finds it natural to begin from Stoic positions. Even more strikingly, many philosophers of the early modern era turn to Stoicism for guidance—far more often than they turn to Aristotle or Plato. Descartes' ethical ideas are built largely on Stoic models; Spinoza is steeped in Stoicism at every point; Leibniz's teleology is essentially Stoic; Hugo Grotius bases his ideas of international morality and law on Stoic models; Adam Smith draws more from the Stoics than from other ancient schools of thought; Rousseau's ideas of education are in essence based on Stoic models; Kant finds inspiration in the Stoic ideas of human dignity and the peaceful world community; and the American founders are steeped in Stoic ideas, including the ideas of equal dignity and cosmopolitanism, which also deeply influence the American transcendentalists Emerson and Thoreau. Because the leading works of Greek Stoicism had long been lost, all these thinkers were reading the Roman Stoics. Because many of them read little Greek, they were primarily reading Cicero and Seneca.

The Stoic influence on the history of literature has also been immense. In the Roman world, all the major poets, like other educated Romans, were acquainted with Stoic ideas and alluded to them often in their work. Virgil and Lucan are perhaps particularly significant in this regard. Later European literary traditions also show marked traces of Stoic influence—in part via the influence of Roman literature, and in part through the influence of philosophers in their own time who were themselves influenced by Stoic thought, but often also through their own reading of the influential works of Cicero, Seneca, and Marcus Aurelius.

Seneca's Stoicism

Seneca identifies himself as a Stoic. He declares his allegiance by repeatedly referring to "our people" (*nostri*)—the Stoics—in his writings. Yet he exercises considerable independence in relation to other Stoics. While he is committed to upholding basic Stoic doctrines, he recasts them on the basis of his own experience as a Roman and a wide reading of other philosophers. In this respect he follows a tradition of Stoic philosophical innovation exemplified most clearly by Panaetius and Posidonius, who introduced some Platonic and Aristotelian elements while adapting Stoicism to Roman circumstances. Seneca differs from previous Stoics by welcoming some aspects of Epicurean philosophy along with other influences.

Seneca is concerned above all with applying Stoic ethical principles to his life and to the lives of others like him. The question that dominates his philosophical writings is how an individual can achieve a good life. In his eyes, the quest for virtue and happiness is a heroic endeavor that places the successful person above the assaults of fortune and on a level with god. To this end, Seneca transforms the sage into an inspirational figure who can motivate others to become like him by his gentle humanity and joyful tranquility. Key topics are how to reconcile adversity with providence, how to free oneself from passions (particularly anger and grief), how to face death, how to disengage oneself from political involvement, how to practice poverty and use wealth, and how to benefit others. All of these endeavors are viewed within the context of a supreme, perfectly rational and virtuous deity who looks with favor on the efforts of humans to attain the same condition of virtue. In the field of politics, Seneca argues for clemency on the part of the supreme ruler, Nero. In human relations, he pays special attention to friendship and the position of slaves. Overall, he aims to replace social hierarchies, with their dependence on fortune, with a moral hierarchy arranged according to proximity to the goal of being a sage.

Seneca's own concerns and personality permeate his writings. The modern reader learns much about the life of an aristocrat in the time of Claudius and Nero, and much about Seneca's personal strengths and weaknesses. At the same time, there is also much in the work that transcends the immediate concerns of Seneca and his period. Some topics that resonate especially with a modern audience are his vision of humans as members of a universal community of mankind, the respect he demands for slaves, his concern with human emotions, and, in general, his insistence on looking within oneself to find happiness. What is perhaps less appealing to the modern reader is the rhetorical elaboration of his message, which features an undeniable tendency toward hyperbole. Most of all, Seneca's own character strikes many readers as problematic. From his own time onward, he was perceived by some as a hypocrite who was far from practicing what he preached. Some of Seneca's writings (in particular, his *Consolations* to Polybius and his mother Helvia, and his essay *On the Happy Life*) are obviously self-serving. As Seneca himself suggests (*Letters* 84), he has transformed the teachings he has culled, in the manner of bees, into a whole that reflects his own complex character.

The Stoics divided logic into dialectic (short argument) and rhetoric (continuous exposition). There is not much to be said on dialectic in Seneca's writings except that he shuns it, along with formal logic in general. Every so often, however, he engages in a satirical display of fine-grained Stoic-type reasoning. The point is that carrying logical precision to excess is futile: it does not make a person any better. Quibbles of all kinds should be avoided, whether they involve carrying through a minute line of argument, making overly subtle verbal distinctions, or indulging in abstruse philological interpretation. While making the point, Seneca makes sure the reader knows he could beat the quibbler at his own game if he wanted to.

We have only sparse details about how the Stoics viewed rhetoric. What is clear about Seneca, however, is that he used the full panoply of Roman rhetorical methods to persuade readers of his philosophical message. His writings are full of vivid examples, stunning metaphors, pointed sayings, ringing sound effects. He knows how to vary his tone, from casual conversation to soaring exhortation and bitter denunciation. He peoples his text with a varied cast of characters: the addressee, the implied audience, hypothetical objectors, friends, opponents, historical figures. He himself hovers over the proceedings as watchful friend and sometime foe. Following Cleanthes, he intersperses poetry into his prose to impel the reader even more forcefully toward the task of self-improvement.

Given Seneca's ethical aims, it is perhaps surprising that he devotes a large work, *Natural Questions*, to physics. Yet the entire work has an overarching ethical aim. As Seneca insists repeatedly, the mind is uplifted by venturing beyond narrowly human concerns to survey the world as a whole. The contemplation of the physical world complements moral action by showing the full context of human action: we see god in his full glory, caring for human lives as he administers the world as a whole. In the spirit of Lucretius (who championed a rival philosophy), Seneca also intersperses ethical messages throughout his physical inquiries. Thus he emphasizes that humans must confront natural events, such as death and natural disasters, with courage and gratitude to god; and he warns against human misuse of natural resources and the decadence that accompanies progress. Of all areas of inquiry, physics affords Seneca the greatest scope for making additions and corrections to Stoic doctrine. He ranges over the whole history of physical inquiries, from the Pre-Socratics to his own time, to improve on the Stoics.

Seneca writes (*Letters* 45.4) that while he believes "in the judgment of great men," he also claims something for his own judgment: previous philosophers left some things to be investigated by us, which they might indeed have discovered for themselves if they hadn't engaged in useless quibbles. Granted that Seneca shows special investigative fervor in his cosmological inquiries, his moral teachings too are a product of his own judgment and innovation. What he contributes is a new vision rather than new theories. Using certain strict Stoic distinctions as a basis, he paints a new picture of the challenges that humans face and the happiness that awaits those who practice the correct philosophy. In agreement with Stoic orthodoxy, Seneca is uncompromising about differentiating between external advantages and the good, about the need to eradicate the passions, about the perfect rationality of the wise person, about the identity of god with fate. What he adds is a moral fervor, joined by a highly poetic sensibility, that turns these distinctions into springboards for action.

The Stoic sage was generally viewed by critics as a forbidding figure, outside the reach of human capabilities and immune to human feeling. Seneca concedes, or rather emphasizes, that the sage is indeed rare; he remarks that the sage is like a phoenix, appearing perhaps every five hundred years (*Letters* 42.1). As he sees it, the sage's exceptional status is not a barrier to improvement; it inspires. Seneca gives real-life immediacy to the sage by citing the younger Cato, opponent of Julius Caesar, as an example. Cato, indeed, is not just any sage; Seneca says he is not sure whether Cato might even surpass *him* (*On Constancy* 7.1). In this he is not blurring Stoic distinctions, but highlighting the indomitable moral strength of a sage. Through Cato and numerous other examples from the Roman past, Seneca fuses the Stoic sage with the traditional image of a Roman hero, thus spurring his Roman readers to fulfill their duties by emulating both at once.

Below the level of sage, Seneca outlines three stages of moral progress, demarcated according to our vulnerability to irrational emotions (*Letters* 75). There is the condition very near to that of being a sage, in which a person is not yet confident of being able to withstand irrational emotions (the so-called passions, *pathê*). Just below it is the stage in which a person is still capable of lapsing, and at the lowest level of progress a person can avoid most irrational emotions, but not all. Below these are the innumerable people who have yet to make progress. Seneca has nothing to say to them; he wants to avoid them, lest he be contaminated. What he does allow is that persons who are still struggling to become good may give way to grief initially; but he insists that this period must be brief. The Stoics talk "big words," he says, when they forbid moans and groans; he'll adopt a more gentle tone (*Letters* 23.4). Still, he insists, these words are "true"; and his aim is to lead, as much as he can, to the goal of a dispassionate attitude toward externals. Like everyone, the wise person is prone to initial shocks—reactions that look momentarily like irrational emotions—but these are involuntary responses to be succeeded immediately by the calmness of judgment. Seneca's sage is kind to others and is filled with a serene joy that has nothing to do with the ephemeral pleasure that other people take in externals.

Looking toward Roman heroism, Seneca portrays moral progress as an arduous struggle, like a military campaign or the uphill storming of an enemy's position. The enemy is fortune, viciously attacking its victim in the form of the most cruel disasters. Its opponent may succumb, but he will have conquered fortune if he resists to the end. In reality, the disasters come from other people or simply from circumstances. Seneca commonly cites death (whether one's own or that of a loved one), exile, torture, and illness. His own life is rich with examples. He goes so far as to advocate adversity as a means of making moral progress, but he also allows (with a view to his own wealth) that favorable circumstances are a help to the person who is still struggling to make progress.

To make progress, a person must not only confront externals but also, above all, look within oneself. Drawing inspiration from Plato, Seneca tells us there is a god inside; there is a soul that seeks to free itself from the dross of the body. Seneca invites the reader to withdraw into this inner self, so as to both meditate on one's particular condition and take flight in the contemplation of god. This withdrawal can occur in the press of a very active life. But it's easier when one is no longer fully caught up in politics, and so Seneca associates moral withdrawal with his own attempt to withdraw from politics toward the end of his life. He insists that he will continue to help others through his philosophical teachings, like other Stoics.

Senecan Tragedy

From Seneca's hand there survive eight tragedies (*Agamemnon*, *Thyestes*, *Oedipus*, *Medea*, *Phaedra*, *Phoenissae*, *Troades*, *Hercules Furens*), not including the spurious *Octavia* and the probably spurious *Hercules Oetaeus*; of the *Phoenissae* there remain only fragments. These dramas have undergone many vicissitudes in fortune throughout the centuries; however, they are no longer criticized as being mere flawed versions of the older Greek dramas in which much of Seneca's subject matter had already been treated. While Seneca's plays were once mined only for the light they shed on Roman Stoic philosophy, for examples of rhetorical extravagance, or for the reconstruction of missing plays by Sophocles and his fellows, the traits that once marked the dramas as unworthy of critical attention now engage us in their own right. Indeed, they are the only extant versions of any Roman tragedy, the writings of other dramatists such as Marcus Pacuvius (ca. 220–130 BCE) and Lucius Accius (ca. 170–86 BCE) having been lost to posterity. It is thus only Seneca's version of Roman drama, translated into English as the *Tenne Tragedies* in 1581, that so influenced the tragedians of the Elizabethan era.

Seneca may have turned his hand to writing drama as early as the reign of Caligula (37–41 CE), although there is no way of determining exactly when he began. Our first reference to the plays comes from a famous graffito from the *Agamemnon* preserved on a wall in Pompeii, but we can only deduce that this was written before the eruption of Vesuvius in 79 CE; it is of little actual use in trying to date the dramas. Stylistic analysis has not provided us with a sure order of composition, though scholars seem to agree that the *Thyestes* and the *Phoenissae* are late efforts. Certainly we are unable to make claims about their dating with respect to the *Essays* and *Letters*, despite the very different tones of Seneca's prose and his poetry—a difference that led some readers, including the fifth-century churchman and orator Sidonius Apollinaris and after him Erasmus and Diderot, to speculate (erroneously) that there might have been two Lucius Annaeus Senecas at work on them rather than one.

This confusion about the authorship of Seneca's writing may seem natural, given the argument that Stoicism fails as a way of life in the dramas. Whether it fails because its adherents are too weak to resist the pull of desire or emotion, because Stoicism itself is too difficult to practice successfully, because the universe is not the locus of a divine providence, or because the protagonists are so evil that they fail to see providence in action, is open to argument; a metaliterary view might even suggest that plotlines inherited from mythology provide the force that condemns a Cassandra or a Polyxena to death at the hands of a Clytemnestra or a Ulysses, with Seneca taking advantage of this dramatic fact to suggest the inexorable workings of Fate and the futility of struggle against it. Consider the *Thyestes* (a topic often dramatized in the Late Republic, though Seneca's version is the only one we have). We meet the eponymous exile as he praises the pauper's life to his children—only the man who drinks out of earthenware cups can be truly happy and without fear, he reminds them—but when invited to return to the palace at Argos by his conniving brother Atreus, the source of his exile, he allows himself to be lured back after only a token hesitation about giving up his newfound equanimity. "Sequor," he says to his son, "I follow you"; but in following his appetite for the luxurious life he does the opposite of the good Stoic.

The rest is, well, the stuff of myth. Dressed in royal regalia, Thyestes sits down to enjoy a hearty stew and some fine red wine, but his satiated belches soon turn into howls of horror as the delighted Atreus informs him of his dinner's provenance: the meal is made up of the dismembered bodies of Thyestes' own sons. Is there an explicit ethical or philosophical message here? If we followed the view of another Stoic, Epictetus (ca. 55–ca. 135 CE), who defined tragedy as what happens "when chance events befall fools" (*Discourses* 2.26.31), we might conclude that the story of Thyestes precisely illustrates the folly of giving in to a desire for power (or haute cuisine). In Seneca's treatment, however, such a clear object lesson seems undermined by a number of factors: the fact that Atreus reigns triumphant as the drama ends; the undeniable echoes of Stoic exhortation in the impotent counsels of Atreus's adviser; and the fragility of civic and religious values—the hellish scene in which Atreus sacrifices the children represents precisely a travesty of sacrifice itself, while *xenia* (the ancient tradition of hospitality) fares still worse. The adviser or a nurse mouthing Stoic platitudes without effect is featured in many of the plays: Phaedra, Clytemnestra, and Medea all have nurses to counsel them against their paths of action, even though their advice is invariably distorted and thrown back in their faces. Creon plays a similar role in the *Agamemnon*.

Other Senecan protagonists have more lasting doubts than Thyestes about the value of earthly success. Oedipus asks: "Joys any man in power?" And unlike his more confident Sophoclean manifestation, he feels the answer is clearly no. From the beginning of the play, the *Oedipus* provides striking contrasts to its Greek precedent, whose emphasis on the discovery of identity yields here to the overwhelming sense of pollution affecting Oedipus. The king, anxious even as the drama opens, worries that he will not escape the prophecy of his parricide, and suspects he is responsible for the plague ravaging Thebes. Despondent, he hopes for immediate death; his emotional state is far different from that of the character at the center of Sophocles' play. Seneca's version also features Creon's report of the long necromantic invocation of Laius's ghost in a dark grove, something absent in Sophocles. Even the sense that the characters' interaction onstage fails to drive the drama makes sense in the context of Seneca's forbidding and inexorable dramatic world. Causality and *anagnorisis* (dramatic recognition) are put aside in favor of the individual's helplessness before what awaits him, and the characters' speeches react to the violence rather than motivate it.

The pollution of the heavens by humans goes against Stoic physics but finds its place in the plays. The Stoics posited a tensional relationship between the cosmos and its parts; according to this view, the *pneuma* or vital spirit that subtends all matter results in a cosmic sympathy of the parts with the whole. "All things are united together . . . and earthly things feel the influence of heavenly ones," as Epictetus (*Discourses* 1.4.1) puts it. But what we see in the dramas is a disquieting manifestation of this *sympatheia*: the idea that the wickedness of one or a few could disrupt the rational and harmonic logos of the entire cosmos represents a reversal of the more orthodox Stoic viewpoint that the world is accessible to understanding and to reason. Thus we see the universe trembling at Medea's words, and the law of heaven in disorder. In the *Thyestes*, the sun hides its face in response to Atreus's crime; in the *Phaedra*, the chorus notes an eclipse after Phaedra's secret passion is unveiled. Horrific portents presage what is to come in the *Troades*. In Seneca's dramas, unlike in Greek tragedy, there is no role for civic institutions or the city to intervene in this relationship. The treatment of the gods is similarly unorthodox. Although Jason calls upon Medea to witness that there are no gods in the heavens, the very chariot in which she flies away is evidence of the assistance given her by her divine father. The gods are there; the problem is that they are unrecognizable.

Seneca's great antiheroes like Medea and Thyestes are troubling not only because they often triumph but because the manner of their triumph can resemble the goal point of the aspiring Stoic: in exhorting themselves to take up a certain stance toward the world, in abandoning familial and social ties, in rejecting the moral order of the world around them, and in trying to live up to a form of selfhood they have judged to be "better," Seneca's tyrants, just like his sages, construct a private and autonomous world around themselves which nothing can penetrate. Not only do they borrow the self-exhortations and self-reproving of the Stoic's arsenal, in which the dialogue conducted with the self suggests a split between a first-order desiring self and a second-order judging self, but they also adopt the consideration of what befits or is worthy of them as a guiding principle—always with a negative outcome.

This leads in turn to a metatheatrical tinge in several of the plays. In the *Medea*, for example, Medea seems to look to prior versions of her own story to discover what exactly is appropriate for her persona, in the same way that Oedipus, after putting out his eyes, remarks, "*This* face befits (an) Oedipus" (*Oedipus* 1000) or that Atreus says of his recipe, "This is a crime that befits Thyestes—and befits Atreus" (*Thyestes* 271). Such metatheatricality seems to draw upon the concern of the traditional Roman elite to perform exemplary actions for an approving audience, to generate one's ethical exemplarity by making sure that spectators for it exist.

And spectators do exist—we, the theater audience or the recitation audience. Scholars have long debated the question of whether Seneca's dramas were staged in antiquity. It is possible, as argued by the nineteenth-century German scholar Friedrich Leo, the tragedies were written for recitation only; inter alia, it would be unusual (but not impossible) to represent animal sacrifice and murder onstage. The question is unresolvable, but whether the original audiences were in the theater or in the recitation room, they shared with us the full knowledge of how the story would turn out, and in this they uncomfortably resembled some of the plotting antiheroes themselves. Indeed, our pleasure in watching Senecan tragedy unfold might seem to assimilate us to the pleasure these characters take in inflicting suffering on one another. In a famous line from the *Troades*, the messenger who brings news of Astyanax's murder reports of the scene of his death—which he has already compared to a theater—that "the greater part of the fickle crowd abhors the crime—and watches it" (1128–29). Here, in the tension between sadistic voyeurism and horror at what the drama unfolds, we can recognize the uncomfortable position of the spectator of Seneca's despairing plays.

Senecan Drama after the Classical Period

The fortunes of Senecan drama have crested twice: once during the Elizabethan period, and again in our own day. Although Seneca himself never refers to his tragedies, they were known in antiquity at least until Boethius (ca. 480–524 CE), whose *Consolation of Philosophy* draws on the themes of Seneca's choral odes. The dramas then largely dropped from sight, to reemerge in 1300 in a popular edition and commentary by Nicholas Trevet, a Dominican scholar at Oxford. Trevet's work was followed by vernacular translations in Spain, Italy, and France over the next two centuries. In Italy, an early imitator was Albertino Mussato (1261–1329), who wrote his tragic drama *Ecerinis* to alert his fellow Paduans to the danger presented by the tyrant of Verona. In England, the Jesuit priest and poet Jasper Heywood (1535–1598) produced translations of three of the plays; these were followed by Thomas Newton's *Seneca His Tenne Tragedies Translated into English* in 1581—of which one tragedy was Newton's own *Thebais*. The dramas were considered to be no mere pale shadow of their Greek predecessors: Petrarch, Salutati, and Scaliger all held Seneca inferior to none on the classical stage. In Scaliger's influential treatise on poetry, the *Poetices libri septem* (1561), he ranks Seneca as the equal of the Greek dramatists in solemnity and superior to Euripides in elegance and polish (6.6).

The Elizabethan playwrights in particular took up Seneca as a model for translation or imitation. T. S. Eliot claimed that "No author exercised a wider or deeper influence upon the Elizabethan mind or on the Elizabethan form of tragedy than did Seneca," and the consensus is that he was right. It is perhaps little wonder that Seneca appealed to an age in which tragedy was seen as the correct vehicle for the representation of "haughtinesse, arrogancy, ambition, pride, iniury, anger, wrath, envy, hatred, contention, warre, murther, cruelty, rapine, incest, rovings, depredations, piracyes, spoyles, robberies, rebellions, treasons, killings, hewing, stabbing, dagger-drawing, fighting, butchery, treachery, villainy, etc., and all kind of heroyicke evils whatsoever" (John Greene, *A Refutation of the Apology for Actors*, 1615, p.56). Kyd, Marlowe, Marston, and Shakespeare all read Seneca in Latin at school, and much of their drama shows his influence in one form or another. The itinerant players at Elsinore in Shakespeare's *Hamlet* famously opine that "Seneca cannot be too heavy nor Plautus too light" (2.2.400–401), but it is Shakespeare's *Titus Andronicus* that shows the greatest Senecan influence with its taste for revenge, rape, decapitation, human cookery, and insanity. Richard III and Macbeth, on the other hand, exemplify the presence of unrestrained, brooding ambition in the power-hungry protagonist. Similarly, in such plays as Thomas Kyd's *The Spanish Tragedy* and John Marston's *Antonio's Revenge* we see the influence of such Senecan fixtures as ghosts speaking from beyond the grave, graphic violence, obsession with revenge, and even structural features such as choruses, use of stichomythia, and division into five acts.

The bleak content of the dramas was often tied to the notion of a moral lesson. Already Trevet's preface to the *Thyestes* argued that the play taught the correction of morals by example, as well as simply offered the audience enjoyment. The Jesuit Martín Antonio Delrio (1551–1608) defended the use of Roman drama in a Christian education by suggesting that it provided a masked instruction in wisdom, as did Mussato before him. Nonetheless, after the middle of the seventeenth century Seneca's drama fell largely into disrepute. The Restoration poet John Dryden (1631–1700) took the opportunity in the preface to his own *Oedipus* to criticize both Seneca's and Corneille's versions; of the former, he wrote that "Seneca [. . .] is always running after pompous expression, pointed sentences, and Philosophical notions, more proper for the Study than the Stage." The French dramatist Jean Racine (1639–1699) used Seneca as a model for his *Phèdre*, but at the same time claimed that his main debt was to Euripides. Not surprisingly, the Romantics did not find much to like in Seneca. Recently, however, an efflorescence of interest in both the literary and the performance aspects of Senecan drama has produced new editions, scholarly monographs, and the staging of some of the plays. Noteworthy here are Sarah Kane's adaptation *Phaedra's Love*, performed in New York in May 1996; Michael Elliot Rutenberg's May 2005 dramatization of a post-Holocaust *Oedipus* at Haifa University in Israel; and a 2007 Joanne Akalaitis production of the *Thyestes* at the Court Theatre in Chicago.

A note on the translations: they are designed to be faithful to the Latin while reading idiomatically in English. The focus is on high standards of accuracy, clarity, and style in both the prose and the poetry. As such, the translations are intended to provide a basis for interpretive work rather than to convey personal interpretations. They generally eschew terminology that would imply a Judeo-Christian moral framework (e.g., "sin"). Where needed, notes have been supplied to explain proper names in mythology and geography.

For Further Information

On Seneca's life: Miriam T. Griffin, *Seneca: A Philosopher in Politics* (Oxford, 1976) and Paul Veyne, *Seneca: The Life of a Stoic*, translated from the French by David Sullivan (New York, 2003). On his philosophical thought: Brad Inwood, *Seneca: Stoic Philosophy at Rome* (Oxford, 2005), and Shadi Bartsch and David Wray, *Seneca and the Self* (Cambridge, 2009). On the dramas: A. J. Boyle, *Tragic Seneca: An Essay in the Theatrical Tradition* (New York and London, 1997); C. A. J. Littlewood, *Self-Representation and Illusion in Senecan Tragedy* (Oxford, 2004); and Thomas G. Rosenmeyer, *Senecan Drama and Stoic Cosmology* (Berkeley, 1989). On Seneca and Shakespeare: Robert S. Miola, *Shakespeare and Classical Tragedy: The Influence of Seneca* (Oxford, 1992) and Henry B. Charlton, *The Senecan Tradition in Renaissance Tragedy* (Manchester, 1946).

Editor's Note

The ten tragedies attributed to Seneca have been here translated by five different translators. As should be evident from the text, the translators have chosen to follow certain conventions and not others (for example, to avoid archaic language; to use blank verse, but no rhyming verse; and to aim at language that was as literal as possible without being awkward). Apart from this they were left to follow their own sense of what terminology suited their own encounter with the original Latin. All five translators were also invited to write their own short translator's introduction to their plays, focusing on what was of the most interest to them; there was no attempt to provide a general overview of all the scholarship on each play, though a suggested reading section follows each introduction.

The transmitted colometry of Seneca's anapests, even when the manuscript families A and E are in agreement, is often problematic, and two important editors (Zwierlein and Fitch) have hewn their own paths in their editions.[1] In this volume, instead of choosing between different modern understandings of the colometry for the choral odes and non-iambic verse, in the few cases where extra line-breaks create an extra line they have simply been reorganized to eliminate the extra line. This simple measure ensures that the line numbers continue in regular succession throughout the play; and while this has the disadvantage of turning a deaf ear to the metrical niceties of the original Latin (which might accommodate trochees and anapests differently from iambic trimeter), the translation gains the advantage of letting students and teachers refer to specific lines in the translation without having to gesture vaguely at some point between, for example, line 720 and line 730. In rendering all ten plays consistent in this way I have occasionally overridden the line divisions of a particular translator, even when that translator has noted that he or she has used a specific Latin edition.

I want to thank all the translators for their patience and flexibility in this very time-consuming and difficult project. All the translations were vetted by external reviewers for the University of Chicago Press, though probably my voice was the one that my collaborators were the most tired of by the end of this process. I hope our general readers will agree that this joint effort has been rewarded by the final result.

Oedipus

The story of the house of Oedipus starts with Oedipus' father, Laius, king of Thebes. An oracle tells Laius that he will be killed by his own son. He and his wife Jocasta therefore give their baby to the royal shepherd Phorbas with instructions to fasten its ankles together and leave it to die on Mount Cithaeron. Phorbas instead hands the baby to a Corinthian shepherd, who gives it to the childless king and queen of Corinth, Polybus and Merope. They raise the baby as their own with the name Oedipus or "Swollen-Foot." When the teenage Oedipus visits Delphi, he is told by Apollo's oracle that he will kill his father and marry his mother, so he does not return home to Corinth. Roaming as an exile in a remote area, Oedipus is driven off a cross-road by an imperious old man in a chariot—King Laius. In his anger he kills the old man. Soon afterward, Oedipus arrives at Thebes and sets the city free from the tyranny of the Sphinx, a ravenous monster who is terrorizing the citizens, by solving her riddle. He is made king and marries the queen, Jocasta, with whom he has a number of children, including Antigone, Ismene, Polynices, and Eteocles.

The drama starts years later when a devastating plague has over-whelmed the city and Oedipus as king attempts to discover the cause so he can eradicate it. The chorus now sings of the deadly effect of this plague on all living things in Thebes. Oedipius' brother-in-law Creon reports that the Delphic oracle says Laius' murderer must leave Thebes before the plague will end, and Oedipus curses the murderer who must be in the city. Tiresias summons Laius' ghost to find out the perpetrator. As Creon announces to Oedipus, it is Oedipus himself. In outrage and disbelief, Oedipus has Creon jailed on charges of collusion with Tiresias to seize the throne. The choral ode that follows is likewise skeptical, suggesting that the cause of the plague is the gods' hostility to Thebes.

Oedipus questions three figures carefully: Jocasta, Phorbas, and the old Corinthian shepherd who was given the baby by Phorbas and handed it over to the king and queen of Corinth. He now realizes that his worst fears have been realized and that the Delphic oracle has come true: he has unwittingly killed his father, Laius, and married his mother, Jocasta. Upon discovering this, Jocasta commits suicide, and Oedipus punishes himself by blinding himself and voluntarily departing into exile, thus removing the pollution from the city.

Introduction

SUSANNA BRAUND

Oedipus, king of Thebes, is one of the giant figures of ancient mythology. Through the centuries his story has inspired works of epic poetry, tragedy, and opera and been famously used in psychology. The complexities of the story have engendered a variety of treatments.[1] And yet, because our culture knows and values Greek tragedy over Roman and because the story of Oedipus is most familiar from Sophocles' play *King Oedipus* (and from Freud's deployment of the myth), we might readily fall into the trap of assessing Seneca's Roman treatment of the myth as secondary, as belated, as a response to Sophocles that struggles under the anxiety of influence. That would be a mistake. There is no evidence that Seneca conceived his tragedies as derived from or competing with those of the Attic tragedians. If we seek any earlier influences on Seneca as a tragedian, we do well to turn to Latin tragedy of the Roman Republican period (which survives only in fragments) and to Ovid's synthesis of Greco-Roman mythology in his epic poem, *Metamorphoses*. But even that is not essential. What is most illuminating is to set Seneca in the context of his own times. Let us ask what influenced him to shape his version of the famous myth as he does and what elements in the play correspond to particular interests of Seneca and his likely audience.

Of the several striking features of Seneca's articulation of his play, most significant is his elaboration of Oedipus' search for knowledge, which is the essence of the story, into three different scenes in addition to the conventional conversation with the shepherds: the report of the Delphic oracle, the divination scene, and the necromancy. Evidence from Seneca's contemporary, his nephew Lucan, suggests that these types of material were in vogue in the mid-first century CE: all three are incorporated into his epic poem on the *Civil War* between Pompey and Caesar, including a necromancy that lasts for half of a book. The divination scene includes a detailed account of haruspicy—that is, an examination of the entrails of the sacrificial animals, a practice that was likely familiar to many of Seneca's audience. Using the correct technical terminology, Seneca imagines details such as the twin heads on the liver (359) and the seven veins (364) that foretell the conflict between Oedipus' two sons Polynices and Eteocles and the attack by the seven champions mustered by Polynices on the seven gates of Thebes. The necromancy in act 3 allows Seneca to depict an inverted form of ritual, again with details designed to horrify his Roman audience: the setting is a grove dark as night, the priest is dressed in black and wearing a wreath of yew (a tree associated with death), the sheep and cattle he sacrifices are black instead of flawless white, he drags them backward to the altar (victims were supposed to approach willingly) and throws them into the fire while still alive instead of slaughtering them first (548–58). Besides all this, the necromancy gives Seneca the opportunity for an atmospheric description of the sinister grove in which the rite takes place; it is clear from similar passages in Ovid and Lucan as well as Seneca's *Thyestes* that this era relished such set-pieces.

Another striking feature is Seneca's unflinching interest in gruesome physiological detail, which manifests itself in the descriptions of the plague reported by Oedipus and the chorus (ode 1) and in the report of Oedipus' self-mutilation as well as in the divination scene. Again, it seems fair to assume that Seneca is here delivering something his Roman audience craved; other poetry of this era shares Seneca's interest in bodily deformation and destruction, including Lucan again, who devotes a lengthy episode to the effects of fatal snake bites. He is surely also competing with other memorable plague narratives in earlier Latin literature—specifically, that which ends Lucretius' epic poem *On the Nature of the Universe* and that which closes the third book of Virgil's *Georgics*.

A third remarkable feature is Seneca's decision to have Jocasta commit suicide on stage (certainly a departure from the conventions of Greek tragedy) by typically masculine means: not by hanging herself but by a sword-thrust. For a Roman audience in the early principate, such a death evoked the famous death during the civil war of the Stoic Cato, who after the battle of Thapsus preferred to commit suicide rather than be spared by Caesar. Seneca deploys this episode with admiration several times in his prose writings, where it represents the ultimate act of self-sufficiency available to the Stoic. To say this is not to imply that Jocasta is a Stoic, but the prominent position of Jocasta's suicide at the climax of the play conveys admiration for her courage. Seneca has seen in the Oedipus myth an opportunity to incorporate plague narratives, a divination, a necromancy, and a memorable suicide.

The theme of knowledge necessarily pervades the play not only in the articulation of the plot but also at the linguistic level. Oedipus' conflicted attitude toward knowledge receives clear expression at line 209—"the mind unsure desires knowledge, fears it too"—and the vocabulary of knowing recurs frequently, often interconnected with the motifs and antitheses of darkness and light, sight and blindness. Another motif closely connected with knowledge, and one also embedded in the ancient myth of course, is that of riddles. In act 1 Oedipus responds to Jocasta's criticisms of his weakness by reminding her that he had dared to face the Sphinx and that he was the only one able to solve her riddle (101–2): "But I untied the word-knots of the oracle, entangled tricks, / the fatal riddle of the beast with wings." His language of untying knots and his image of himself as solver of riddles recur as he seeks the cause of the plague. He urges Creon to report the obscure response of the oracle by saying, "Oedipus alone can understand enigmas" (216); he invites Tiresias to "untie / the oracle's response" (291–92); and he asks "soul-mate wife" to "unravel" his "perplexities" (773). But it turns out that his solving the new riddle of the plague and of Laius' murderer only renders him, in the words of Laius' ghost, "an evil all entwined, / a monster more entangled even than his Sphinx" (640–41). The final riddle in the play is one that he poses to himself in the speech reported by the messenger (926–57)—namely, how to find a punishment that is appropriate to his crimes: "You must find a way / to roam not mingling with the dead and buried, and yet / banished from the living. You must die, but not as much as father" (949–51). His solution is, of course, to pluck out his eyes.

Other key elements in Seneca's handling of the Oedipus myth

that are foregrounded by this kind of reiteration are specifically Roman and specifically Senecan. First is a concern with kingship, a theme that occurs in most of Seneca's tragedies and in many other texts of the early principate, where good kings are contrasted with tyrants. Oedipus remarks on the "deceptive blessing" of kingship in his opening words (6–11); Jocasta appeals to the obligation of courage that goes with kingship in her first speech (82–86); Oedipus asserts that kings "must guard the well-being of kings" (239–43) as he institutes the search for the murderer of Laius and he later uses his absolute power to compel Creon to speak (518–29). Finally, in the dialogue with Creon in which Oedipus asserts that Creon is ambitious to replace him as king (668–706), Seneca delivers several of his typical *sententiae* (pithy points) about kingship: "He who is too much afraid of hatred / is incapable of ruling. It's fear keeps kingdoms safe," and "He who wields the scepter cruelly and tyrannically / dreads his victims. Fear rebounds against its instigator" (703–6).

A second motif is typical of Seneca's Stoic vocabulary and ideas: the fickleness of Fortune and the fixity of fate. Nowhere is this more explicit than in the final ode, which starts (980): "By fate we are driven—so yield to fate!" Oedipus' resistance to his fate—his heroic efforts to foil the oracle—are shown to be useless. In other words, the Oedipus story is recruited as evidence for the Stoic view of predetermination/predestination. Oedipus of course is aware of his vulnerability to Fortune (8–11) and has a sense that fate has something awful in store for him right from the start (28–36). Creon knows better than Oedipus does that he cannot alter his lot (681), and Jocasta urges Oedipus not to hurry to find out his fate when she says, "Without your challenge let the fates unfold themselves" (832). Once he understands his true identity, Oedipus depicts himself as an innocent victim of Fortune (934), a sentiment reiterated by Jocasta in further *sententiae* at line 1019: "The blame belongs to fate: no one is made guilty by his fate." In other words, Oedipus never gains the equanimity of the Stoic sage who is able to endure anything and everything that fate and Fortune throw at him, a topic explored in depth by Seneca in his essay on the wise man's endurance (*De Constantia Sapientis*).

Also treated from a Stoic perspective, the theme of Nature and her laws emerges strongly from Seneca's handling of the play. For the Stoics, the ideal life was one lived "in accordance with Nature"; for Seneca, the inversions and perversions of Nature are signs of moral as well as cosmological chaos. Oedipus in his horror at the predictions of the oracle has made every effort to keep Nature's laws intact, as we hear early in the play when he explains the motivation for his self-imposed exile from Corinth (12–26). Corresponding to this at the close of the play is Oedipus' realization that Nature "inverted / her established statutes in the case of Oedipus alone, / devising novel births" (he means the children he has fathered on his mother), and he accordingly requests an unnatural punishment for his unnatural crime: "to be allowed to live again, and die again, / to be reborn repeatedly, so every time you'll pay / with different punishments" (942–47). But the fullest and most shocking depiction of the perversion of Nature comes in the divination scene, when Manto is describing to her father Tiresias the strange formation of the sacrificial heifer's entrails (366–73):

> Altered is the natural order, nothing in its proper place,
> but everything is back to front. On the right side
> lie the lungs, filled with blood, no room for air.
> The left is not the region of the heart. The caul does not
> conceal the entrails' folds of fat with soft embrace.
> Nature is inverted. Even in the womb no law persists:
> let me investigate the reason for such stiffness in its organs.
> What monstrosity is this? A fetus in a virgin heifer!

The breaking of the boundaries set by Nature is a theme typical of Senecan tragedy—it is a crucial theme in his *Thyestes*, for example—but here it is pervasive. The elision of proper barriers occurs in Oedipus' first speech, in his description of the effects of the plague, which is indiscriminating in its victims (young and old, fathers and sons), which kills a man and his wife on their wedding day, which produces funerals without lamentation because they have no tears left, which sees parents burying their children, which fells mourners during funeral processions, which makes people burn the bodies of their kin on strangers' pyres, which produces so many casualties that there is no land left for graves and not enough timber to supply the pyres (54–68). The same motif of the disruption of natural boundaries recurs in the final scene as Jocasta prepares to kill herself with the words, "Because of you, incestuous woman, / the decency of human law is jumbled and destroyed" (1025–26). She boldly articulates the unnatural relationships—her dead husband was also her husband's father—and logically targets "the fertile womb that bore me sons and husband" (1034–39).

The rules that should govern kinship relations are in Seneca's *Oedipus* couched in the essentially Roman framework of *pietas*, a word hard to translate but which denotes proper respect toward one's parents, one's nation, and one's gods. In this play, the obligations imposed by *pietas* drive Oedipus as he attempts to do the right thing. Seneca introduces the motif (the words translating the noun *pietas* and the adjectives *pius* and *impius* are emphasized) as early as line 19, where he writes "*pro misera pietas*!" or "Unhappy *love of kin*!" Oedipus fears the "*wicked* blaze of incest" (21) predicted by the oracle but has unwittingly produced "*unnatural* offspring" (639), which leads the ghost of Laius to promise "*unnatural* warfare" (646) to crush his incestuous house.

Ironically, in his curse on the murderer of Laius, Oedipus uses exactly this vocabulary of *pietas* (257–63):

> may he find no peaceful shelter, no trusty hearth,
> no land to offer him a welcome in his exile.
> May shameful marriage and *unnatural* offspring bring him
>   pain.
> May he with his own hand even slay his father
> and may he do—there cannot be a heavier curse—whatever
> I have run away from.

Still, after the announcement of Polybus' death, Oedipus believes in his innocence: "*without offense* I now can raise to heaven / hands undefiled, that need to fear no crimes" (790–91). Once he has discovered how wrong he is, "he lays his *sinning* hand upon his sword-hilt" (935) in his first impulse to kill himself, but then he realizes that although this might make atonement to his father it would leave unpaid his debts to his mother, his children, and his "grieving fatherland" (936–41), a conceptualization of obligation that is quintessentially Roman. The *pietas* motif makes its final appearance in the play's last speech when Oedipus shockingly calls Apollo, the god of the oracle, a "liar" because Jocasta's death was not foretold. His mother's death has made him even more guilty than he had feared; though unwillingly and unwittingly, he has "outdone the *wickedness* of fate" (1042–46). Seneca's language of *pietas* is designed to resonate for his Roman readers. There is much more to be said about Seneca's *Oedipus*, but I hope I have shown how rich and well-crafted the play is when studied in its Roman context as the literary creation of a Stoic philosopher of the early principate.

In terms of language, it is not easy to capture the effect of the intellectual and physical horrors of Seneca's Latin, and I have done my best while remaining faithful to the Latin in the same number of lines as the Latin. To achieve this I have used what may seem a rather compact and muscular English idiom, since Latin typically uses fewer words than English—for example, it uses "a" and "the" where Latin uses neither. Where possible, I have tried to reproduce effects of word order and enjambment, although this is very hard when translating from an inflected language such as Latin into English where word order rather than word form determines meaning. I have also tried to reflect the nuances of vocabulary, especially in terms of the repetition of key words, variation, strained language, and the striking collocations which abound in Senecan drama. One characteristic of Seneca's dramatic language is his deployment of *sententiae*, pithy generalizations (examples include 804 and 910–11), which demand a matching compression in English.

Seneca uses a variety of meters. The monologues and passages of dialogue are almost entirely in iambic trimeters; I have aimed at a broadly iambic rhythm for these, with lines that have between five and eight strong beats. The choral passages are in various lyric meters and I have tried to convey the shift from regular iambics by using anapaestic or dactylic meters or irregular metrical patterns. For a modern audience, the choral passages, which are static, flowery, and studded with mythological and geographical allusions, will seem alien, while Seneca's highly-educated Roman audience would instantly have recognized the style. I find it significant that Ted Hughes, in his adaptation of the play, which otherwise maintains a close relationship to the Latin text, abandons the idea of a formal hymn at this point and has his chorus chanting (and presumably dancing as they chant) a weird song "against the dead." His 1968 translation (published by Faber & Faber in 1969) may valuably be read as a complement to my translation, for Hughes attempts to create a brutal contemporary English version of Seneca's Latin. Hughes deploys vivid and insistent iterations, nearly all of them stark monosyllables, to encapsulate the themes of the play: sick, plague, dead, stench, rot, fear, father, mother, blind, dark, blood, roots, twist, noose, ropes, knots, tangle, riddle, black (all these established during the first two acts), dig, and stab.

Suggested Reading

Ahl, Frederick. 2008. *Two Faces of Oedipus*. Ithaca.

Boyle, Anthony J. 2011. *Seneca:* Oedipus. Oxford.

Braund, Susanna. 2016. *Seneca:* Oedipus. London.

Busch, Austin. 2007. "*Versane Natura Est?* Natural and Linguistic Instability in the *Extispicium* and Self-blinding of Seneca's *Oedipus*." *The Classical Journal* 102: 225–67.

Davis, Peter J. 1991. "Fate and Human Responsibility in Seneca's *Oedipus*." *Latomus* 50: 150–63.

Henry, Denis, and B. Walker. 1983. "The *Oedipus* of Seneca: An Imperial Tragedy." In *Seneca Tragicus: Ramus Essays on Senecan Drama*, edited by A. J. Boyle, 128–39. Berwick.

Hughes, Ted. 1969. *Seneca's* Oedipus. London.

Poe, Joe P. 1983. "The Sinful Nature of the Protagonist of Seneca's *Oedipus*." In *Seneca Tragicus: Ramus Essays on Senecan Drama*, edited by A. J. Boyle, 140–58. Berwick.

Oedipus

LUCIUS ANNAEUS SENECA

TRANSLATED BY SUSANNA BRAUND

DRAMATIS PERSONAE

OEDIPUS, king of Thebes
JOCASTA, wife of Oedipus and queen of Thebes
CREON, brother of Jocasta
TIRESIAS, blind seer of Thebes
MANTO, daughter of Tiresias
OLD CORINTHIAN, messenger from Corinth
PHORBAS, shepherd of the king's flocks
MESSENGER
CHORUS of Thebans

The drama takes place outside the palace of King Oedipus at Thebes. An altar stands before the palace.

ACT 1

OEDIPUS

(*To himself.*)

Now night is driven out. A hesitating Sun returns
and lifts his beam,[1] shrouded with a filthy cloud.
Bringing somber light with his fire that heralds grief,
his view will be of houses wasted by devouring plague:
the day will show the devastation of the night.
Does anyone rejoice in kingship? A deceptive blessing:
how many evils you conceal behind a smiling mask!
As elevated ridges always catch the gales,
and as the rocky crag that juts into the massive strait
is pounded by the surge, however calm the sea, 10

so the heights of power lie exposed to Fortune.
How well I did to flee the scepter of my father Polybus![2]
Freed from my anxieties, an exile, fearless, wandering,
I stumbled (sky and gods I call to witness) into kingship.
My fears are monstrous: that my sire be slaughtered
by my hand. Of this the Delphic laurels tell me,[3]
and impose on me another, greater, crime.
Is there an atrocity that's greater than a murdered father?
Unhappy love of kin! I am ashamed to speak my fate:
20 Phoebus threatens son with father's bed,[4]
a terrifying union, a wicked blaze of incest.
This was the fear that drove me from my father's kingdom;
for this fear I left my hearth, a fugitive.
Too little trusting in myself, I kept your laws
secure, Nature. When one dreads calamity,
still one fears what seems unthinkable.
Everything induces panic; in myself I have no confidence.
At this very moment, fate is planning some assault on me.
What else to reckon, when this plague so deadly
30 to the Theban people with such widespread devastation[5]
spares me alone? For what evil am I being saved?
Among the ruins of the city, deaths which must be wept
with tears continually renewed, the massacre of Thebes,
unscathed, I stand apart—to answer Phoebus' accusation,
I suppose! Did you expect that with your crimes so great
you would receive a healthy kingdom? My guilt pollutes the sky.
No gentle breeze with cooling breath caresses hearts
that gasp with heat, no kind west winds are moving,
but Sun intensifies the scorching Dog-Star's fires,[6]
40 pressing hard upon the Lion of Nemea.[7]
The rivers are leached of water, the foliage of color.
Dirce's spring is parched;[8] the trickle of Ismenos[9]
hardly wets the naked channel with its meager flow.
Obscurely through the sky slips Phoebus' sister;[10]
the world is gloomy, blanched beneath a light that's overcast.
No star flashes out from cloudless nights,

but a heavy black miasma broods upon the earth.
A hellish look has veiled the sky-gods' citadels
and homes on high. The ripened wheat withholds
its harvest and, although its tall ears quiver, 50
the golden crop is barren, dying on parched stalks.[11]
No group is exempt or free from this destruction,
but every age and sex alike collapses.
The deadly plague unites the young with old and fathers
with their sons. A single blaze cremates the marriage-bond,
and funerals occur without complaints and bitter lamentation.[12]
Yes, the unremitting slaughter of this great calamity
has dried their eyes: as ever in extremes of misery,
their tears have died. An ailing father bears one victim
to the final fire, a mother, crazed, conveys her son, 60
then hurries back to bring another to the same death-pyre.
And in the middle of their grief, fresh grief arises,
and its own procession falls around the corpse.
Then people burn the bodies of their kin with strangers' flames—
the fire is stolen; the wretches have no sense of shame.
No individual graves protect the hallowed bones—
to burn them is enough—but far too few are turned to ash.[13]
There is no land for graves, the woods refuse the pyres'
needs now.
No prayers avail, no skill relieves the stricken:
healers fall as victims, the plague drags down assistance. 70

(*Jocasta enters.*)

I stretch my hands in supplication, prostrate at the altars,
asking for an early fate, so I may anticipate
my fatherland's collapse, and not be last to fall,
not be the final victim in my kingdom.
O powers above, too pitiless, O heavy fate!
How can it be that I alone of this whole people am denied
the death that is ubiquitous? Turn your back upon the kingdom
blighted by your deadly hand. Leave the tears, the deaths,
the poisonous infections of the air you carry with you,

80 disastrous visitor. Get out of here, right now, belatedly—
even to your parents![14]

JOCASTA

Husband, what's the point of weighing down
your troubles with complaints? The essence of a king, I think,
is to grasp adversity, to stand more firmly
and courageously with steady foot the more unsure
his situation, the more his mighty power slips and slides.
A real man does not retreat from Fortune.

OEDIPUS

The charge and brand of cowardice is utterly remote.
My manhood is a stranger to ignoble fears.
With unsheathed weapons facing me, with terrifying violence
90 of war engulfing me,[15] I would be martialing
my hands to fight, boldly to confront the wild giants.[16]
I ran not even from the Sphinx when she was weaving words
in hidden measures: I withstood the monstrous prophetess' bloodied
gaping jaws, the ground all bleached with scattered bones.[17]
And when from crag above, already menacing her prey,
she flexed her wings and, like a savage lion,
roused her threats with lashes of her tail, I asked her
for the riddle.[18] From above, she gave a terrifying shriek,
she snapped her jaws, and, hating the delay, her talons
100 clawed the rocks in eagerness to tear my guts.
But I untied the word-knots of the oracle, entangled tricks,
the fatal riddle of the beast with wings.

(*To himself.*)

Why, you fool, do you now pray, too late, for death?
You had your chance to die. You have your prize of glory,
your reward for slaughtering the Sphinx—the scepter.
I see—it is that cunning monster's dreadful dust
that wages war on us again—that scourge I slaughtered
now lays waste to Thebes. One deliverance still is left—
if Phoebus can reveal some path to our deliverance.

CHORUS OF THEBANS

You are ruined, race of Cadmus, noble-born, 110
all your city too. Pitiable Thebes,
you see your lands bereft of farmers.
That fighting force of yours is cropped by death,
Bacchus,[19] your comrades to the furthest Indies,
who dared to ride through eastern plains
and plant your banners there, where earth begins.
They saw the Arabs, rich with groves of cinnamon,
they saw the horseman's arrows turned around,
the trickster Parthian's dangerous back.[20]
They trod the shore of reddening sea,[21] 120
where Phoebus shows his rising and reveals
his light, staining naked Indians
with nearness of his flame.
Heirs of an unconquered line, we are dying,
sinking in the grip of savage fate.
Death's procession wends its way, continually renewed:
the lengthy mourning line troops hurriedly
toward the ghosts, but the grim procession
jams—the seven gates do not open wide enough
for the crowds that seek their graves. 130
The heavy carnage rises, corpses crushing
corpses in their piles.
First affected by the blast were slow-foot sacrificial flocks.
The woolly sheep could hardly graze the fertile grasses.
The priest had taken up his stand to strike his victim:
while his hand, upraised, prepared a blow unerring,
the bull, his gilded horns aglow,
collapses, limp. His slackened neck
yawned open from the weighty strike:
no gore; what stained the blade was a disgusting 140
ooze, flooding from the black gash.
The charger faltered as it ran and fell
midcircuit, threw its rider
over tilting shoulder.

Cattle lie abandoned in the fields;
as the herd declines, the bull wastes away.
The herdsman weakens as his stock dwindles,
dies among emaciated steers.
No ravening wolves now terrorize the stags,
150 roar of angry lion subsides,
ferocity is gone from shaggy bears,
lurking snake has lost her venom:
parched, she dies, her poison dry.
No shadows on the dusky hills are cast
by woods adorned with their own foliage,
no fields grow green with soil's bounty,
no vine bends low its branches,
heavy with its own god:[22]
nothing is untouched by our calamity.
160 The mob of sisters with their brands of Tartarus[23]
has smashed the bolts of Erebus deep down,[24]
and Fire-River has changed his course[25]
and blended Styx with waves of Sidon.[26]
Black Death opens wide its greedy gaping
jaws and fully unfolds its wings.
The ferryman who guards the murky rivers[27]
with his roomy boat, though tough
with vigorous old age, can hardly move
his arms, exhausted by continual poling,
170 tired of ferrying the masses newly come.
Still more: they say the Hound has burst[28]
his chains of hellish iron and roams[29]
our world, that earth has roared,
that through the sacred groves have flitted[30]
human phantoms more than human size, that twice
has Cadmus' forest quaked and shed its snows,[31]
that twice has Dirce's spring been stained by blood,
that in the silent night around the walls of Amphion[32]
the howls of dogs were heard.[33]

Death takes a strange and dreadful form, 180
more terrible than death! Our listless limbs
are paralyzed by numbing lethargy, the sickly
face is flushed, and tiny rashes
mark the skin. Then a fiery heat
burns the body's very citadel,
distending cheeks with copious blood.
Eyes are fixed, a demon fire[34]
feeds upon the limbs, ears are ringing,
black gore drips from flaring nostrils,
ruptures veins to make them gape. 190
A persistent grating cough racks
the inmost guts, and now they constantly
clutch close the rocks that cool them.
You people now released by houses emptied
of their guardians, you seek the springs
but only feed your thirst by gulping down the water.
Crowds lie stretched among the altars,
praying for death, the only thing the gods
are ready to bestow. They seek the shrines,
not to placate the powers by votive offerings, 200
but in their wish to glut the gods with death.[35]

ACT 2

CHORUS OF THEBANS

(*Creon enters.*)

Who is that, with hurried step heading for the palace?
Is Creon here, glorious in lineage and deeds,
or does my ailing mind see false for true?
Here he is, in answer to our prayers, Creon.

OEDIPUS

I shake with dread, in terror of the tilt of fate.
My anxious breast is faltering between twin feelings:
while the mix of joy and hardship lies in doubt,

the mind unsure desires knowledge, fears it too.
210 O brother of my wife, if you bring any help for us
in our distress, speak out with hastened voice.

CREON

The oracle's response is tangled in uncertainty.

OEDIPUS

Uncertain help, to those in trouble, is no help at all.

CREON

The god of Delphi always hides his secrets
in convoluted twists.

OEDIPUS

Speak, uncertain though it be.
Oedipus alone can understand enigmas.[36]

CREON

The god commands atonement of the murder of the king
by banishment as vengeance for the death of Laius.[37]
Not till then will day run shining in the sky
220 or offer healthy draughts of unpolluted air.

OEDIPUS

And who *was* the killer of the famous king?
Name the one that Phoebus means, so he may pay the penalty.

CREON

I pray that I may safely tell the horrifying sights and sounds:
paralysis has settled through my limbs; chill, my blood congeals.
When with humble foot I entered Phoebus' hallowed shrine
and ritually raised my reverent hands in prayer to his power,
the twin tops of Parnassus,[38] white with snow, roared fiercely;
Phoebus' laurel swayed and trembled, shook the shrine,
and suddenly the hallowed water of Castalia's spring stood
still.[39]
230 The prophetess of Leto starts to shake her bristling hair,[40]
to be possessed by Phoebus, frantic. She is not yet at the cavern,
when a more than human sound shoots out with mighty crash:
"Benevolent stars will return to the Thebes of Cadmus
if as a fugitive the visitor leaves Ismenian Dirce,

guilty of murdering the king, known to Phoebus from infancy.
The joys from that criminal murder will not linger long for you:
war you will wage on yourself, war to your children too
you will bequeath, vilely returned to maternal origins."

OEDIPUS

What I plan to do in obedience to the gods' advice
should already have been done for the dead king's ashes, 240
preventing any treacherous violation of his hallowed scepter.
More than anyone, a king must guard the well-being of kings;
none that fears him when alive will miss him when he's dead.

CREON

Anxiety about the dead man was dispelled by greater fear.

OEDIPUS

Could any terror stop the duty owed by loyalty?

CREON

Yes: the Sphinx and the fatal threats of her monstrous riddle.[41]

OEDIPUS

Now, by divine command, the crime must be atoned for.
I pray to all you gods who look benign on kingship:
you, you, controller of the laws of the hurtling universe,
and you,[42] the greatest glory of the cloudless sky, traversing 250
with your changing course the signs that number twice
times six[43]
unrolling the slow centuries with your rapid wheel,
and you, his sister, always facing toward your brother,
Phoebe, wanderer by night, and you, the master of the winds,[44]
driving azure horses over the expanses of the deep,
and you, the governor of halls that lack the light:
attend![45] The man by whose hand Laius fell[46]—
may he find no peaceful shelter, no trusty hearth,
no land to offer him a welcome in his exile.
May shameful marriage and unnatural offspring bring him 260
pain.
May he with his own hand even slay his father
and may he do—there cannot be a heavier curse—whatever

I have run away from. There will be no room for pardon.
I swear this by the kingship I now wield as a visitor,
by the kingship that I left, by my household gods,
by you, great father Neptune, doubly playing
with your shallow waves upon my land from either side.[47]
And you[48]—come yourself, as witness to my words,
rouser of prophetic lips of Cirrha's seer:[49]
270 Exactly as I hope that father has a peaceable old age,
that he resign his final day secure on his high throne,
that Merope know marriage-blaze with Polybus alone,
so I hope that no reprieve will rob me of the guilty man.
But in what location was the monstrous crime committed?
Tell me: did he die in open warfare or by ambush?

CREON

While on his way toward Castalia's leafy groves, that holy place,
he trod a path enveloped in dense thickets,
where the road in triplets branches out into the plains.
One cuts through the land of Phocis, loved by Bacchus,
280 where tall Parnassus leaves the fields,
his two peaks seeking sky with gently rising slope.
Another goes toward the land of Sisyphus with its two seas,[50]
heading for Olenian fields.[51] The third track snakes
through a winding gorge, grazing wandering waters,[52]
and cleaves the icy shallows of the river Olmius.[53]
Here a sudden band of brigands set upon him, unsuspecting.[54]
They were armed and carried out their crime unseen.

(*Tiresias and Manto enter; throughout this scene*
Manto carries out Tiresias' instructions.)

Most opportunely, roused by Phoebus' oracle,
Tiresias comes hurrying, though slowed by shaky knees,
290 and with him Manto, leading on the man deprived of light.

OEDIPUS

You are sacred to the gods, the closest font to Phoebus, untie
the oracle's response. Tell us whom it seeks for punishment.

TIRESIAS

You need not be surprised, you who are great of soul,
that my tongue is slow to speak, that it seeks delay.
For a man who lacks his sight, much of truth is hidden.
But I shall follow where my fatherland, where Phoebus
calls me:
fate must be rooted out. If my blood were young
and warm, I would take the god into my breast.
To the altar drive a bull whose back is gleaming white
and a heifer on whose neck the curving yoke has never weighed. 300
You, my daughter, guide your father lost for light,
report the telling tokens of the fate-revealing rite.

MANTO

A perfect victim stands before the hallowed altar.

TIRESIAS

To our ritual call the gods with the ceremonial words
and pile the altar high with gift of oriental incense.

MANTO

I have now heaped incense on the sky-gods' sacred hearth.

TIRESIAS

And the flame? Is it seizing on its lavish feast already?

MANTO

Suddenly it blazed with light and suddenly died down.

TIRESIAS

Did the fire take an upright stance, clear and bright,
lifting an unsullied peak straight toward the sky, 310
unfolding wide its topmost crest into the air?
Or does it snake around the sides, uncertain of its course,
and falter, murky with undulating smoke?

MANTO

The flame kept changing, varying its look.
As Iris,[55] bringer of the rain, entwines herself
with many colors, spanning a huge tract of sky
and heralding the storm-clouds with her painted bow—
you would be unsure what color is or is not there—

so it was erratic: azure mixed with orange flecks,
320 then red like blood, fading into blackness finally.
But look! The fire is fighting and dividing
into two, the embers of a single sacrifice
are splitting in hostility—sire, I shudder as I watch.
The wine we offered as libation changes into gore[56]
and dense smoke wreathes the king's head
and settles thicker still around his face
and blocks the dingy light with a dense cloud.
Father, tell us what it is.

TIRESIAS

What can *I* tell,
reeling through the tumult of my mind, aghast? What
330 am I to say? These are evils terrible, but hidden deep.
The powers like to manifest their rage by unambiguous signs.
What is it that they want to be disclosed
and yet do not, concealing their fierce anger?
Something shames the gods. Quickly, bring the victims close
and sprinkle on their necks the salted meal.
Do they undergo the ritual touch of hands
with calm expression?

MANTO

As the bull, positioned facing east,
raised his head up high, he panicked at the daylight
and in terror turns his face away, flinching from the rays.

TIRESIAS

340 Is a single wound enough to thrust them to the ground?

MANTO

The heifer wrapped herself around the blade when it was offered
and fell down by a single wound. The bull, though, after suffering
two blows, is staggering here and there erratically,
hardly yielding up his struggling breath in his exhaustion.[57]

TIRESIAS

Does the gore spurt quickly from a narrow wound
or does it well up slowly in the gashes driven deep?

MANTO

A stream is pouring through the path of where the heifer's breast
gapes wide. For the bull, its heavy wounds are stained
with just a meager shower: the blood runs backward,
copiously pouring out of face and eyes.[58] 350

TIRESIAS

These unpropitious rites arouse great terror.
But describe to me the entrails' unambiguous signs.

MANTO

My father, what is this? The organs are not quivering, as is
usual,
pulsing in a gentle motion, but they make my whole hand
shake, and from the veins fresh gore is jumping out.
Diseased, the heart is withered through and through, and lies
submerged.
The veins are livid. The guts are largely missing,
and the putrid liver oozes with black bile
and here protrude two heads identically bulging—
invariably an omen that is bad for solitary power. 360
But one transparent membrane covers both
these cloven heads, refusing to conceal secrets.[59]
The side that omens ill rears up with sturdy strength,[60]
extending seven veins, but they are all cut off
by a slanting ridge, preventing them from turning back.
Altered is the natural order, nothing in its proper place,
but everything is back to front. On the right side
lie the lungs, filled with blood, no room for air.[61]
The left is not the region of the heart. The caul does not
conceal the entrails' folds of fat with soft embrace. 370
Nature is inverted. Even in the womb no law persists:
let me investigate the reason for such stiffness in its organs.

What monstrosity is this? A fetus in a virgin heifer!
And not positioned in the usual way, it fills its mother
in a foreign place. With a moan it moves its limbs,
its feeble body twitching with convulsive stiffness.
Livid gore has stained the entrails black—
and the mangled torsos try to walk along—
and a disemboweled body rises up and menaces the ritual
380 attendants with its horns—its entrails slip out of my hands.
That noise that struck your ears was not the lowing
of the cattle, herds are nowhere sounding out in terror:
it's the fire on the altar bellowing, the hearth quaking.

OEDIPUS

Expound the meaning of those signs from the terrifying
rite. I shall drink your words with ears unperturbed.
Extremities of evil can dispel anxiety.

TIRESIAS

This evil that you look for help with—you will envy it.

OEDIPUS

Tell the one thing that the sky-divinities want known:
who defiled his hands with the murder of the king?

TIRESIAS

390 The name cannot be summoned either by the birds
that cut through heaven's heights on buoyant wing, or by entrails
torn from living breasts.[62] We must try another way.
He himself must be evoked from regions of eternal night,
released from Erebus to point the finger at the murderer.
We must unseal the earth, entreat the unforgiving
power of Dis,[63] fetch out to here the population
of infernal Styx. Tell us who this ritual is assigned to,
since for you, the holder of the kingdom's highest power,
it is taboo to see the shades.

OEDIPUS

This task asks for you, Creon:
400 my kingdom looks to you in second place.

(*Creon leaves.*)

TIRESIAS

While we unlock the barriers of deepest Styx,
let the people's hymn sound out in praise of Bacchus.

(*Oedipus, Tiresias, and Manto leave.*)

CHORUS

Bacchus, with hair streaming out and circled with bobbing ivy,
your delicate hands wielding the thyrsus of Nysa,[64]
luminous beauty of heaven, come here
in response to the prayers
that your glorious Thebes
with its suppliant palms offers you.
Turn your girlish head this way as a blessing,
with your star-bright face drive away rain-clouds 410
and grim threats of Erebus
and devouring fate.
You glory in binding your hair with spring-season flowers,
in wrapping your head with Tyrian turban,[65]
in wreathing your soft brow with berries of ivy,
in tossing your streaming locks in disarray,
in bringing them under control again by tightening a knot.
Like this, in fear of your angry stepmother[66]
you grew up by taking a shape that was false,
pretending to be a girl with blonde hair, 420
a girdle of saffron fastening her dress.
That is why you delight in such soft attire,
hanging folds and trailing robes.
You were seen, seated on your chariot of gold,
when you steered your lions in your long gown,
by the whole vast region of the eastern world,
by those that drink from the Ganges and shatter
the ice of Araxes.[67]
You are followed by elder Silenus on his vile donkey,[68]
his bulging temples circled by garlands of ivy. 430
Your unruly initiates celebrate your secret mysteries.
Your escort, the Bassarid troop,[69]

has pounded the earth with their dance,
now on Edonian Pangaeum,[70] now on the Thracian
peak of Pindus.[71] Now your unscrupulous maenad,
Ogygian Iacchus' companion,[72]
has come among Cadmean mothers,
438 a sacred fawnskin girdling her flank,
441 in her hand brandishing lightly the thyrsus.[73]
439 The mothers have loosened their hair,
440 their breasts made frantic by you.
442 Finally, after the mangling of Pentheus' shape,
the Thyads,[74] their bodies released from the frenzy,
were shocked to see their atrocity.
The aunt of shining Bacchus is queen of the ocean's realm,
Ino, the daughter of Cadmus, surrounded by dancing bands of Nereids;[75]
and a boy-child, a newcomer, kin of Bacchus, holds dominion
over the mighty ocean's waves, no insignificant power, Palaemon.[76]
When *you* were a boy you were kidnapped by a Tyrrhenian band,[77]
450 and Nereus settled the swelling sea,
changing the azure waters to meadowlands.
Then came the plane-tree, greening with spring-season foliage,
and groves of laurel, beloved by Phoebus.
The chatter of birds sounds through the branches.
The oars are covered in evergreen ivy,
vines are entwining the mastheads,
a lion from Ida roared in the prow,[78]
a tiger from Ganges is crouched in the stern.
Then the panicking pirates swim in the sea
460 and once in the water they are transformed:
first from the brigands their arms drop away,
their chests then collapse to meet with their bellies,
miniature hands hang down at their sides,
and, with backs curving, under the waves they dive,
slicing the sea with their crescent tails.

Retreating, the sails are followed by curving dolphins.
In Lydia, Pactolus carried you on its rich stream,[79]
taking its waters of gold down between burning banks.
Massagetans,[80] who blend their goblets of milk with blood,
unstrung their bows in defeat and their Getic arrows.[81] 470
The power of Bacchus was felt by the kingdom of axeman
Lycurgus,[82]
and by the Zalacians' ferocious lands,[83]
and by those wandering peoples, buffeted
by neighboring Boreas,[84] and tribes
that Maeotis washes with icy wave,[85]
and those viewed from the zenith above
by Arcadian star and by twofold wagon.[86]
He tamed the scattered Gelonians,[87]
stripped of their weapons the virgin warriors:
with faces downturned they fell to the earth, 480
the squadrons of Thermodon,[88]
they finally laid their light arrows down
and turned into maenads.
Sacred Cithaeron streamed with the blood[89]
from Ophionian slaughter.[90]
The daughters of Proetus made for the woods,[91] and Argos
paid homage to Bacchus, with his stepmother present.[92]
Naxos encircled by the Aegean
gave him to marry a virgin abandoned,[93]
making up for her loss with a better husband. 490
From the dry pumice-rock
flowed Nyctelian liquor:[94]
its chattering streams cut through the meadows.
Deep drank the earth of the juices so sweet,
shining white fountains of snowy-white milk
and thyme-fragranced Lesbian wine.
Bacchus' new bride is escorted to heaven:
Phoebus is singing the ritual hymn
with his locks flooding over his shoulders;
twin Cupids are brandishing torches. 500

At Bacchus' arrival, Jupiter has set aside
his weapon of fire, loathing his thunderbolt.[95]
As long as the luminous stars of the ancient universe keep on
their course,
as long as the Ocean embraces the globe in his circle of waves
and as long as the Moon at the full recovers the fires she let slip,
as long as Lucifer heralds the sun's morning rising[96]
and as long as the Bear up above knows nothing of azure
Nereus,[97]
we shall adore the bright-shining face of our lovely Lyaeus.[98]

ACT 3

(*Oedipus and Creon enter from opposite sides.*)

OEDIPUS

Although your face alone displays the signs of grief,
510 tell out the name: with whose life can we appease the gods?

CREON

"Speak!" is your command—but fear advises silence.

OEDIPUS

If the fall of Thebes is not enough to sway you,
the collapse of power of your kinsfolks' house must.

CREON

You will long not to know what you so seek to know.

OEDIPUS

Ignorance is useless as a remedy for troubles.
Will you really bury information that could save the state?

CREON

When the medicine is foul, one shrinks from being healed.

OEDIPUS

Tell me what you've heard, or you'll be broken by dire suffering
and learn how far the violence of an angered king can go.

CREON

520 Kings always hate the words expressed at their command.

OEDIPUS

I'll have you sent to Erebus, a worthless sacrifice for all,
if you do not reveal the secrets of the rites. Speak out!

CREON

Allow me to be silent. Can any lesser freedom
be requested from a king?

OEDIPUS

Often, freedom that is mute
can do more damage to a king and kingdom than free speech.

CREON

When silence is not allowed, then what is anyone allowed?

OEDIPUS

Silence is subversive after the command to speak.

CREON

Then I ask that patiently you hear the words you have
compelled.

OEDIPUS

Was any person ever punished for speaking under pressure?

CREON

Far off from the city is a grove all dark 530
with ilex trees, near Dirce's watered glen.
A cypress thrusts its head above the towering woods
and with its ever greening bulk it binds the grove;
and an ancient oak tree stretches crooked branches
rotten with decay. Devouring age has broken off
the flank of one; the other, tumbling, with its root
now failed, is suspended, propped up by another's beam.
Here is laurel with its bitter berries, slender linden trees,
Paphian myrtle and the alder soon to stir its oars[99]
across the boundless sea, and rising to the sun 540
the pine tree, offering its knotless flank to western winds.
At the center stands a massive tree: with weighty shade
it overwhelms the lesser woods and stands sole guardian
of the grove by spreading out its branches in a wide embrace.

Beneath it water grimly pools, of light and sunshine
ignorant, and numb with chill perpetual;
a muddy swamp surrounds the sluggish spring.
When the aged priest set foot inside the grove,
there was no delay: the place provided instant night.
550 Then the earth was trenched and flames just seized from pyres
were tossed above the pit. The priest is shrouded
in funereal garb and brandishes a frond.
A mourning vestment overflows his feet;
the ancient, drab and all unkempt, advances;
poison yew-tree wreaths his silver hair.
Black-fleeced sheep, dark cattle too, are dragged
backward. Flames ransack the funeral feast
and in the deadly fire the beast is twitching, still alive.
Next he summons up the ghosts and you, king of the ghosts,
560 and the keeper of the gates of Lethe's lake.[100]
He recites a magic incantation and, menacing
in frenzied tones, he chants the spell that coaxes or compels
the flitting shades. He makes a blood-libation to the fire-pit
and burns the beasts intact and soaks the hole
with copious gore. He offers a libation too
of snowy milk and with his left hand pours on wine,
repeats his incantation and, his gaze fixed on the earth,
he conjures up the ghosts with voice more sonorous and crazed.
Hecate's pack then bayed. Three times the gullies resonated
570 with mournful noise; all the earth was throbbing as the ground
was jolted from below. "They have heard me!" said the priest.
"The words I uttered are fulfilled! Dark Chaos is breached:[101]
hell's population is granted passage to the upper world."[102]
The whole wood cringed, its foliage bristling,
strong oaks were fissured, and a shudder shook
the grove in its entirety, the earth shrank backward
and from deep within it groaned: maybe Acheron could not
easily endure the breaching of its hidden depths;
maybe earth itself, to make a pathway for the dead,
580 resounded as its structure cracked; or else three-headed

Cerberus, enraged and furious, shook his heavy chains.
Suddenly the earth yawns wide: it opened up
into a boundless gulf. With my own eyes I saw the pallid gods
among the shades; with my own eyes, the stagnant lakes
and quintessential night. My frozen blood congealed
and clogged my veins. Out jumped a ferocious troop,
arrayed full-armed, the serpent brood in its entirety,
the squads of brothers sown from Dirce's dragon-teeth.[103] 588
Then a savage Fury screeched, and sightless Rage,[104] 590
and Horror, anything and everything the deathless shadows
breed and hide. Grief, plucking out his hair;
Disease, feebly holding up his weary head;
Age, burdened with herself; and looming Fear;
and Plague, the greedy scourge of the Ogygian people.[105] 589
My courage failed—and even she,[106] familiar with the old man's
rites and powers, stood aghast. Undaunted, bold from lack
of sight, her father summons up the bloodless throng
of cruel Dis: and straightaway, like flitting clouds,
they flutter, sniffing in the breezes of the open sky.
More than all the falling leaves put out by Eryx's mount;[107] 600
more than all the flowers that Hybla bears at spring-time's
height,[108]
when swarming bees are massed in tight-knit globe;
more than all the waves that the Ionian Sea demolishes;
more than the all birds that leave their winters, fleeing
icy Strymon's threats,[109] to cut through sky,
exchanging Arctic snows for Nile's warmth—
so many were the throngs the wizard's call elicited.
In a panic, shivering souls seek out the hiding-places
in the shady grove. First to emerge out of the ground,
his right hand grasping by the horns a wild bull, 610
was Zethus, with him Amphion, a lyre in his left hand,
with his sweet music charmer of the rocks.[110]
Niobe stood among her sons,[111] safe in her arrogance at last,
holding up her head all vehement with pride
and counting up her shades. Then, a mother worse than her,

Agave in her frenzy,[112] and behind her the entire band
that portioned up their king. Behind the Bacchants follows
Pentheus, mangled but still raging, keeping up his threats.
At long last, after many, many summons, one lifted up
620 his skulking head and, sitting far off from the crowd,
he hides himself. The priest insists, and doubles
his Stygian prayers, till he succeeds in bringing the concealed face
into the open—Laius. I shudder as I say it.
There he stood, a ghastly sight, with smears of blood across his limbs,
his filthy hair all matted with disgusting dirt,
and then in frenzied tones he says: "You family of Cadmus,
wild, delighting ever in the murder of your own,
shake your thyrsus, rip apart your sons with hands
fanatic—this would be better. Thebes' greatest crime
630 is mother-love.[113] My fatherland, you are the victim not of wrath
divine, but crime. You are afflicted, not by south wind[114]
bringing grief with his oppressive blast, not by the earth
with parching breath, by rainy air too little sated,
but by your blood-stained king, who, as reward for savage slaughter,
claimed the scepter and—unspeakable—the bedroom of his father,[115]
638 who thrust himself right back into his origins, and had his mother
bear to him unnatural offspring and (something wild beasts hardly do)
640 sired brothers for himself. He is an evil all entwined,
a monster more entangled even than his Sphinx.
You! You! Wielding the scepter in your blood-stained hand—
You I'll hound, and all your city, I, your father unavenged,
and with me I shall bring the Fury, bridesmaid at your bedding,
I'll bring her as she cracks her lash, I'll overturn this family

of incest, and with unnatural warfare I shall crush this house.
So, Thebans, from your borders with all speed expel the king
and chase him into exile, anywhere. With his deadly step
let him leave your land, and it will then renew its grasses,
greening with the flowers of spring; pure air will be restored 650
by the living breeze, and to the woodlands beauty will return.
Doom and Plague and Death and Toil, Decay and Pain,
his fitting entourage, will leave along with him;
and he himself will long to quit our land
with hurried step, but I shall shackle him severely
and hold him back. Uncertain of his way he'll creep along,
fumbling with an old man's stick his dreary path.[116] Thebes,
deprive him of his earth; I, his father, will take away his sky."

OEDIPUS

An icy quivering has pierced my bones and limbs.
Exactly what I feared I'd do I am accused of having done— 660
but Merope still wed to Polybus refutes the marriage-bed
atrocity, and Polybus alive and well
acquits my hands. Each parent clears me from the charge
of murder and of incest. What room is left for guilt?
And Laius—Thebes was mourning for his disappearance
long before I stepped upon Boeotian soil.[117]
Is the old man telling lies, or is some god oppressing Thebes?
Ah! Now I've got you—partners in a cunning plot:
the priest invents those charges, using gods to shield
his deceit, and to you he promises my scepter. 670

CREON

To me? To have my sister then deposed from power?
If inviolable loyalty to my kinsfolks' hearth
did not keep me firmly in the rank I have,
that eminence would terrify me—always
anxious to excess. But you—may you safely shed
this burden without it crushing you as you depart:
it will be safer for you now to set yourself in lower place.

OEDIPUS

What? Are you urging me to voluntarily resign
my weighty kingship?

CREON

This is advice I'd give to men
680 still free to make a choice about their rank:
but you already have your fate, and that you must endure.

OEDIPUS

To praise the humble life and speak of sleep and leisure—
that's the surest route for someone who desires to rule.
Often it's the restless ones who make a mask of rest.

CREON

So all my years of loyalty are not enough to clear me?

OEDIPUS

Loyalty provides disloyal people with a chance to injure.

CREON

Freed from royal responsibilities, right royal benefits
I reap: my family has influence among the throng
of citizens and no day ever follows night without
690 the generosity of my kinsman's scepter
flowing over toward my hearth. Through my favor
many people have security and finery and lavish feasts.
What could I imagine missing from a life so fortunate?

OEDIPUS

The one thing that *is* missing. Blessings never have a limit.

CREON

So like a guilty man, I must fall with case unheard?

OEDIPUS

Did *you* listen to my testimony of *my* life? No.
Did Tiresias conduct a hearing of *my* case? No. Yet
I'm seen as guilty. You two set the pattern; I just follow it.

CREON

And if I am innocent?

OEDIPUS

Kings often fear suspicions
as if they were certainties.

CREON

If groundless terrors scare him, 700
real terrors he deserves.

OEDIPUS

Any suspect, once set free,
will hate. So—all that is suspicious has to fall.

CREON

That breeds hatred.

OEDIPUS

He who is too much afraid of hatred
is incapable of ruling. It's fear keeps kingdoms safe.

CREON

He who wields the scepter cruelly and tyrannically
dreads his victims. Fear rebounds against its instigator.

OEDIPUS

(*To guards.*)

You there! Keep the guilty man well-guarded in a rocky
dungeon.
Myself, I'll make my way back to my royal hearth.

(*Guards escort Creon away; Oedipus goes into the palace.*)

CHORUS

Oedipus, you're not the cause of such terrible jeopardy,
it is not your fate that's making a target of Labdacus' family;[118] 710
no, it's the gods' inveterate rage
that persecutes us. The grove of Castalia
offered its shade to the traveler from Sidon[119]
and Dirce's spring watered the Tyrian settlers
from the time when the son of mighty Agenor,
tired of chasing to the ends of the earth what Jupiter stole,
fearfully halted under our tree,

humbling himself to the one who had robbed him.
Instructed by warnings from Phoebus to follow
720 a wandering heifer who'd never been governed
by ploughshare or lumbering wagon's curved yoke,
he abandoned his roaming and gave to his people
a name from that ill-omened cow.
From that time onward, the earth has produced
new monstrosities, always.
Either a serpent, emerged from deep gullies,
hisses around the antique timbers;[120]
towering over the pines and Chaonian trees[121]
it raised up its head of azure
730 while its bulk was left sprawled on the ground.[122]
Or else earth, teeming full with unnatural progeny,
poured out an army: the summons to war sounded out
from coiled horn; the trumpet's curved bronze
blasted its piercing blare [and][123]
they deployed for the first time their tongues
and their mouths, till then inarticulate,
to utter their war-cries in voices unknown.[124]
Armies of kinfolk people the fields.
The progeny, fitting the seed it was sown from,
740 measured out life in a single day,
born only after the passage of Lucifer,[125]
dying before the rising of Hesperus.
The newcomer shudders at such great monstrosities,[126]
fearing the warfare this fresh population brings,
till the soldiery in their ferocity fell
and their earth-mother saw her nurslings,
newly brought forth, returned to her breast.
May that be an end to citizen atrocity!
May those battles of brothers be knowledge enough
750 for Hercules' Thebes.
What else? There's the fate of the grandson of Cadmus,[127]
when the horns of a long-lived stag
covered his forehead with branches so strange,[128]

when his hounds gave chase to their very own master.
Hurtling away from the woodlands and mountains
raced swift-foot Actaeon. His step ever faster
while ranging through glades and through boulders,
he shies from the feathers wafted by breezes,[129]
avoiding the snares that he set himself,
till in a tranquil pool's water 760
he saw reflected his horns and his animal face,
the pool where the goddess of modesty all too ferocious
had bathed her virginal limbs.[130]

ACT 4

OEDIPUS

My mind revolves these troubling thoughts, renews its fears.
The gods above, the gods below, declare that Laius died
by crime of mine, but in its innocence my mind resists,
denying it: it knows itself much better than do the gods.
Yet my memory creeps back, along a trail now faint:
a man I met who fell when struck by my stick
and passed to hell,[131] but he began it, an arrogant old man 770
who rammed the younger with his chariot, far away from
Thebes,
where the land of Phocis splits the roads in triple fork.

(*Jocasta enters.*)

My soul-mate wife, unravel my perplexities, I pray:
when Laius died, what was his span of life?
Did he perish in the prime of vigor or in broken age?

JOCASTA

Between old age and youth, but closer to old age.

OEDIPUS

Did numerous companions surround the royal flank?

JOCASTA

Most went astray, perplexed by how the road divided.
The task kept just a few in loyalty beside the chariot.

OEDIPUS

780 Did any of the escort meet the same fate as the king?

JOCASTA

One shared his lot, thanks to his loyalty and courage.

OEDIPUS

(*To himself.*)

I have the guilty man: the number tallies, and the place—

(*To Jocasta.*)

but add the time.

JOCASTA

Ten harvests have been reaped since then.

(*Old Corinthian enters.*)

OLD CORINTHIAN

Corinth's people summon you to the kingdom
of your father: Polybus has gained eternal rest.

OEDIPUS

How cruelly Fortune batters me from every side!
Come, expound the fate by which my father fell.

OLD CORINTHIAN

A gentle sleep released his aged soul.

OEDIPUS

My sire lies dead, without a trace of murder.
790 I declare: without offense I now can raise to heaven
hands undefiled, that need to fear no crimes.
Yet—there remains the portion of my fate that terrifies me more.

OLD CORINTHIAN

Your father's kingdom will dispel your every fear.

OEDIPUS

I would claim my father's kingdom; it's my mother that I dread.

OLD CORINTHIAN

You fear your parent? She longs for your return
anxious, in suspense.

OEDIPUS

It is my love keeps me away.

OLD CORINTHIAN

You'll leave her widowed?

OEDIPUS

You touch exactly on my fears.

OLD CORINTHIAN

Speak out the buried dread that weighs upon your mind.
I am expert at rendering to kings a loyal silence.

OEDIPUS

Delphi's warning makes me dread a marriage with my mother.[132] 800

OLD CORINTHIAN

Cease your empty terrors and abandon those vile forebodings. Merope was not your real parent.

OEDIPUS

What does she gain from raising an adopted child?

OLD CORINTHIAN

Kings' children are the tie that binds proud loyalty.

OEDIPUS

Tell how you know the secrets of her bedroom.

OLD CORINTHIAN

When you were small, these hands of mine conveyed you to your mother.

OEDIPUS

You conveyed me to my mother—but who to you?

OLD CORINTHIAN

A herdsman, underneath Cithaeron's snowy ridge.

OEDIPUS

And what chance was it took you to those forests?

OLD CORINTHIAN

I was on that mountain, herding my horned flocks. 810

OEDIPUS

Now tell me the specific marks upon my body.

OLD CORINTHIAN

Your soles had been pierced through by iron;
you got your name from the swollen maiming of your feet.[133]

OEDIPUS

Who was the man who gifted you my body?
I need to know.

OLD CORINTHIAN

The herdsman of the royal flocks.
Beneath him served a lesser band of herdsmen.

OEDIPUS

Tell me his name.

OLD CORINTHIAN

The early memories of aged men
grow feeble, failing from exhaustion and from long decay.

OEDIPUS

Can you recognize the man from his appearance and his face?

OLD CORINTHIAN

820 Perhaps I could: a faded memory buried deep by time
can often be revived by a tiny prompt.

OEDIPUS

All the herds were driven to the sacred altars earlier,
with their guardians: go, slaves, and quickly
call the man who is responsible for all the flocks.

JOCASTA[134]

Whether this concealment is the work of reason or of fortune,
let things stay hidden always that for so long have been hidden.
The man who digs it up is often damaged by the naked truth.

OEDIPUS

What damage greater than all *this* can possibly be feared?[135]

JOCASTA

Great it is, be sure of it, the thing you seek with such great effort.
830 The issue is between the well-being of the state and of the king,
an even contest. Keep your hands well clear.
Without your challenge let the fates unfold themselves.

OEDIPUS

It's not a good idea to disturb a happy situation;
but there's no risk in stirring desperate circumstances.

JOCASTA

Are you seeking something nobler than the lineage of kings?
See that you not recoil from the father you discover.

OEDIPUS

Certainty is what I seek, even if of blood regrettable:
so set am I on knowing.

(*Phorbas enters.*)

—Here is the aged elder,
once controller of the royal flock,
Phorbas.

(*To Old Corinthian.*)

Do you recall the old man's name or face? 840

OLD CORINTHIAN

My mind welcomes his appearance. That face of his
is neither totally familiar nor again unknown to me.

OEDIPUS

(*To Phorbas.*)

While Laius ruled the kingdom, did you, his servant,
herd the ample flocks beneath Cithaeron's tracts?

PHORBAS

Cithaeron, fertile with fresh pasturage, always
offers summer meadows to our flock.

OLD CORINTHIAN

Do you know me?

PHORBAS

My wavering memory hesitates.

OEDIPUS

Was some boy-child handed on by you, once, to this man?
Speak out. You hesitate? Why does color change your cheeks?
Why do you search for words? The truth detests delay. 850

PHORBAS

You stir up matters clouded by time's lengthy passage.

OEDIPUS

Speak, or pain will drive you to the truth.

PHORBAS

I gave that man a useless gift, a baby.
He could not have lived to see the light of day.

OLD CORINTHIAN

Don't say that: alive he is—and he will stay alive, I pray.

OEDIPUS

Why do you allege the baby that you handed on could not survive?

PHORBAS

A slender shackle, driven through both feet,
pinned his legs together. A swelling born inside the wound
was burning the boy's body with a foul infection.

OEDIPUS

(*To himself.*)

860 Why seek further? Fate is standing close already.

(*To Phorbas.*)

Inform me who the baby was.

PHORBAS

My loyalty forbids.

OEDIPUS

Bring fire, someone! Flames will soon expel your loyalty.

PHORBAS

You'll seek the truth through ways so bloody?
Pardon, please.

OEDIPUS

If I seem wild to you,
beyond control, revenge lies ready in your hands:
tell the truth. Who *was* he? Sired by what father?
Born from what mother?

PHORBAS

Born from your own wife.

OEDIPUS

Earth, gape wide! And you, the king of darkness,
lord of shades, into deepest Tartarus carry off
this backward interchange of stock and offshoot. 870
Citizens, heap rocks upon my monstrous head,
slay me with your weapons: let sons and fathers at me
with the sword, let husbands, brothers, arm their hands
against me, let the plague-sick people snatch up
brands from pyres to hurl at me. I walk, the evil of the age,
abomination of the gods, destruction of the sacred law,
already, on the day I drew my first raw breaths,
deserving death.

(*To himself.*)

Now's the time to restore your courage keen,
now, the time for daring that is worthy of your crimes.—
Go, go quickly, make for the palace with hurried step: 880
congratulate your mother that her house is swelled by
offspring.[136]

CHORUS

If my fate I could fashion
to match my desire,
my sails I would trim to the light west wind,
keeping the yard-arms from shaking beneath
the force of a heavy blast.
May a breeze flowing
moderately, gently, not veering direction,
conduct my ship fearless;
may a life without danger convey me, 890
running along on a middling course.
In fear of the Cnossian king,[137]
while seeking the stars in his madness,
trusting his novel devices,

striving to outdo the genuine
birds and asking too much
of his wings that were false,
the boy stole the name of the strait.[138]
Older and cannier, Daedalus
900 balanced a middling path,
hovering midway beneath the cloud,
awaiting his fledgling—
as the bird who's escaped
from the threat of the hawk assembles
her brood all scattered by fear—
till the boy moved his hands in the sea,
hands all entwined in the fetters[139]
from his audacious journey.
To exceed the mean
910 is to teeter precarious.
But what's this? The doors creak,
and, grieving, a slave of the king
batters his head with his hand.—
Tell us what news you bring.

ACT 5

MESSENGER

When Oedipus had grasped the fate foretold for him,
his monstrous parentage, when he'd condemned himself
as guilty of the crime, with grim intent he headed for the palace
and with hurried step he went inside the hateful rooms;
just as a Libyan lion rages through the fields,
920 tossing tawny mane with threatening brow.
His face is wild with fury, glaring are his eyes,
he groans and mutters deeply, icy sweat glides over
all his limbs, he's foaming at the mouth, rehearsing threats,
his mighty anguish, buried deep, now overflows.
Savagely within his soul he's plotting—something huge

and matching his own fate. "Why do I delay my punishment?"
he says. "Someone should attack this criminal breast
with steel or crush me down with stones or blazing flame.
What tigress or what bird of prey will pounce
upon my guts? You yourself, accursed Cithaeron, 930
encompasser of crimes, from your forests launch
your wild beasts at me, unleash your maddened dogs—
now bring Agave back.[140] My mind, why fear death?
Only death can save an innocent from Fortune."[141]
This said, he lays his sinning hand upon his sword-hilt,
draws the blade. Then: "Is this it? Can you atone for crimes
so heinous with a penalty so quick, and settle all your debts
with a single thrust? You die—and this will satisfy your
father—
but what about your mother and your children, brought so
wrongly
into the world, what will you give your grieving fatherland, 940
which with its vast collapse is paying for your crime?
You cannot pay your debts. Let that same Nature, who inverted
her established statutes in the case of Oedipus alone,
devising novel births, be altered for my punishment.
May you be allowed to live again, and die again,
to be reborn repeatedly, so every time you'll pay
with different punishments.—But use your wits, you miserable
man:
what cannot happen more than once must happen over time;
your choice must be a long, slow death. You must find a way
to roam not mingling with the dead and buried, and yet 950
banished from the living. You must die, but not as much as
father.
Do you hesitate, my mind?"—And a sudden drenching shower
overwhelms his face and floods his cheeks with tears:
"Are tears enough? Is this paltry liquid all my eyes
will shed so far? They must accompany their tears,
driven from their sockets. These married eyeballs

must be dug out right away." He spoke. He raves with anger:
his features are ablaze with menace and ferocious fire,
his eyeballs almost jumping from their sockets;
960 his face is violent, reckless, fierce, enraged,
intent alone on digging: with a groan and terrifying roar
he gouged his fingers deep into his face. His glaring eyes start forth
to meet them; tracking their familiar hands with eagerness
and of their own accord, they meet their wounds halfway.
Greedily with hands like hooks he probes his sockets,
rips and wrenches out entirely, from their deepest roots,
both his eyeballs. In the holes his hands are clinging,
buried deep, with fingernails scratching out
the hollow spaces of the eyes and empty sockets.
970 His rage is impotent, his frenzy out of bounds:
so awful is the risk of daylight. He lifts his head,
surveys the sky's expanse with hollow eyeballs,
and tests his night. He snaps the shreds still hanging
from the mess of dug-out eyes and calls triumphantly
to all the gods: "Now spare my fatherland, I pray.
Now justice has been done by me and I have paid my debts.
I have found a night at last that fits my marriage-bed."
A ghastly shower floods his face and from the torn-out veins
his mangled head spews streams of blood.

CHORUS

980 By fate we are driven—so yield to fate!
The threads of the spindle of destiny
cannot be changed by our troubled anxieties.
All of our sufferings, all of our actions,
for we mortals on earth, come from above.
Lachesis keeps to her distaff's decrees,
which she has wound with her pitiless hand.[142]
Existence proceeds on its track preordained.
Our first day already determines our last.
Even god cannot change what is rushing along

in the mesh of cause and effect. 990
Each individual's sequence of destiny goes on its way
and no prayer can alter it.
Many are damaged by their terror alone;
many have met with their fate while shunning their fate.[143]
The doors gave a sound. Here he is, with no guide
to help as he struggles along on his journey,
bereaved of the light.

OEDIPUS

All is well, it's over now: I've paid in full my debts to father.
I like this darkness. Which god is it, at last appeased,
that drenches my head with this black cloud? 1000
Which god forgives my crimes? I have escaped the gaze of
daylight.
Nothing, father-slayer, do you owe to your own right hand:
it is the light that's run from *you*. This face is right for Oedipus.

CHORUS

Oh look! With speeding step Jocasta has rushed out,
ferocious, frantic, just like the Theban mother when,[144]
aghast and raving, she had torn her son's head off
—and realized it. She hesitates to speak to him, the
ruined man,
wants to, fears to speak. Now shame has given way to misery,
but her first words are sticking in her throat.

JOCASTA

What am I to call you?
Son? You shake your head? You *are* my son. That shames you?[145] 1010
Speak, my son, although you'd rather not. Why turn away your
head
and empty face?

OEDIPUS

Who's stopping my enjoyment of my darkness?
Who gives me back my eyes? That is my mother's voice, my
mother's!
My efforts are entirely gone to waste. It isn't right for us

monstrosities to meet again. The wide, wide sea should
separate us,
a distant land should keep us far apart, and if there is another
world suspended under this one, facing unfamiliar stars
and distant sun, then one of us should go there.

JOCASTA

The blame belongs to fate: no one is made guilty by his fate.

OEDIPUS

1020 Spare your words now, Mother, spare my ears,
I pray you, by these remnants of my mutilated body,
by my blood's ill-omened guarantee,[146]
by all that's right and wrong in our relationship.[147]

JOCASTA

Why so numb, my mind? Why do you refuse to pay the penalty
for crimes you shared? Because of you, incestuous woman,
the decency of human law is jumbled and destroyed.
Die! Use the sword to drive out your abominable spirit.
Even if the father of the gods himself, who shakes the world,
should hurl at me with savage hand his shimmering weapons,[148]
1030 I could never pay a retribution equaling my crimes,
a monstrous mother. Death is my resolve; the way of death
I must discover. —Come, then, if you really are a father-slayer,
help your mother—this is left, the last part of your task.—

(*Oedipus does nothing.*)

Then let me seize his sword. —By this blade my husband
Died. —Why use a name that is not true? —He was
my husband's father. —Shall I drive the sword
into my breast, or bury it deep inside my naked throat?
You know not how to choose the wound? Target this, my hand,
this, the fertile womb that bore me sons and husband.

(*Jocasta stabs herself.*)

CHORUS

1040 She lies slain. Her hand is dying as it wounds;
the flood of gore has forced the sword out too.

OEDIPUS

You, fate-declarer, you, the god who guards the truth,[149]
I rebuke you: my father was my only debt to fate.
Twice a parent-slayer, guilty more than I had feared,
I have killed my mother. It is by my crime that she is dead.
You liar, Phoebus, I have outdone the wickedness of fate.

(*To himself.*)

With nervous step now follow paths you cannot see.
Setting feet down warily to make your tracks,
steer your blinded night with faltering hand.
No, hurtle forward, slipping, sliding as you walk, 1050
go, get out, get on your way! —Stop! Don't fall upon your
mother!

(*To the Thebans.*)

Look, all of you in body weary, burdened by disease
and dragging fainting hearts, I flee, I'm leaving.
Lift up your heads. Behind me comes a sky
of gentler nature. Whoever on the sickbed clings
to slender life may lightly breathe the living
draughts of air. Go, carry help to the abandoned.
The deadly infections of this land I take away with me.
Destructive Fates, the quaking shudder of Disease,
and Wasting, and black Plague, and raging Agony, 1060
come with me, with me. You are the guides I choose.

Hercules Mad

This play, which comes first in both the major manuscript traditions of Seneca's tragedies, is modeled principally, though loosely, on Euripides' *Heracles*. In both versions, Hercules is on the point of completing the last labor assigned to him by the tyrant Eurystheus, which is to bring up from Hades the three-headed guard dog Cerberus. Hercules and his family, including his mortal father Amphitryon, his wife Megara, and his children, have been residing at Thebes, the home city of Megara (she is the daughter of the king, Creon).

In Hercules' absence, Lycus, who hails from nearby Euboea, has killed Creon and assumed the throne; to secure his position (and in the belief that Hercules himself is dead), Lycus seeks to marry Megara, and only when she refuses does he decide to slay all of Hercules' kin, lest the sons reclaim the kingship. (Euripides, however, makes no mention of the wooing of Hercules' wife.) At this juncture, Hercules returns, together with Theseus, whom he has rescued from the underworld, and while Theseus describes Hades in detail (this again is absent from Euripides' version), Hercules goes off to kill Lycus. Upon his return, more than two thirds into the play, Hercules begins to show signs of the madness that will cause him to kill his own wife and sons.

In Seneca's treatment, this comes as no surprise: in the prologue, Juno announces her intention to punish Hercules, whom she resents as one of Jupiter's bastard sons, in just this way. Hercules' madness is the result of the sudden intervention of the goddess "Frenzy," sent by Juno (along with Iris, the messenger goddess), to destroy his wits. When he recovers from his bout of insanity, Hercules is understandably distraught, but is persuaded by his father to continue living, and in the end takes refuge, at Theseus' invitation, in Athens.

Introduction

DAVID KONSTAN

In Euripides' drama, it is the shock of Hercules' triumphant return from Hades and rescue of his family, which gives way in turn to his utter mortification, that produces the tragic effect. Critics have long debated whether the hero's madness is a symptom or consequence of his violent nature or an arbitrary affliction that merely reveals humanity's universal vulnerability to chance. Recently, for example, Robert Emmet Meagher has affirmed that "Herakles' madness neither required then nor requires now any elaborate explanation for those who have taken part in the insane rampage of war"; he is a "trauma victim," and his rampage is but an extension of his general savagery.[1] Kathleen Riley, in turn, takes the opposite view: "There is nothing in Euripides' portrait of the sane hero to suggest that killing is attractive to him or that his normal use of violence is excessive."[2] On either interpretation, Hercules' sudden fall may well arouse pity in the audience, as well as the fear that they themselves might suffer such a calamity: the story is well calculated to induce the emotions that Aristotle deemed appropriate to tragedy.

By contrast with Euripides, Seneca's version seems so charged with rhetoric and even bombast as to turn the hero's suffering into a matter for wonder or awe rather than something that spectators could readily perceive as pertaining to themselves. But it is clearly a mistake to judge Senecan drama by the criteria of Aristotle or of Greek tragedy. For one thing, as a good Stoic, Seneca will not necessarily have approved of stimulating passions such as pity and terror. Gregory Staley (2010, 95) has recently argued that Seneca's vivid imagery "may arouse our emotions, but these are only preliminary and involuntary." Staley is referring to Seneca's account, in *On Anger* (2.2.6), of a class of responses that are not emotions (*adfectus*) strictly speaking but rather "the initial preliminaries to emotions" (*principia proludentia adfectibus*)—that is, what in Greek are called *propatheiai* or "pre-emotions." Seneca defines these as "motions that do not arise through our will" (*motus qui non uoluntate nostra fiunt*) and are therefore irresistible and do not yield to reason. They include such responses as shivering or goose bumps when one is sprinkled with cold water, aversion to certain kinds of touch, the rising of one's hair at bad news, blushing at obscene language, and vertigo produced by heights. Further, they include reactions to comic stage shows (*ludicra scaenae spectacula*), historical events, songs and martial trumpeting, horrible paintings, and the sight of punishments (even when deserved—thus differing from Aristotle's notion of pity as a response to unmerited misfortune) as well as contagious laughter and sadness (this last is no more genuine grief, says Seneca, than, the frown evoked by seeing a shipwreck in a mime [*ad conspectum mimici naufragii*]).[3] What these various reactions have in common is that they do not depend upon assent, and therefore do not qualify as true emotions, according to the Stoics.[4] Staley (2010, 74) concludes: "If the emotional pull we feel in response to vivid events is not really emotion in the full Stoic sense of that word, then it cannot really be harmful." In producing involuntary shock or horror rather than fear, which requires our assent to the proposition that we face a genuine danger, Seneca leaves it in the power of the audience to make or withhold the cognitive judgments that are essential to a true emotion.

A second consideration in evaluating Seneca's drama is that Hercules was regarded by the Stoics as a model of virtue. Seneca himself compares Cato to Hercules and Odysseus as Stoic heroes (*On the Constancy of the Sage* 1.2.1; cf. *On Peace of Mind* 1.16.4), and the Stoic Cornutus, a freedman of one of Seneca's relations who assumed the family name Annaeus and was tutor to Seneca's nephew, Lucan, wrote in his *Compendium of the Traditions of Greek Theology* (an allegorical account of Greek myths): "Heracles is the rationality (*logos*) in things as a whole, in accord with which nature is strong and powerful. . . . He is named perhaps from the fact that he pertains to heroes, since he is the one who causes noble men to be celebrated (*kleïzesthai*). For the ancients used to call 'heroes' those who were powerful in their bodies and souls and who were believed, for this reason, to partake of the divine race" (31). Did Seneca mean his Hercules to represent the virtues of the Stoic sage, who fearlessly conquers external threats to mankind and learns even to overcome the greatest harm of all, a temporary lapse of sanity to which even the sage is susceptible (cf. Cicero, *Tusculan Disputations* 3.11)?[5] Or is Hercules a mixed figure, as John Fitch (1987, 21n19) argues, powerful to be sure, and successful in eliminating many evils from the world, but at the same time an arrogant, hubristic, indeed megalomaniacal figure "whose madness arises from his own psyche"?[6] Where learned and perceptive critics of Seneca differ so radically, it is prudent to wonder whether the question of Hercules' character may be poorly formulated. Roland Mayer, an astute scholar in his own right, has sought to resolve the dilemma in what may seem a drastic manner: "Now to my mind there is no solution to such disagreements, thanks to Seneca himself, whose dramatic competence is not something we should yet take for granted. . . . We are presented with automata, puppets who rarely if ever come off their strings" (1990, 273). But a puppet Hercules could well have been endowed with a simple or uniform character, for good or ill. If we accept that speechifying and over-the-top rhetoric, laced with recondite and sometimes enigmatic allusions to earlier texts and traditions, are part of the fabric and indeed the fun of Senecan tragedy, we can still recognize that a purely virtuous protagonist would have made for a dull drama. As Plutarch observes in his essay *How a Youth Should Listen to Poems* (25D), the charm of poetry lies in excitement and surprise (*to empathes kai paralogon kai aprosdokêton*), and to this end it requires dramatic changes of fortune and variety of events, for "what is simple lacks passion and narrative movement" (*to d'haploun apathes kai amuthon*). This is why good people, and even gods when they involve themselves in human affairs, are not consistently successful and free of fault, since this would yield a tale without the shock of danger and struggle (*akindunôn kai anantagônistôn*).

Seneca's characters speak with the epigrammatic flair that he manifests in his prose writings as well; but they also seek to express the inexpressible, to make vivid extreme conditions like the landscape of Hades or passions like Juno's vindictiveness, to reproduce the voice of madness and the limitless sorrow that ensues upon the realization that one has slain one's family, or to depict the insensitivity of a tyrant who woos the daughter of the man he has just murdered. The very notion that a mortal may be made a god—no longer outlandish in imperial Rome, where deceased emperors might attain divine honors—would seem to demand new resources of language. In this respect, I see a kind of modernism in Seneca's plays, akin to that of Lucan's epic on the civil war: an effort to capture the strangeness of the new world in which he lived rather than to normalize it through the use of classical diction and restraint.

I omit comment here on the vexed question of whether and how Seneca's tragedies were performed, referring the reader to the general introduction to this volume. I have no doubt that they could be acted, and one possible venue is in the villas of the wealthy, who could hire or train their own troupes; the theatrical decor of third and fourth style Pompeian wall painting might serve as a perfect backdrop for such performances.

There are two main manuscript traditions of the tragedies, and these seem to have parted company fairly early. Both will have undergone not just corruption but also correction in the course of transmission, and the choice between one or the other (or, where neither provides good sense, subsequent emendations) depends on subtle intuitions of Senecan style. In a number of places, Otto Zwierlein's Oxford Classical Text of Seneca's plays,[7] which appeared the year before Fitch's edition of the *Hercules*, adopts a different and perhaps preferable reading, but where—as almost always—I felt that Fitch's text was acceptable I followed it. I have also relied heavily on his immensely learned commentary, which clarifies many difficult points in the drama. My own notes provide only bare identifications of characters and places mentioned or alluded to in the play. I have not included a guide to pronunciation, but I observe the traditional rule of sounding consonants and long vowels as in English, with accent on the penultimate syllable where that is long and, when it is short, on the preceding syllable; thus Cocytus, the river in Hades, is pronounced "Co-SI-tus" (long "I"), Ixion is Ix-I-on, Alcides is Al-CI-des (in all these cases, the accent falls on the second-to-last syllable).

The translation is in verse: iambic pentameters for the dialogue portions, which in Latin is registered in the six-beat iambic senarius that is customary for conversation, and the shorter tetrameter (or ballad meter) for the choruses, for which Seneca employs a variety of lyric meters. I have tried to preserve the rhetorical flavor of Seneca's language and many of the internal repetitions and echoes that run like leitmotivs throughout the play. I believe the reader can feel confident of the fidelity of my translation to the original; I dearly hope that it also reads like English and that it provides no obstacles to being staged.

Finally, I wish to express my deep gratitude to John Fitch, who kindly read through the entire translation, offering kind encouragement and numerous improvements and saving me from more errors than I dare recall. Shadi Bartsch added her wise suggestions, and the anonymous reader for the University of Chicago Press provided detailed and helpful comments.

Suggested Reading

Fitch, John G. 1987. *Seneca's* Hercules Furens: *A Critical Text with Introduction and Commentary*. Ithaca.

Graver, Margaret. 2007. *Stoicism and Emotion*. Chicago.

Hall, Edith. 2008. "Introduction: A Lost Chord of Ancient Culture." In *New Directions in Ancient Pantomime*, edited by Edith Hall and Rosie Wyles, 1–41. Oxford.

Mayer, Roland. 1990. "Seneca's Hercules." Review of Fitch 1987. *Classical Review* 40: 272–74.

Staley, George A. 2010. *Seneca and the Idea of Tragedy*. Oxford.

Zanobi, Alessandra. 2008. "The Influence of Pantomime on Seneca's Tragedies." In *New Directions in Ancient Pantomime*, edited by Edith Hall and Rosie Wyles, 227–58. Oxford

Zimmermann, Bernhard. 2008. "Seneca and Pantomimus." In *New Directions in Ancient Pantomime*, edited by Edith Hall and Rosie Wyles, 218–27. Oxford.

Zwierlein, Otto. 1984. *Senecas Hercules im Lichte kaiserzeitlicher und spätantiker Deutung: Mit einem Anhang über "tragische Schuld" sowie Seneca-Imitationen bei Claudian und Boethius*. Wiesbaden.

Hercules Furens

LUCIUS ANNAEUS SENECA

TRANSLATED BY DAVID KONSTAN

DRAMATIS PERSONAE

JUNO, sister and wife of Jupiter
AMPHITRYON, husband of Alcmene and stepfather of Hercules
MEGARA, wife of Hercules and daughter of Creon
LYCUS, tyrant of Thebes who took Creon's throne
HERCULES, son of Jupiter and Alcmene
THESEUS, king of Athens
CHORUS of Thebans

The drama takes place in front of the royal palace at Thebes. There is an altar on the stage.

ACT 1

JUNO

I, Thundering Jupiter's sister[1]—for what other name
is left me, once his wife?—have abandoned him, forever
faithless, and the precincts of the upper air;
driven from the heavens, I've ceded place to rivals.
I must inhabit earth: my rivals occupy
the sky. Here the Bear,[2] high constellation in
the lofty region of the frozen pole, guides
Greek fleets; there, where day lengthens in early spring,
there shines the bull that bore Europa of Tyre
through waves.[3] Here widely wandering Pleiades 10
display the troop that's feared by boats and sea.[4]
Orion, menacing of sword, here scares
the gods,[5] and golden Perseus has his stars.

There sparkle the twin Tyndarids' bright stars and
those at whose birth the shifting earth stood fast.[6]
Nor did just Bacchus or his mother reach
the gods:[7] lest any part be free of vice
the night sky wears the garland of the Cnossian girl.[8]
But I complain too late: how often has
20 that one fierce dire Theban land, bestrewn with
sinful daughters, made a stepmother of me.
Let Alcmene rise victorious and take my
place, and her son with her seize the promised
stars—for whose birth the world dropped a day
and Phoebus shone late on the Eastern sea,
ordered to hold his light still sunk in the Ocean[9]—
my hatred still won't quit: my furious mind
will drive my forceful rage, and savage pain
will wage eternal wars with peace destroyed.
30 What wars? Whatever horrid thing the hostile
earth creates, what sea or air has borne,
terrible, dire, plaguey, dreadful, wild,
is crushed and tamed. *He* overcomes and thrives
on evils, profits from my rage. He turns
my hatred to his praises. When I ordered things
too cruel, I but confirmed his father, gave his
fame room. Where the Sun brings back or sets the day,
tints either Aethiopian with his near flame,[10]
his dauntless courage is worshipped and he's called
40 a god worldwide. Now monsters fail me, it's
less work for Hercules to carry out
commands than for me to command; he gladly
takes orders. What king's fierce decrees can harm
that violent youth? He bears as arms the things
he feared and slew: he comes clad in the lion
and the hydra, and lands never welcome him enough.
Look! He smashed the threshold of infernal
Jove and bore that conquered king's spoils back
50 to those above:[11] I saw it, saw him flaunt

the brother's trophies to his sire, the hellish
night dispelled, Hades laid low. Why not drag off Dis
himself, bound, crushed, in chains, whose lot equaled
Jupiter's, whose rule captured hell and laid bare Styx?
It's little to come back, the shades' own law — 49
has died. The way back from the ghosts below
is bared, the holies of dire Death lie in
the open. But he, bold with the shades' burst jail,
triumphs over me and with a prideful hand
leads the dusky dog through Argive towns.
At the sight of Cerberus I saw daylight falter, — 60
the Sun afraid; a shudder seized me too:
seeing the conquered beast's three necks I feared
what I'd commanded. But I complain too much at
trivia: I should fear for heaven, lest he who
beat the depths attack the heights; he'll snatch his
father's scepter. He'll not, like Bacchus, come
slowly to the stars: he'll seek a route of ruin, want
to rule an empty sky. He swells with proven
might, and by carrying the heavens, he knows
his strength can master them:[12] he placed his head beneath — 70
the world, the task of that vast bulk bent not
his back, the axis of the sky sat better on his neck.
His firm shoulders bore the stars and heavens and
me, as I pressed down: he seeks a pathway to the gods.
Go, my anger, go and crush him as he plans
great things, fight, slash him, you yourself, with your
own hands. Why delegate such hate? O beasts,
be gone! Let Eurystheus himself,[13] tired of ordering, be
idle! Send forth the Titans who dared burst
Jove's empire, open the abyss of Sicily's peak: — 80
let the Doric land tremble at the giant released
and free the fierce fiend's buried neck,[14]
may the Moon on high conceive still other beasts.[15]
But he beat them! You seek an equal to Alcides?[16]
There's none but he—let him war with himself!

Eumenides,[17] roused from the deepest floor of hell,
Come! Let your fiery hair spray flames, your cruel
hands strike snaky blows. Go now, proud man,
and seek the seat of gods, despise what's human.
90 You think you've fled the Styx, the feral ghosts?
Here I'll show you the shades below.
I'll summon discord's goddess,[18] buried in
deep gloom beyond the exile of the guilty:
an obstructing mountain's huge gorge walls her in.
I'll draw and drag from Hades' lowest realm
whatever's left: detested Crime will come
and fierce Impiety licking its own blood,
Error, and Madness ever armed against
itself—*this* agent must my pain exploit!
100 Handmaidens of Hades, start! In frenzy shake
the burning pine, let Megaera bring the throng
bristling with snakes and with a grievous hand
snatch up a vast beam from a burning pyre.
Do this, demand vengeance for the sullied
Styx. Strike your chests, let a harsher fire
burn your minds than fumes in Aetna's forge.
For Alcides to be driven, his wits snared,
stirred up by a grand madness, you first must
rave. Why, Juno, do *you* not yet rage?
110 My sisters, first whirl me, me, drive me from
my mind, if I plan to do something suited
to a stepmother. No, let my wish change:
I pray he may come back, see his boys safe
and return strong of arm. I've found the day
when the hated courage of Hercules can help me.
Did he conquer me? Then may he conquer himself and wish,
to die, though returned from those below. May it serve me
now that he's born of Jove. I'll stand by, aim
his hand so the arrows sent from the string leave[19]
120 true, I'll guide the madman's darts, at last
I'll favor the fighting Hercules. When the crime's complete

his father may admit those hands to heaven.
Wars must now be roused: the day glows and
the bright Sun's rising from the saffron east.

CHORUS[20]

Now a few faint stars shine in the sloping sky;
night, quelled, draws in its roaming fires as
light's reborn. The
morning star drives the radiant host;
The icy sign of the lofty pole,
Arcas' Bear with seven stars, 130
calls the light, the wagon's turned.[21]
The Sun borne on its sky-blue steeds
looks out from topmost Oeta. Thickets
famous for Cadmean Bacchantes,
sprayed with daylight, redden; Phoebus'
sister flees,[22] but she'll return.
Hard toil rises, stimulates
every worry, opens houses.
The shepherd in the icy frost
plucks pale fodder, the herd's set loose. 140
In the open field a calf plays freely,
and its brow is still unbroken;
the idle mothers fill their udders;
a kid, frisky, rambles nimbly
in soft grass, his moves uncertain.
Perched upon the highest branch, one
yearns to spread wings to the new sun,
shrill amid the screeching nestlings—
the concubine of Thrace;[23]
around her cries a mingled flock, 150
affirms the day with varied hum.
The sailor, unsure of his life, trusts sails to winds,
breezes filling the loose furls.
Another, perched on weathered rocks,
arranges his deceptive hooks

or leaning forward
observes the prize with tightened hand:
the line feels the trembling fish.
This for those with the tranquil repose
160 of a blameless life,
a home happy with its own,
a little. Huge hopes roam in cities,
and anxious fear.
One man, sleepless, haunts the proud
entries and harsh doors of kings;
another endlessly adds up blessed riches,
gazes at his treasures,
a pauper midst his piled-up gold.
The people's favor exalts this one,
170 a mob more shifting than the waves,
he's crazed and puffed up by a breeze;
another peddles frenzied lawsuits in the raucous forum,
evilly hires out ire and speeches.
Secure repose has known but few,
who, mindful of fleet time, hold fast
to moments never to return.
While fate allows, live happily.
Life rushes at a rapid run,
and with the speeding day
180 there turns the wheel of the headlong year.
The stern sisters use up their wool,[24]
and their threads do not spin backward.
But the race of humans goes to meet
a swift fate, unsure of itself:
on purpose we seek the Stygian stream.
You hasten with too bold a heart,
Alcides, to visit the sad ghosts:
The Fates arrive at a fixed time.
None may dally when once bidden,
190 none may postpone the written day:
the urn receives the summoned throngs.

Let Glory deliver one to lands
aplenty and loquacious Fame praise him through all cities,
raise him equal to the sky and stars,
may another ridehigh
in a chariot; as for me, may my land shelter
me in a safe secluded home.
Gray age comes to the sluggish,
and the paltry fortune of a tiny home
rests secure in humble station. 200
Proud courage tumbles from on high.
—But Megara, sad, with hair undone,
comes escorting her small flock,
and, slow with age, Alcides' father enters.

ACT 2

AMPHITRYON

Great ruler of Olympus, lord of heaven,
set now at last a limit to harsh toils,
an end to ruin. No day has ever shone
secure for me. The end of one evil is
a step to one to come. No sooner is he back,
a new foe's ready; even before he reaches 210
happy home he goes commanded to
another war. No rest, no time is vacant,
save while he's given orders. A hostile Juno's
pursued him from the very start: was the infant's
age exempt? He conquered monsters before
he could know them. Snakes with crested heads
brought near twin mouths, to which the infant crawled,
staring at the serpents' fiery eyes
with mild and placid gaze, and with serene
expression did he suffer their tight coils 220
and crush their swollen throats with tender hand,
rehearsing for the Hydra. Maenalus'
swift beast,[25] flaunting a head decked with much gold,

was caught at a run; the lion, Nemea's great
scare, was squashed groaning in Herculean arms.
Why cite the Thracian herd's grim stables and
the king given as fodder to his own horses,
or the bristly Maenalian boar that used to shake
the Arcadian woods on Erymanthus' dense cliffs,
230 or the bull, no small scare to a hundred towns?
Amid the far-off flocks of Hesperia's folk
the tri-form herdsman on the Spanish shore
was slain, the prey driven from the farthest west;
Cithaeron set to pasture the cattle Ocean knew.
Ordered to enter the region of the summer
sun, the scorched domain that midday roasts,
he split the mountains on both sides, and cracked
that barrier, making a wide path for the rushing sea.
Assailing next the homes of the opulent grove
240 he snatched the golden spoils of the wakeful snake.
What? Did he not conquer Lerna's vicious beast
by fire, that multiple scourge, and teach it to die,
and strike from the very clouds the Stymphalids
that used to dim the daylight with drawn wings?
The unmarried queen of Thermodon's race, of ever
solitary bed, did not defeat him,
nor did the Augean stables' filthy task
repel hands bold for every brilliant deed.
What good were those? He's gone from the world he saved.
250 The lands sense that the author of their peace
is absent. Lucky and successful crime's
called virtue, good men acquiesce to guilty,
right lies in arms, fear stifles laws. With my
own eyes I saw sons fall, defenders
of their father's reign, by a brutal hand,
and him, last heir of noble Cadmus, die.[26]
I saw the royal ornament ripped from his head
and his head with it. Who'd weep enough for Thebes?
Land fertile of gods, what master makes you quake?

The land from whose fields and fecund folds young 260
warriors, risen sword in hand, did stand,[27]
whose walls Amphion, son of Jove, built up,
attracting stones with tuneful harmonies,
to whose town the father of gods came not just once,
deserting heaven, this town which has received
and made and perhaps (be it pious to say!)
will make gods, is oppressed by a filthy yoke.
Brood of Cadmus and Ophion's race,
where have you sunk? You fear a clueless outcast,
who lacking his own country weighs on ours. 270
He who hunts down crimes on land and sea
and broke cruel scepters with his just hand is gone;
slave now, he bears what he forbids there to be,[28]
and the outcast Lycus holds Herculean Thebes—
but won't keep holding! *He*'ll come and seek revenge,
rise suddenly to the stars; he'll find or make
a way. I pray, arrive safe and return,
at last come victor to your vanquished home.

MEGARA

Rise up, husband, dispel the darkness,
sunder it with strength. If there's no path back and 280
the road is closed, split the world, return, and
send forth with you whatever black night
holds, just as you once stood and sought
a plunging path for a swift stream,
when Tempe,[29] cliffs pulled down, sliced by huge force,
lay open; stricken by your chest the mountain
fell both ways,[30] and through its collapsed mound
the Thessalian torrent ran by a new route;
just so, seek your parents, children, country,
burst out and take the bounds of nature 290
with you, restore what greedy time has hidden for
so many rounds of years, drive forth the throngs
who fear the light, forgetful of themselves.

They're spoils not fit for you if you bring back
just what was ordered. But I speak too proudly,
unknowing of our fate. Where is that day
when I'll hold you and your right hand and grumble
at your slow return and how you forgot me?
To you, O leader of the gods, unbroken bulls will
300 bring their necks by hundreds; mistress of the
grain,[31] to you I'll grant arcane rites; with mute
faith Eleusis silently will toss its long torches
for you. Then I'll deem my brothers' lives
restored to them, my father flourishing
as he rules his realm. But if some greater power
keeps you shut in, I follow: defend us all
by your safe return or drag all down with you.
—You'll drag us down, no god will raise your broken family.

AMPHITRYON

O sharer of our blood, preserving with
310 chaste faith brave Hercules' own bed and brood,
have better thoughts in mind and rouse your spirit.
He'll surely come, just has he does from every task, and
greater still.

MEGARA

What the wretched too much want
they easily believe.

AMPHITRYON

No, what they too much
fear they think can never be changed or removed:
the belief of the fearful always tends toward the worse.

MEGARA

Submerged and buried and pressed down by the whole
world, what path has he to those above?

AMPHITRYON

The same he had when through the torrid zone
320 and sands that surged just like a troubled sea
he escaped the straits that twice ebbed, twice returned,

and when, abandoning his ship, he stuck
caught fast in Syrtes' shallow shoals,
and though the boat was fixed, overcame the sea on foot.[32]

MEGARA

Unfair fortune rarely spares the greatest
virtues. No one can long expose himself
to such frequent dangers safely; he whom chance
has often passed it someday lights upon.
But look! Cruel, with threats upon his face,
his stride matching his mind, brandishing 330
in his right hand a scepter not his, comes Lycus.

LYCUS

Though ruling the rich spaces of the Theban
town and all the fertile soil that sloping
Phocis circles,[33] all that Ismenos waters,
all that Cithaeron sees from its high peak,
and narrow Isthmus splitting the twin straits,
I have no ancient rights, as a lazy heir
to a father's house; no noble forefathers
nor lineage renowned with high titles,
but famed valor. Who boasts of lineage 340
praises what's not his. But a stolen scepter's held
with trembling hand: all safety lies in steel.
What you know is held despite the will of citizens,
the drawn sword protects. Rule is not stable
in another's stead. But one person can
underpin my strength, if conjoined by royal
bed and wedlock: Megara. My newness will
acquire tone from her famed stock. I do not think
she'll refuse and spurn my couch, but if
she stubbornly and rashly denies me this, 350
it's settled: I'll raze utterly the whole house of
Hercules. Will ill-will and the people's voice stop me?
Kingship's chief art is to put up with ill-will.
Let's try, then; fortune's given me the chance;

for she, head veiled in her sad robing,
stands by the guardian gods, and the
real father of Alcides sticks to her side.

MEGARA

What novelty is this one planning, our race's
ruin and plague? What is he trying to do?

LYCUS

Bearing the brilliant
360 name of a royal line, receive, kind lady,
my words with patient ear for a brief while.
If mortals always bore eternal hates,
and rage, once spurred, never left their hearts,
the lucky staying armed, the unlucky striving to,
wars will leave nothing behind. Farms will then lie waste
in barren lands, torches will be set to roofs,
deep ash will cover buried nations.
To want peace restored is useful for the victor,
required for the vanquished. Partner of my
370 reign, come, let's ally our minds. Receive this pledge of
faith: take my hand. Why silent, with that harsh look?

MEGARA

I, take a hand stained with my father's blood and
twin murders of my brothers? The east will sooner
quench the day and the west bring it back,
sooner there'll be faithful peace twixt snow and flame,
and Scylla will join Sicily's flank to Italy,[34]
far sooner will swift Euripus with its shifting
tides stand still, slowed by the Euboean sea.
You took my father, kingdom, brothers, home,
380 country—what more is there? One thing's left me,
more dear than brother, father, kingdom, home:
hatred for you: I grieve that mine's in common
with the people—how small is my part in it!
Be lordly and puffed up, cherish your high pride;
an avenger god tracks proud ones from behind.

I know the Theban kingdom: why mention mothers
who suffered and dared crimes?[35] Or the twin evil,
the mingled name of husband, son and father?
Or brothers' double armies and double pyres?
Niobe, proud mother, turned stiff with grief, 390
and drips, a sad stone, on Phrygian Sipylus.
Even Cadmus, raising his grim crested head,
measured out the Illyrian realm in flight
and left long tracks as his body dragged behind.
These models wait: be master as you please,
till our rulers' routine fortune calls on you.

LYCUS

Come, stop the wild words of your rage and from
Alcides learn to endure the orders of kings.
Though I wield a scepter that I seized as victor
and rule everything with no fear of laws, since weapons 400
overpower them, I'll say some words in my defense.
Your father fell in the bloody fray? Your brothers
fell? But arms observe no measure, nor can
the drawn sword's rage be lightly tempered
or repressed. Blood gladdens war. But he
fought for his realm, while I was driven by
a shameless greed? The outcome of war is queried,
not the cause. But let all memory now pass away.
When the victor's laid down arms, it's right that
the vanquished lay down hate. I'm not asking that 410
you worship me as king on bended knee.
I'm pleased you take your ruin with grand pride.
You're a wife worth a king: let's join our beds.

MEGARA

A cold shiver runs through my bloodless limbs.
What outrage have I heard? I didn't quake
when crash of war resounded round our walls,
and peace was ruptured; I intrepidly bore all.
I quake at marriage: now I seem a slave.

Let chains weigh down my body, let my death be drawn
420 out slowly with long hunger. There's no force
will vanquish my loyalty. Alcides, I'll die yours.

LYCUS

Your husband, sunk in hell, prompts pride?

MEGARA

He reached hell so that he might reach the heights.

LYCUS

The weight of the immense earth presses him down.

MEGARA

One who has carried the sky will feel no weight.

LYCUS

You will be forced.

MEGARA

One who can be forced does not know
how to die.

LYCUS

Say rather what royal gift
I should prepare for our wedding.

MEGARA

Your death or mine.

LYCUS

You're insane—and you will die.

MEGARA

I'll run to meet my spouse.

LYCUS

430 To you a slave is stronger than my scepter?

MEGARA

How many kings has that slave given to death!

LYCUS

Why then does he serve a king and bear the yoke?

MEGARA

Remove harsh orders, what will courage be?

LYCUS

To be thrown to beasts and monsters, you deem courage?

MEGARA

The role of courage is to tame what all men dread.

LYCUS

Hell's darkness presses down that boaster.

MEGARA

Not gentle is the road from earth to stars.

LYCUS

What father bore him, that he hopes to live among immortals?

AMPHITRYON

Silence, poor wife of great Hercules;
it's my role to restore his father and true lineage 440
to Alcides. After that colossal
man's many famous deeds, after he's subdued
everything the Sun sees as he sets and rises,
after so many monsters tamed, Phlegra bespattered
with impious blood,[36] and the gods defended—his
father's not yet clear? We make believe it's Jove?
Trust Juno's hate.

LYCUS

Why outrage Jove?
The mortal race cannot be joined to the heavens.

AMPHITRYON

That is the common source of many gods.

LYCUS

Had they been slaves before they became gods? 450

AMPHITRYON

Apollo fed flocks, a shepherd in Pherae.[37]

LYCUS

He didn't wander exiled through all regions.

AMPHITRYON

Yet an outcast mother bore him on shifting land.[38]

LYCUS

Did Phoebus fear fierce monsters or wild beasts?

AMPHITRYON

A serpent first stained the arrows of Apollo.

LYCUS

You don't know what grave evils the baby endured?

AMPHITRYON

The child cast out by lightning from his mother's
womb soon stood beside his lightning father.[39]
Did he who guides the stars, who shakes the clouds,
460 not hide as infant in the hollow of an eroded cliff?[40]
Such great births have a troubled price; it's always
cost a great deal that a god be born.

LYCUS

Whom you see wretched, know that he's a man.

AMPHITRYON

Whom you see brave, don't call him wretched.

LYCUS

Can we call him brave from whose shoulders the lion skin
fell, and was made a gift for a girl, whose club fell, and
whose body was spangled in a Sidonian dress?[41]
Can we call him brave whose bristly hair was soaked
in nard, who clapped his hands, renowned for glory,
470 to the unmanly sound of cymbals, wearing on
his fierce brow a barbarian diadem?

AMPHITRYON

Tender Bacchus does not blush to have loosened
his locks or to wield with delicate hand
the dainty thyrsus, when with no bold stride
he trails a gown adorned with gold from the east.
It's usual for courage to relax after so much work.

LYCUS

To this Eurytus' ruined house bears witness,[42]
and droves of virgins seized in the style of cattle!

No Juno, no Eurystheus ordered this:
this was his doing.

AMPHITRYON

You don't know all: 480
Eryx[43] smashed by his own gloves was his own
doing, and with Eryx the Libyan Antaeus,
and the hearth awash in murdered guests
that justly drank the blood of Busiris;
his doing that Cycnus, impervious to wound
and sword, was forced to endure his death intact,
and multiform Geryon was conquered by him alone.
You'll be among them—though they did not sully marriage
with adultery.

LYCUS

What's good for Jove's good for
a king: you gave Jove a wife, now you'll give one to a king;[44] 490
you'll teach your daughter-in-law what she already knows:
to follow the better man when even her husband approves.
But if she staunchly snubs being joined in wedlock,
I'll acquire noble offspring even by force.

MEGARA

Creon's shades and house of Labdacus,[45]
impious wedding torch of Oedipus,
grant now the accustomed fate to matrimony.
Now, gory daughters-in-law of King Aegyptus,
now come, hands tainted with much blood: the total's
short one Danaid—I'll complete the crime. 500

LYCUS

Since you're set on turning down marriage with me
and menace a king, you'll see what a scepter can do.
Go ahead, embrace the altar: no god will snatch you from me,
not even if Alcides could ride victorious
to the gods above, heaving the world aside.
—Pile up wood, and let the temple, toppled

on the suppliants, burn, let one pyre be kindled
to consume the wife and her whole brood.

AMPHITRYON

As Alcides' father, I beg this gift of you,
510 fitting for me to ask: that I fall first.

LYCUS

A man who'd punish everyone with death
doesn't know how be a tyrant. Inflict variety:
don't let the wretched die, but force the happy to.
While the pyre rises with beams for the fire,
I will honor the seas' lord with votive rite.

AMPHITRYON

By the highest power of spirits, ruler and father of
gods, at whose hurled shafts all humans tremble,
curb the impious hand of the cruel king. —Why do I
vainly pray to gods? Wherever you are, son,
520 hear! Why does the temple teeter, shaken by
sudden shifts? Why does the ground roar? From
deep down sounds a hellish crash. We're heard!
It's it, it is the sound of Hercules' tread!

CHORUS

Fortune jealous of brave men,
What unfair gifts you grant the good!
That Eurystheus should reign in easy leisure,
but Alcmene's son in all his battles
must fight monsters with the hand that held the sky,
slice and reslice a serpent's fecund necks,
530 bring apples back from swindled sisters,[46]
when the snake watching those rich fruits
gave his wakeful eyes to slumber.
He came to Scythia's nomad houses
and tribes who are strangers to their homelands,
he trudged the strait's deep-frozen surface,
the silent sea with muted shores.

The hard waters there lack waves,
and where boats once spread their sails,
unshorn Sarmatians tread a path.[47]
The sea stands but shifts with yearly seasons, 540
supports a ship, then a man on horseback.
There she who rules the unmarried race,
binding her sides in a golden girdle,
stripped her body of its noble spoils,
her shield and the bands of her snowy breast,
looked up at her conqueror on bended knee.
What hope drove you to the steep underworld,
to travel boldly the way of no return,
and to see Sicilian Persephone's realm?
There, no waters with swollen waves 550
surge with south or western winds,
there Tyndareus' twins,[48] now stars,
do not rescue fearful ships;
the sea stands still with black eddies,
and when pale Death with greedy teeth
has brought to the ghosts the unnumbered folk,
so many crowds cross with one oarsman.
May you conquer wild Styx's laws,
the irrevocable distaffs of the Fates!
The king who here rules many peoples 560
attached you with his pestilential hands,
wielding his three-pronged weapon,
when you brought war to Nestor's Pylos.[49]
When injured with a light wound, he fled;
the lord of death was scared of dying.
Break free of fate by force! Let a view of light
open to the sad shades, let the blocked border
grant easy paths to the upper world!
With song and suppliant prayer Orpheus
could bend the pitiless lords of shades, 570
when he claimed back his Eurydice.
The song that drew woods, birds, and stones,

that gave rivers pause, and at whose sound
wild beasts stood still, soothes those below
with unfamiliar tones, and echoes
loudly in the realm of silence.
Furies weep for the Thracian girl,[50]
gods not prone to tears weep also,
and the judges with scowling brows
580 who question crimes and grill the once accused
sit weeping for Eurydice.
Death's lord at last says, "We're beaten;
go to those above, on this condition:
you march behind as your husband's partner,
you don't look back at your wife till
the bright day has revealed the gods and
Spartan Taenarus' gate is near!"
True love hates delay and cannot bear it:
as he rushed to see his gift, he lost it.
590 —The realm that could be conquered by song
is a realm that can be conquered by force.

ACT 3

HERCULES

Ruler of cherished light and heaven's jewel,
who orbit with your flaming chariot
both spheres and show your bright head to the broad[51]
lands—Phoebus, if your eyes have seen what's banned,
grant pardon: on orders I brought to the light
the world's secrets.[52] You, lord and father of gods,
hide your gaze by interposing lightning.
You who with second scepter rule the seas,
600 seek your lowest waters. Let any who from above
see earth and fear to be defiled by a strange
form, turn eyes away, raise faces to the sky,
avoid the monster. May two observe this evil:

I who fetched it, she who ordered. Earth's not
wide enough for to punish me with labors,
given Juno's hate. I saw things inaccessible
to all, unknown to Phoebus, the dark spaces that
the lower pole granted the infernal lord; and if
I'd liked the third lot's place, I could have
reigned. The void of eternal night, and 610
something worse than night and the grim gods
and fate I conquered; I defied death and came back:
what's left? I saw and laid bare the shades of hell.
If there's more, Juno, give it: you've too long allowed
my hands to rest; what do you order to be conquered?
But why do hostile soldiers hold the temple,
and fearful arms besiege the holy threshold?

AMPHITRYON

Do my prayers deceive my eyes, or has
that tamer of the world and pride of Greeks
left the silent house with its grim haze? 620
Is that my son? My limbs are numb with joy.
My son, Thebes' sure salvation, though late,
do I hold you released back to the world, or do I
take joy in an empty ghost, deceived? Is it you? I know
the muscles, shoulders, famed hands and tall trunk.

HERCULES

Why this squalor, Father, my wife draped
in mourning, children covered in such shameful
filth? What affliction weighs upon the house?

AMPHITRYON

Your father-in-law's killed, Lycus has power
and seeks to kill your children, father, wife. 630

HERCULES

Ungrateful land, did no one come to help
Hercules' house? The world I defended watched
so great a crime? But why waste the day in protest?

Let him die, though not my match; my courage must bear
this stain,[53] and Lycus must be Alcides' final foe.
I run to spill my enemy's blood; stay back,
Theseus, lest some sudden force attack.
War summons me: defer embraces, Father,
defer them, wife. Let Lycus inform Hades
that I've now returned.

THESEUS

640 Queen, drive from your eyes
that tearful look, and you, your son now safe,
control your falling tears. If I know Hercules,
Lycus will pay the price owed Creon. "Will pay" is
slow; he's paying. This too is slow: he's paid.

AMPHITRYON

May some god, who can, favor our prayer and
help our ailing state. Tell me, my great son's
noble friend, the sequence of his deeds,
how long the way that leads to the sad ghosts,
how hell's dog submitted to harsh chains.

THESEUS

650 You force me to recite things horrid even
now I'm safe: I've still no firm trust in the
life-giving air. My eyesight's slack, my dull
vision scarcely bears the alien light.

AMPHITRYON

Theseus, conquer what fear remains deep in
your breast, don't cheat yourself of the best fruit
of toils: that which was hard to suffer is sweet to
recollect. Recount the dread events.

THESEUS

I pray to heaven's every law, and to you who rule the roomy
realm,[54] and you, whose mother sought you vainly
660 round all Aetna: let me safely divulge
what's justly hidden and buried in the earth.

Sparta's land supports a noble cliff
where Taenarus with dense woods hems the sea.
Here hated Hades' house opens its jaws,
the high cliff gapes and in an immense cleft
a huge hollow opens with wide throat
and offers a broad road to all the nations.
The path does not at first start in blind darkness;
a faint glow from behind of light relinquished
and a doubtful glimmer of the stricken sun[55] 670
fade and trick the sight; just so the early or late
day is apt to give light mixed with night.
From there spread broad zones with empty spaces, where
the entire human race can sink down and enter.
To go is not laborious: the road itself leads down.
As currents often snatch unwilling ships,
so the downhill breeze and greedy chaos urge us on,
and clinging shades don't let you ever turn your
footsteps back. Within, calm Lethe flows,[56]
its gulf immense, with placid shallows, ousting cares. 680
Lest a too great an opportunity for return lie bared,
she coils her sluggish stream with many bends,
just as the wandering Maeander mocks its
uncertain waters and yields to itself, then
flows on, unsure if it should seek shore or spring.
The filthy marsh of slow Cocytus sprawls;
here a vulture, there a baneful owl moans,
the grim portent of the dire screech owl resounds.
Blackening foliage bristles with dark leaves;
the place of sluggish Sleep and its overhanging yew; 690
bleak Famine lies there with emaciated jaws,
and tardy Shame conceals its guilty face.
Fear and Terror, Death and gritting Pain
and black Grief follow, shivering Sickness, Wars
girt in steel; secluded at the end
slow Age assists its steps with walking stick.

AMPHITRYON

Does any land bear grain or wine?

THESEUS

Lush fields do not sprout verdantly, ripe
crops do not wave in gentle Zephyr's breeze,
700 no forest has fruit-bearing boughs; a sterile
desolation rots deep through the ground,
and foul earth languishes in eternal mold,
the sad finale of things and the world's end.
The air hangs unmoving, black night sits on the listless
world; all things are horrid with decay:
the place of death is worse than death itself.

AMPHITRYON

What about the one who rules the darkness with his scepter:
from what seat does he curb the flimsy crowd?

THESEUS

There's a place in a dark recess of hell
710 that thick fog swathes in deep shadows. Here, from
one spring flow opposing waters; the one,
as if at rest (gods swear by it), conveys
the sacred Styx's silent stream. But wild,
with great commotion, Acheron sweeps and churns
stones with its flow, impassable for sailing
back. The facing halls of Dis are circled
by this double stream, his huge house sheltered
by a shady grove. The tyrant's threshold
hangs over a vast gorge: this is the road
720 for shades, gate of the realm. A field lies round it
where, sitting with proud mien, he sorts fresh souls.
Dour is the god's majesty, and stern his brow,
yet it bears tokens of his brothers and so great
a race; his face is Jove's, but when thundering.
A great part of his savage tyranny is
the lord himself, whose looks are feared
by the fearsome.

AMPHITRYON

Is the rumor true that judgments are
pronounced, though late, on those below, and the guilty
who've forgot their crime pay the due price?
Who is that guide of truth and judge of right? 730

THESEUS

No one commissioner sits on a high chair,
issuing late verdicts to the scared accused:
Minos of Cnossus attends one court, Rhadamanthus,
yet another, Thetis' father-in-law hears in a third.[57]
What each has done he suffers; the crime seeks out
its author, the guilty's punished by his own example.
I've seen bloody generals locked in jail,
a headstrong tyrant's back torn by commoners'
hands. He who, peacefully in power, though lord
over lives, keeps his hands innocent, rules 740
mildly with unbloodied sway, and spares
souls: when he's filled the long span of a lively
life, he attains the skies, or, blessed,
the happy places of the Elysian woods,
a future judge. Abstain from human blood
O you who rule, *your* crimes are punished
in greater measure.

AMPHITRYON

Does a fixed place keep the guilty
under lock? And, as rumor says, do cruel torments
tame the impious with eternal bonds?

THESEUS

Ixion,[58] twisted, is spun on a rapid wheel; 750
a huge stone sits on the neck of Sisyphus;
the old man in midstream pursues the water
with dry throat: the liquid laps his chin;
when it's roused trust in one so oft deceived,
the water disappears in his mouth, fruit fails his hunger.
Tityos grants the bird eternal feasts,

in vain the Danaids convey full urns;
Cadmus' impious daughters wander madly,
the greedy bird gives fright to Phineus' table.

AMPHITRYON

760 Now describe my son's noble fight. Did he
bring back a willing uncle's gift or booty?

THESEUS

A deadly rock hangs over the slow water,
where the sluggish stream is torpid, its waves stunned.
A foul old man, horrid in dress and mien,
guards this river and ferries the fearful ghosts.
His unkempt beard is straggly, a knot constricts
his ugly cloak, his gaunt eyes glint; the ferryman
himself directs his bark with a long pole.
Bringing to shore his boat empty of load,
770 he seeks more shades. Alcides demands passage;
Dread Charon, as the crowd gives way, exclaims:
"Where go you, bold one? Stay your hastening stride."
Refusing any delay, Alcmena's son
subdues the sailor shoved by his own pole
and boards the boat. The skiff that could hold hordes
sank down beneath one man. The boat sits heavier,
gulps Lethe on both sides, as its gunwales rock.
Conquered monsters tremble, savage Centaurs
and Lapiths warmed for battle with much wine.[59]
780 The labor that was Lerna seeks the remotest coves
of Styx's marsh and dunks its fecund heads.
Next the house of greedy Dis appears.
Here the fierce Stygian dog that guards the realm
alarms the shades, tossing its triple heads
with awesome noise. Snakes lick the head, filthy
with slime: its mane bristles with vipers and
a long reptile hisses at its coiled tail.
Its rage matches its shape: sensing steps,
with a shake of the serpents it lifts its shaggy tuft,

and strains for the emitted sound with ears erect, 790
used to hearing even shades. As Jove's son
stood nearer the cave, the dog, unsure, sat still,
and both felt fear. Look! With a deep bark it scares
the silent places. A menacing snake hisses
at every shoulder. The horrendous voice's din
coming from three mouths appalls even the blessed
shades. But *he* then looses from his left the fierce jowls
of his cloak, holds in front the Cleonaean
head, and shields himself with its huge hide;[60]
wielding the great club in his conquering hand 800
here, there, he whirls it with incessant strokes,
doubles the blows. The vanquished dog has dropped
defiance, wearied, it's lowered all its heads,
and leaves its cave entirely. Parked on their thrones,
both lords take fright and bid it be led off;
when Alcides asked, they gave me too as gift.
Then stroking by hand the monster's hefty necks,
he chains it with meshed steel. Forgetting itself,
the dim realm's wakeful guard dog tamely droops
its ears, submits to being led, accepts 810
its master, docile, with its muzzle lowered,
and thumps both sides with its snake-bearing tail.
Once it arrived at Taenarus' rim, and the glow
of strange light struck its eyes,[61] though conquered
it regains its nerve and furiously rattles the
huge chains. It almost carried its victor off,
it budged him from his stance and dragged him down.
Then Alcides looked to my hands too,
and, hauled with twice the strength, we brought into
the world the dog raging with wrath and trying 820
to fight in vain. And when it saw bright daylight,
viewed the pure regions of the shining pole,
[night rose, and it turned its eyes toward the ground,]
it shut its eyes, drove out the hated day,
turned its gaze backward and laid every neck

upon the earth. Then under Hercules' shadow
it hid its head. —But a dense crowd arrives
with glad cries, wearing laurel on its brow,
and sings the well-earned praises of great Hercules.

CHORUS[62]

830 Eurystheus, born with hastened childbirth,[63]
had bid you delve into the world's foundation.
his labors' number was short this only,
to despoil the king of the third realm.
You dared enter the blind entrance,
where the road leads to the far ghosts,
grim and scary with its black forest,
but busy with huge attending throng.
As many people as walk through cities
avid for a new theater's games,
840 or rush to the Elean Thunderer[64]
when the fifth year brings round the rite,
or the crowd that visits secret Ceres,
when the season comes for night to grow long,
and balanced Libra, desiring calm sleep,
houses Phoebus' chariot, and when,
their homes abandoned, Attic initiates
hurry quick to honor the night:
so great a crowd is led through
the mute fields. Some step slowed by age,
850 sad and tired of their long lives;
some at a better stage still run;
virgins not yet yoked to marriage,
boys with tresses not yet cut,
an infant just taught the word mother:
For them alone, so they fear less,
the night can be eased with torches in front.
The rest go grimly through the dimness.
What's your mind like, when light is far,
and each one, grieving, senses that

his head is covered by the whole earth? 860
Thick chaos and foul darkness hover,
night's sickly color, and the repose
of a silent world, and empty clouds.
May old age bring us there late!
No one comes too late to a place from which
once he's arrived, he can never return.
What good is it to hasten harsh fate?
This whole crowd roaming in great lands
will go to the ghosts and set sail
on slow Cocytus. All that sees 870
sunset or sunrise grows for your benefit:
be kind to those who'll come! We're prepared for you,
Death.
You may be sluggish, we are hastening;
the hour that first gave life snatches it away.
Thebes' happy day is here.
Touch altars, suppliants,
slay sleek sacrifices;
let girls with husbands mingled
lead solemn choruses,
tenants of fertile fields 880
relax, put down the yoke.
By Hercules' hand there's peace
from east to west, and where
the sun, holding the middle,
denies shadows to bodies.
Whatever soil is lapped
by Tethys' long circuit,[65]
Alcides' toil has tamed.
He crossed hell's streams and returned,
with those below subdued. 890
Now no fear remains;
nothing lies past those below.

(*To Hercules.*)

For sacrifice, crown your untrimmed hair
with the cherished poplar.

ACT 4

HERCULES

Lycus struck the ground, face down, laid low
by my avenging hand. Each partner of the
tyrant fell next, partner in his punishment too.
As victor I will sacrifice to father and gods,
and honor the due altars with slain victims.
900 You, partner, helper of my toils, I pray you,
warlike Pallas, in whose left hand the aegis
casts fierce threats with petrifying face;
may Lycurgus' and the Red Sea's conqueror come,[66]
bearing spear point covered with green thyrsus,
and the twin powers, Phoebus and Phoebus' sister
(sister more apt for arrows, Phoebus for lyre),
and any brother of mine who lives in heaven,
but not brother from stepmother.[67] Summon here
fat herds; whatever fragrance Indians
910 reap in fields and Arabs pluck from trees,
bring to the altars, let rich fumes pour forth.
Let the poplar tree adorn my hair, an olive
branch with native foliage will crown you,
Theseus: my hand will exalt the Thunderer;
you'll revere the city's founders and rough
Zethus' woodland cave and Dirce's famous
stream and the Tyrian home of the immigrant king.[68]
Put incense on the flames.

AMPHITRYON

First cleanse your hands,
Son, drenched in blood of murdered enemies.

HERCULES

920 Would I could in libation pour the blood
from his head, the head hateful to the gods! No fluid

more welcome could have stained the altars;
no greater or richer victim can be slain[69]
for Jove, than an unjust king.

AMPHITRYON

Pray that your father
end your toils, that rest at last and respite
be given to the weary.

HERCULES

I'll myself pronounce
prayers worthy of Jove and me. May sky, earth, sea
stay in their place, the eternal stars steer orbits
unimpeded, deep peace nourish nations.
May toil in the harmless countryside use all 930
the steel, and swords lie hidden, may no violent
storm perturb the straits, no fire leap from
an angry Jove, no river nursed on winter
snow drag off the upturned farms. May poisons
cease, and no herb swell with noxious sap,
and may no cruel and savage tyrants
reign. If earth is yet to bear some evil
even now, let it make haste, and if it grooms
some monster, may it be mine. But what's this? Darkness
has hemmed the day. It's cloudless, but Phoebus moves 940
with face obscured. Who's driving the day backward,
forcing it to its source? Why does this strange night
bring forth its black head, why do so many stars
fill the sky in daytime? See! My first labor,
Leo, shines in no small part of heaven
and wholly seethes with rage, ready to bite.
He'll seize some constellation; he stands with gaping
mouth, menacing, breathes fire, turns red, and tosses
the mane on his neck; what sickly autumn and frigid
winter bear round in the frozen zone 950
he'll leap in one bound, strike, and crush the neck
of the spring bull.

AMPHITRYON

What sudden ill is this?
Son, why do you turn stern looks here and there,
and see with a fictive sky with confused eyes?

HERCULES

Earth is conquered, swollen seas have yielded,
the infernal realms have suffered my assaults.
But heaven's untouched, toil worthy of Alcides.
Let me be carried high to the summits of the sky,
and reach the ether: my father promised me the stars.
960 What if he says no? Earth can't hold Hercules,
at last restores him to those above. See! The
whole band of gods calls me, spreads wide the gates,
she alone bands it. Do you receive me and unlock the sky?
Or must I pull proud heaven's portal down?
Do you still waver? I'll take off Saturn's chains,
and I'll loose my grandfather against
my impious father's reckless reign. Let mad Titans
plan war as I lead. I'll bring stones and trees,
rip out with my hand cliffs full of centaurs.
970 I'll force a way with twin peaks to the gods:
let Chiron see his Pelion beneath Ossa;[70]
Olympus piled as third step will reach heaven
or it will be hurled.

AMPHITRYON

Banish those thoughts
unspeakable; repress the crazy impulse of
your mind that's barely sane, however great.

HERCULES

What's this? Noxious giants are wielding arms.
Tityos forsakes the shades, and as he totes his mangled,
hollow breast, how close to heaven he's stopped!
Cithaeron totters,[71] high Pallene trembles,
980 Tempe shrivels. One giant's seized Pindus' cliffs,
another Oeta, and Mimas rages horribly.[72]

A flaming Fury shrills with flourished whip,
thrusts ever closer to my face stakes
scorched in pyres. Savage Tisiphone,
head fenced in snakes, has shut the door, unguarded
after the dog was snatched, with a torch before.
But look—the children of the hostile king,
Lycus' wicked seed, are hiding. This hand
will restore you to your hateful father. Let my
bowstring spew swift arrows: thus should darts of 990
Hercules be launched.

AMPHITRYON

Where has blind madness
struck? He's flexed his huge bow, tips drawn tight,
undone his quiver, the arrow is shot and hisses as it flies,
the barb escapes midneck, a wound is left
behind.

HERCULES

I'll flush the other children out,
and all their hiding places. Why delay? A greater
war awaits me at Mycenae: the Cyclops'
stones must be overturned and toppled by my hands.[73]
Let my club go this way and that,[74] knock
the bolt down, smash the posts, let the roof supports 1000
be struck and fall, the whole palace light up. I see hidden
here an evil father's son.

AMPHITRYON

See, he begs,
voice piteous, stretching tender hands to a father's knees.
A vile crime, grim, horrible to see!
He's seized the child as he pleads, spun him madly
two, three times and hurled him; his head makes contact,
the roof is wet with his spattered brain. But wretched
Megara, protecting in her bosom her smaller son,
flees like a mad one from her hiding place.

HERCULES

1010 Though you take refuge in the Thunderer's bosom,
this hand will seek you everywhere and catch you.

AMPHITRYON

Run where, poor woman? Seeking what escape
or shelter? Nowhere's safe if Hercules
is hostile. Hug him, rather, try to soothe him
with wheedling prayer.

MEGARA

I pray, refrain now,
husband. Know me! This child reflects your looks and
bearing; see how he extends his hands?

HERCULES

I've grabbed my stepmother: come, pay the price,
free Jove, weighed down by a shameful yoke. But let this
1020 little monster die before its mother.

AMPHITRYON

Where are you going, madman? Will you shed your own
blood? The frightened babe dies at his father's
fiery look, before the wound: fear's snatched
his soul. The heavy club's now aimed against his wife.
He's smashed her bones, her maimed body lacks a head,
it's nowhere to be seen.

(*To himself.*)

Do you dare to watch this? Your old age
has lived too long. If grief offends you, you have death
at the ready.

(*To Hercules.*)

Here! plunge the arrows in my breast,
or turn your club that's smeared with gore of monsters:
1030 be rid of your false father, a stain upon your
name, lest his cries drown out your glory.

CHORUS

Why thrust yourself, old man, in the way of death?
Where are you heading, madman? Run and hide,
in safety: remove one crime from Hercules' hands.

HERCULES

Good: the shameful king's house is wiped out.
To you, wife of great Jove, I've slain this herd
as offering. Gladly I've fulfilled vows worthy
of you; Argos will provide other victims.

AMPHITRYON

You've not yet done, my son; finish the rite.
The victim stands at the altar, awaits your hand, 1040
neck bowed: I provide it, come to it, insist on it—
kill me! What's this? Does my eyesight stray, grief
blunt my vision? Do I see Hercules'
hands tremble? His face slips into sleep,
his tired shoulders sink as his head droops.
Knees bent, he now falls wholly to the ground,
like an ash felled in the forest or a breakwater
that'll give the sea a harbor. Are you alive,
or has that madness that sent your family to death
killed you too? It's sleep: his breath goes in and out. 1050
Let him have time for rest, so that deep sleep can check
the disease's force and ease his oppressed heart.
Slaves, move his weapons, in case he seizes them while raving.

CHORUS[75]

May the sky mourn, and the great father of the high sky,
and bountiful earth
and the shifting waves of the mobile sea,
and you above all, who over lands and tracts of sea
pour your rays
and chase the night with your lovely face,
O blazing Sun. 1060
With you, Alcides saw your settings and your risings,

and has known both your homes.
Release, O gods, release his wits
from such great savagery; guide his mind, turn it to better.
You too, O Sleep, tamer of evils,
the mind's repose,
the better part of human life,
winged offspring of star-bearing mother,
sluggish brother of harsh Death,
1070 mixing false with true, sure herald
of the future, yet the worst,
O peace of the world and haven of life,
light's repose and night's companion,
who come alike to king and slave,
and force mankind, afraid of death,
to learn of the long-lasting night:
be calm and gentle, and soothe his weariness,
hold him locked in heavy torpor;
may sleep tie down his untamed limbs,
1080 nor leave his savage breast before
his former mind regains its way.
See—stretched on the ground
he spins cruel dreams in his fierce heart.
The scourge of this great danger is still not overcome.
Used to resting his tired head on his heavy club,
he seeks its weight with empty hand,
tossing his arms in futile motions.
He's not expelled yet all the fever,
just as a wave, vexed by a stout
1090 south wind, maintains its long-drawn roiling
and still swells when the breeze has ceased.
Drive out your mind's insane billows,
may duty and valor return to the man.
Or better may his
mind be stirred by frenzied motions,
blind error keep on as it began:
only madness can now make you innocent.

The closest fate to untainted hands is
not to know the crime.
May his chest resound, pounded by Hercules' own palms, 1100
may his blows beat with vengeful hand
the shoulders used to holding up the sky.
May the ether hear his desperate groans,
the queen of the black world hear them,
and savage Cerberus,
his neck bound in huge chains,
skulking in his deepest cave.
May chaos echo with sad clamor,
and the broad deep's open waves,
and the air, though 1110
it had felt your arrows once to a better end.
A breast besieged by such great evils
must not by be struck lightly;
let three realms resound with one beat.
You too, the splendid weapons on his shoulder,
arrow brave and quiver heavy, slung for so long,
lay cruel blows on his fierce back;
may the wood, his mighty stick,
scourge his strong arms and
burden his chest with its harsh knots: 1120
may his weapons grieve for such great pain.
—You, children, no partners in your father's glory,
avenging savage kings with wounds,
not taught to twist your limbs upon
the Argive wrestling ground, brave with glove, brave with bare
hand—
though already bold
to balance in sure hands the light dart
issued from the Scythian quiver,
and to pierce deer, saved by fleeing,
and the flanks of beasts not yet with mane. 1130
Go, to the Stygian haven, go
O harmless shades,

whom at the first threshold of life
atrocity and a father's madness crushed.
Go, unlucky brood of children,
on the sad path of a well-known labor:
go and see the angry monarchs.

ACT 5

HERCULES

What place is this, what region, what quarter of the
world? Where am I? At the rising sun or at the
1140 axis of the frozen Bear? Is this the limit
the far land of the western sea gives Ocean?
What air do I breathe? What ground lies under my fatigue?
Surely I'm back: why do I see gory bodies,
a house in ruins? Has my mind not yet cast off
the infernal images? Does the deathly throng
engage my eyes even after my return?
I'm ashamed to say it: I'm afraid; my mind
forebodes something, some great iniquity.
Where are you, father? Where my wife, proud of
1150 her troop of sons? Why is my left side bare
of the lion's spoils? Where has my covering gone,
that's a soft bed too for Hercules' sleep?
Where are my arrows, and my bow? Who could remove my
armor
with me alive? Who captured such great spoils,
who didn't fear the very sleep of Hercules?
I'd like, yes like to see my conqueror.
Up, courage! What new son has my father spawned,
deserting heaven? At whose birth did a night stall
longer than mine? —What horror do I see?
1160 My sons lie slaughtered in bloody murder,
My wife is slain. What Lycus rules this realm?
Who's dared to stir up such great crimes in Thebes

when Hercules is back? Whoever dwells in
Ismenus' land,[76] or Attic fields, or the tract
of Trojan Pelops beaten by twin seas,
help! Expose the author of this cruel slaughter!
Let my wrath fall on all: he is my foe
who won't point out my foe. Alcides' conqueror,
do you hide? Come out, whether you're avenging
the cruel Thracian's brutal chariot, Geryon's 1170
herd or Libya's lords; there's no delay in
fighting. Look, I stand here stripped, you can
attack me unarmed, with my own arms. —Why do Theseus
and my father avoid my gaze? Why do they hide their
faces? Put off weeping! Tell me who sent my family
all at once to death. Why silent, Father?
You speak, then, Theseus; Theseus, by your faith!
Both are mute, conceal shamed faces, furtively
shed tears. In such great misfortune what cause is there
for feeling shame? Has the Argive city's reckless 1180
master or dying Lycus' hostile platoons
overwhelmed us with so great a ruin?
I pray you, father, by the glory of my
deeds and the ever helpful power of your
name, speak! Who destroyed our house? To whom
have I fallen prey?

AMPHITRYON

May these evils pass in silence.

HERCULES

So I be unavenged?

AMPHITRYON

Revenge oft harms.

HERCULES

Has anyone borne such great evils idly?

AMPHITRYON

He who's feared worse.

HERCULES

Is there something, Father

1190 worse than these, or graver, that can be feared?

AMPHITRYON

How small the part of your ruin that you understand!

HERCULES

Pity me, Father, I spread my suppliant hands.
What's this? He shuns my hands. Some crime hovers here.
Where's this blood from? What is that arrow wet with
a child's death? It's stained with Hydra's blood.
I see my shafts now, I don't ask about the hand that did this!
Who could bend that bow or what hand flex
that string that scarcely yields to me when drawn?
Father, I return to both of you: is this crime mine?
They're silent—it is mine.

AMPHITRYON

1200 The grief is yours,
the crime's your stepmother's; this calamity lacks guilt.

HERCULES

Now thunder, Father, from every zone in rage;
You've forgotten me, but avenge at least with tardy
hand your grandsons. Let the starry sky
resound, and heavens hurl flames here and there.
May Caspian cliffs and the greedy eagle tug
at my bound body:[77] why is Prometheus' rock
vacant? Why is Caucasus' steep flank vacant,
with its huge peak, bare of trees, that
1210 feeds beasts and birds? The Symplegades
that constrict the Scythian Sea should stretch
my hands, tied on either side upon the deep,
and when in turn the rocks meet and expel
skyward the sea between, cliffs closing on each side,
may I lie there, the mountains' sleepless hindrance.
Why not pile up a mound built of heaped wood

and burn this body drenched with impious blood?
So be it: I'll give back Hercules to hell.

AMPHITRYON

His breast is not yet free of stunned commotion,
and has changed its target: as fury does, 1220
it rages at itself.

HERCULES

Dire home of Furies,
prison of those below and zone ordained for
the guilty throng! If there's exile that hides
past Erebus, unknown to Cerberus
and me, conceal me there, O Earth; I'll go and
stay at hell's far edge. O too wild breast!
Who, children, can lament you worthily,
scattered through all the house? My face, hard with
suffering, does not know how to weep. Give my bow
here, my arrows here, give here my huge club. 1230
For you I'll shatter my darts; and for you, son,
I'll break my bow; for your shade my heavy
club will burn; my quiver, packed with arrows
of Hydra's poison, will go upon your pyre. Let my
weapons pay the price. You too, stepmother's hands,
disastrous for my weapons, I shall burn.

AMPHITRYON

Whoever's given error the name of crime?

HERCULES

Huge error often has earned the rank of crime.

AMPHITRYON

This needs a Hercules: bear this load of suffering.

HERCULES

My shame's not so far gone, so quenched by madness that I'd 1240
put all nations to flight with my godless appearance.
Arms, arms! I beg you, Theseus, quickly give me
back those that were taken. If my mind's sane,

put weapons in my hands; if madness remains,
Father, stand back: I'll find a path to death.

AMPHITRYON

By our family's holy rites, by the right
of both my names, whether you call me father
or stepfather, by my white hairs, which good men
should revere, spare my forlorn old age,
1250 I pray, and weary years; preserve yourself,
sole prop of our fallen house, sole light in my calamity,
preserve yourself! None of your labors' benefits
reached me: I always feared the monsters or
the risky sea; every savage king in all the
world, with guilty hands or altars, is my
fear. As father of one always gone,
I want the joy and touch and look of you.

HERCULES

No reason why I should detain my life
or linger longer in this light. I've lost
1260 all goods: mind, arms, fame, wife, sons, hands,
even madness. No one can heal a polluted
soul; the crime must be cured by death.

AMPHITRYON

You'll kill your father.

HERCULES

I'll die to prevent it.

AMPHITRYON

In front of your father?

HERCULES

I've taught him to watch evil.

AMPHITRYON

Look rather to your deeds, recalled by all,
and ask pardon of yourself for a single crime.

HERCULES

Shall he who pardoned none pardon himself?

I did glorious deeds on orders. This one is
mine. Help me, Father, if love moves you,
or sad fate, or my valor's damaged splendor; 1270
bring out arms, let Fortune by my hand
be conquered.

THESEUS

A father's prayers are capable
enough, yet be moved by my tears as well.
Rise up and crush misfortune with your normal
vigor. Now regain your spirit that's
unequal to no ill; now you must act with
huge bravery: don't let Hercules rage!

HERCULES

If I live, I've done crimes; if I die,
I've borne them. I rush to purge the world: long since
a monster, evil, savage, pitiless, and wild 1280
has been confronting me. Come, hand, try and attempt
this giant task, greater than twelve labors.
You hang back, coward, brave only against children
and scared mothers? If I'm not given arms,
I'll tear down all of Thracian Pindus' woods,
I'll burn Bacchus' groves, Cithaeron's cliffs
along with me, or the whole palace with its
homes and lords; I'll pile on my body
the Theban temples with all their gods, be buried
with the town upturned, and if walls dropped 1290
on my strong arms are too light a weight,
if swamped by seven gates I'm not crushed enough,
I'll turn upon my head the entire mass
that sits midsky and separates the gods.

AMPHITRYON

I give back your arms.

HERCULES

Words worthy of Hercules'
father. Look, my boy fell by this shaft.

AMPHITRYON

Juno shot this arrow with your hands.

HERCULES

I'll use it now.

AMPHITRYON

See how my wretched heart
quakes with fear and pounds my troubled breast.

HERCULES

The arrow's fitted.

AMPHITRYON

1300 Look, now you'll do the crime
willing and knowing.

HERCULES

Speak: what do you bid me do?

AMPHITRYON

I ask for nothing; my pain is secure.
You alone can save my son for me,
but you can't take him. I've escaped the greatest fear,
you cannot make me wretched: happy, yes.
Decide what you decide, so long as you know
your case and your fame are balanced on the edge:
you live, or else you kill me. This insubstantial soul,
wearied with age nor less weary with ills,
1310 I hold back at my lips. Who'd grant a father
life so slowly? I'll bear no more delay,
I'll plunge the fatal sword into my punctured breast.
Here, here will lie the crime of a sane Hercules.

HERCULES

Stop now, Father, stop, withdraw your hand.
Valor, yield; accept a father's command.
Let this too join the labors of Hercules.
I'll live! Theseus, lift from the ground my father's
afflicted limbs. My polluted hand shuns loving
contact.

AMPHITRYON

I happily embrace this hand,
I'll lean on it and walk, hold it to my sick 1320
chest and drive out pain.

HERCULES

As exile, what place
can I seek? Where hide, be buried in what earth?
What Tanais or Nile,[78] what Tigris ripping
with Persian waves, ferocious Rhine or
turbulent Tigris awash with Spanish gold
can cleanse this hand? Even if cold Maeotis
pours its arctic sea on me and all of
Ocean cascades through my hands, the crime will
stick deep. Impious, to what lands will you
withdraw? Will you seek east or west? I am 1330
known everywhere, I've lost a place for exile.
The world rejects me, the stars turn and follow
slanted orbits, the very Sun saw Cerberus
with a kinder gaze. O Theseus, faithful soul,
find a distant, secret, hiding place.
Since you when judging others' crimes forever
cherish the guilty, give thanks and recompense
for what I've earned. Return me back to
the shades below, and reinstate me as captive
of *your* chains. That place will hide me—but 1340
that place too knows me.

THESEUS

My land awaits you.
There Mars put again his hand to arms,
absolved of murder.[79] That land, Alcides, calls you,
that's used to rendering the gods innocent.

Hercules on Oeta

Hercules has just conquered the town of Oechalia to get to the king's daughter, Iole, and has killed her father and brother. The princess has been sent to his home in Trachis, where his current wife Deianira lives. As the play opens, Hercules boasts of having brought land and sea under his dominion everywhere: he is ready for deification. A stark contrast is provided by the chorus of grieving Oechalian women, including Iole, who lament Hercules' brutality.

In Trachis, Deianira in turn voices her rage against Hercules for this latest infidelity. The nurse tries to calm her, but Deianira is even ready to kill her husband. To divert her into another plan of action, the nurse suggests magic instead, and Deianira remembers the love potion given to her by the centaur Nessus. Although he had tried to rape her, and was killed in the process by Hercules, he gave her some gore from his wounds as he lay dying and claimed it would win back her husband from any future rivals for his love. A robe is smeared with this philter and sent to Hercules via the messenger Lichas.

A choral ode expressing sympathy for Deianira's plight is halted by the queen's sudden appearance: belatedly, she fears the philter may be poisonous. At this moment her son Hyllus arrives from Oechalia and announces that when Hercules donned the robe, it began to eat his flesh. Hercules killed Lichas in rage and is now being carried home. Deianira makes preparations for her suicide.

Hercules is brought in, in agony, and condemns Deianira despite her suicide. He wants to attack his disease as he has attacked his other enemies, but it is within him. He realizes his death is in accordance with a prophecy heard long ago and prepares to die in a way that befits his glory. At his instructions, a pyre is built on Mt. Oeta. The chorus is not sure if he is ascending to the heavens or going to the underworld, but Philoctetes returns from Oeta and describes the bravery with which Hercules immolated himself. His mother Alcmene is overcome by grief but hears Hercules consoling her from the heavens.

Introduction

DAVID KONSTAN

Scholarly opinion is divided on whether to assign this play to Seneca himself or to some unknown imitator of his tragic style.[1] It is included and comes last in both the major manuscript traditions, in ninth place or, in the tradition that includes the certainly spurious *Octavia*, in tenth (in this latter it is given the title *Hercules Oetaeus*, just as the first play in the series is called *Hercules Furens*; the former tradition labels both simply *Hercules*). The main arguments against authenticity have to do with its length (it is the longest play to survive from classical antiquity), repetitiveness, and rhetoric (which sometimes seems exaggerated even by Senecan standards); in addition, some passages appear to draw on plays recognized as genuine (especially *Hercules Mad*), and there are also some subtle features of style, diction, and meter in which *Hercules on Oeta* differs from Seneca's other tragedies. Nevertheless, the question remains open. My own view is that the play might well be by Seneca but be incompletely revised and so lack the compactness and some of the refinement of his other tragedies.

The closest model for Seneca's play is Sophocles' *Women of Trachis*, in which Hercules brings back Iole as a slave after sacking her city and installs her in his home to the distress of his wife, Deianira. To recover his love, Deianira prepares a potion given to her by Nessus, the centaur who volunteered to carry her across a swollen river and who, when he attempted to rape her, was slain by Hercules with an arrow dipped in the Hydra's poison. The potion, made from Nessus' blood, in fact carries the same poison, and when Hercules dons the cloak that Deianira doused in it, his flesh is consumed and he realizes in his final agony that this death was fated (he also orders his son Hyllus to marry Iole). In the meantime, Deianira, having realized her error, kills herself. The dramatic tension is produced by the conflict between good intentions, strong passions, and unreliable information. Deianira is a decent woman, willing to tolerate Hercules' long absences and philandering, and even when she is threatened by a rival in her own home, she represses any anger and seeks only to inspire love in her wayward husband. Iole herself maintains a dignified silence. The boy Hyllus, when he learns what has happened to his father, berates his mother violently, which contributes to her decision to commit suicide; but when he learns—too late—the truth, he regrets his words and tries to persuade Hercules that she is innocent. Hercules is something of a brute: destroying a city to satisfy his lust, insensitive to his wife's situation (he sends a messenger ahead to inform her of his arrival while he attends to sacrifices), self-absorbed, domineering, and full of fury—understandably, given the pain he endures when the poison takes hold. But he is also mysterious, seemingly reserved for some higher destiny (although Sophocles does not allude to his apotheosis); in the end, Hyllus declares: "No one can foresee what will happen, but what has happened now is pitiable for us, shameful for the gods, and most difficult of all to him who, of all men, bore this torment" (1270–74 in Sophocles' play).

Nothing could be more different than Seneca's treatment of much the same episode (for convenience, I will speak here of the play as Seneca's). In Sophocles' play, the audience first sees Deianira, who is worried about Hercules' long absence. She learns of his arrival via a messenger, and when Iole is brought on stage, Deianira is led to believe that she is merely one captive among others, and indeed she pities her. Only later is she informed that Hercules destroyed Iole's city out of desire for her, and at this point Deianira begins to fear for her marriage. Even so, her reaction is mild. She knows that Hercules has had adulterous affairs before this, but she accepts the fact passively: "It is not decent (*kalon*) for a sensible woman to be angry," she declares (552–53; cf. 543 on Deianira's inability to "grow wroth" [*thumousthai*] with Hercules for his behavior). The chorus consists of young Trachinian women, who are sympathetic to her plight. Hercules himself appears, carried in on a litter, nearly four fifths into the play, already in his death throes. Seneca, by contrast, gives the prologue to Hercules, who rehearses his various services to mankind with spectacular braggadocio. After a chorus in which the advantages of a humble life are proclaimed, the first to speak is Iole, who, far from keeping silent like her Sophoclean counterpart, laments her misfortune in tones that might well arouse Deianira's pity; the chorus, which consists here of the slave women captured along with Iole by Hercules, do what little they can to comfort her. But when Deianira herself appears, it is as a woman afire with jealousy, and she immediately decides to murder Hercules. This is no submissive wife who disapproves of any expression of anger; Seneca's Deianira is more like Euripides' Medea, dangerously passionate, wholly unafraid despite her nurse's warnings of Hercules' unconquerable might. Indeed, Deianira's situation is not unlike that of Medea: each has a husband who threatens to displace her by taking another wife; and indeed, both succeed in destroying their husbands, even if Deianira ends up doing so inadvertently, by sending Hercules a garment that she believes is steeped in a love potion rather than poison: and yet, a poisoned robe is the same means by which Medea kills Jason's would-be bride along with her father, the king of Corinth. If one might imagine that Sophocles' Deianira at some unconscious level wished for Hercules' death (her trust in the dying Nessus' gift is all too naïve), Seneca's heroine does so openly and in full awareness, and it is only when the nurse suggests that a magic brew might serve to reignite Hercules' love that Deianira consents to a switch of plan and remembers the serum that Nessus gave her, not foregoing a vivid description of the occasion which alone ought to have roused her suspicions.

When Hyllus enters to announce the effect of the poison on Hercules, Deianira is appalled and decides on suicide, and she sticks to her resolve even though in Seneca's version Hyllus immediately realizes that her offense was accidental and tries to dissuade her from harming herself. Given her murderous disposition shortly before, this shift may seem dramatically implausible, but once Deianira has imagined that Hercules might again be brought to love her and reject Iole, it is understandable that she should be distraught at what she has accidentally done, and she knows that her situation now is hardly tenable. All Seneca's characters are emotionally overwrought. But the effect they produce on the audience is less one of sympathy and concern than one of shock and awe: how powerfully these people feel, how vast the stage on which they stride! When Hercules returns to the scene, he is in no way humbled by his pain or the prospect of death; on the contrary, he is as proud and boastful as he was at the beginning of the play, and his recognition that he is defeated by the poison is in dramatic counterpoint to his former bravado. Whereas Sophocles was content to leave the final scene of Hercules' agony to a dialogue between the hero and his son, Seneca squeezes every ounce of pathos out of it by also bringing in Alcmena, Hercules' mother. And just when you thought you'd seen it all, in comes Philoctetes with a long speech about Hercules' death and transfiguration on the pyre. But not even this is enough: at the very end, after all the weeping and wailing for the dead hero, Hercules appears in the sky to explain that he has been divinized and that there is no need to mourn for him (his epiphany is reminiscent of the conclusion to Sophocles' *Philoctetes*). There is none of the doubt about divine benevolence or concern for humanity that marked the finale of Sophocles' *Women of Trachis* or the sense of human solidarity in the face of our sad or at least unpredictable destiny. Seneca's *Hercules on Oeta* ends in the triumph of a great spirit amidst the universal admiration of lesser beings who nevertheless participate in some measure in the transcendent glory of the hero.

The Hercules of *Hercules on Oeta* is the most consistently courageous and virtuous character in all of Senecan drama, despite his apparent intention to make Iole his mistress (and his attack on her city with this purpose in mind) and his violent murder of Lichas (this modeled on Sophocles), who is innocent of any wrongdoing. It is perhaps no wonder that it is placed last in the manuscripts, as a kind of crowning manifestation of heroic grandeur. Given that Hercules was regarded by the Stoics as a kind of ideal or model of the sage, celebrated by Seneca himself and by his elder contemporary Cornutus (see the introduction to *Hercules Mad*), this play comes closer than any other to dramatizing what a Stoic hero might be like, in apparent contrast to his portrayal in *Hercules Mad*, where he slaughters his own family in a fit of insanity. Here, it is his great services to humanity that stand out, even if, much of the time, Hercules does say so himself: the prologue sets the scene for the final apotheosis. But the transformation of the traditional warrior figure into one who comes to understand and accept his fate occurs over time, and most particularly in the latter part of the drama, first in the course of his exchanges with his mother and his son and above all in his behavior on the pyre as reported by Philoctetes, who now assumes the task of comforting Alcmena. If Seneca (or, more neutrally, the author of *Hercules on Oeta*) had recourse to some other source than Sophocles' *Women of Trachis* for this part of his tragedy, as he may well have for the characterization of Deianira as a vengeful heroine in the image of Medea, he has deployed it effectively in the service of a larger story line in which passion mellows into acquiescence to the larger plan of things.[2]

The rhetorical pyrotechnics of Seneca's dramatic style are an acquired taste. Modern English tends to favor a kind of dry, journalistic simplicity, save in religious discourse, where fire-and-brimstone preachers may still avail themselves of the higher registers (most people don't even know what "brimstone" means these days, but the resonances are enough to inspire terror). Senecan artistry does not shy away from calling attention to itself: it aspires to grandeur rather than to plainness or prettiness. Performed properly, Seneca's verses retain their power to move an audience, and whatever one's view of whether and how the tragedies were intended to be staged, there is no question that they were meant, like all declamatory literature in antiquity, to be read aloud and vigorously.

I have consulted various texts while preparing this translation, and my version is unavoidably eclectic. When the two main manuscript traditions, labeled A and E, offer discrepant readings, it is often impossible to decide between them, and editors are sometimes moved to emend even where they agree. I have been influenced by the commentary of Daniela Averna (2002), who adopts a generally conservative approach, preferring a transmitted reading rather than a modern emendation or rearrangement of lines, but her text is occasionally vitiated by unmetrical lines. The Oxford edition by Otto

Zwierlein (1986) and the Loeb edition by John Fitch (2004) are more adventurous in this regard, and often, even where I have not followed their readings, I suspect that they are right for reasons either of style or logic.[3] I have indicated significant places where Zwierlein or Fitch (or both) adopt a different reading from the one I have elected, to facilitate comparison with their texts, but readers should be warned that I have not attempted to produce anything like a complete apparatus or concordance.

As in my translation of the *Hercules Mad*, my notes offer only the information needed to identify characters and places mentioned or alluded to in the play, with occasional indications of pronunciation. The translation is in verse, by and large iambic pentameter, but freely admitting the longer iambic hexameter (and even heptameter) when it seemed impossible to reduce Seneca's basic twelve-syllable line to ten syllables in English. Choruses are handled variously, sometimes rendered in pentameters, more often in shorter lines to register the metrical distinction between chorus and dialogue in the original. The translation is line for line, subject to slight displacements, rarely running over more than two verses, where English syntax requires a different word order from Latin. My intention has been to render the Latin faithfully, even literally, while at the same time producing a version that is readable and sounds as though it might have been composed originally in English. The reader must judge the extent to which I have succeeded in reconciling what must seem like contrary objectives.

Finally, I wish to express my deepest gratitude to Scott Smith, who selflessly read through the entire manuscript with consummate care, and offered hundreds of suggestions and corrections (a great many in the latter category) that have materially improved both the accuracy and style of this translation. I can only hope that this version is up to the standard that he himself has set in his translations of other tragedies of Seneca. I am profoundly indebted as well to Shadi Bartsch and to the anonymous referee for the University of Chicago Press, both of whom provided invaluable comments on matters of style and substance and improved my version in countless places.

Suggested Reading

Averna, Daniela. 2002. *Lucio Anneo Seneca:* Hercules Oetaeus; *Testo critico, traduzione e commento*. Rome.

Fitch, John G. 1987. *Hercules Furens: A Critical Text with Introduction and Commentary*. Ithaca.

———. 2004. *Seneca: Tragedies II*. Cambridge, MA.

King, Christine M. 1971. "Seneca's 'Hercules Oetaeus': A Stoic Interpretation of the Greek Myth." *Greece & Rome* 18: 215–22.

Marcucci, Silvia. 1997. *Analisi e interpretazione dell'* Hercules Oetaeus. Pisa and Rome.

Rosenmeyer, Thomas G. 1989. *Senecan Drama and Stoic Cosmology*. Berkeley.

Walde, Christine. 1992. *Herculeus labor: Studien zum pseudosenecanischen Hercules Oetaeus*. Frankfurt am Main.

Zwierlein, Otto. 1986. *L. Annaei Senecae tragoediae*. Oxford.

Hercules Oetaeus

LUCIUS ANNAEUS SENECA

TRANSLATED BY DAVIS KONSTAN

DRAMATIS PERSONAE

HERCULES
CHORUS of Oechalian maidens
IOLE
NURSE
DEIANIRA
CHORUS of Aetolian maidens
HYLLUS
ALCMENA
PHILOCTETES

Most of the drama is set in front of Hercules' palace in Trachis, though Ode 1 seems to be sung near the destroyed city of Oechalia, where Iole is from.

ACT 1

HERCULES

You who sowed the gods, whose lightning, launched
from your hand, both houses of the Sun perceive,[1]
you may rule carefree now: I've brought peace for you
to anywhere the Sea prevents the land's extension.[2]
No need to thunder: treacherous kings, cruel tyrants
are laid low. I've smashed whatever ought to have been
blasted by your lightning. But to me, Father,
heaven's still denied.[3] I've surely shown myself
worthy of Jupiter everywhere, and that you're my father
she—my stepmother[4]—testifies. Why do you weave delays? 10
Am I feared? Will Atlas be unable to uphold the skies
if Hercules as well is loaded on him?

Why, Father, why deny me still the stars? Death, for one,
released me to you: every evil has surrendered
that earth or sea or sky or hell has sired.
No lion prowls the cities of Arcadia,[5]
the Stymphalian bird's been shot, there's no Maenalian beast.
The dragon's killed, spattering his golden grove,
the Hydra has laid down its might, I've smashed the herds
20 that Hebrus knows, grown fat on blood of guests,
and carried off the spoils of the Thermodontian foe.
I've seen the fates of the silent ones, and didn't just come back
alone:
the trembling daylight saw dark Cerberus
and he in turn the Sun. Libyan Antaeus
gains back his breath no more, Busiris has fallen
before his own altars, Geryon's been spattered by a single hand,
and so has the bristling bull, that terror to a hundred towns.
Whatever the hostile earth has borne has fallen,
laid low by my right hand. I've left the gods
30 no scope for rage. If the world denies me beasts,
and my stepmother her anger—then give the father,
even the stars, to the brave son. I do not ask you to show the
path.
Merely allow me, Father: I'll find the way.
Or if you fear the earth will conceive monsters,
let it rush any sort of evil up while earth still holds
and sees Hercules. For who else will attack evils,
who throughout the Argive towns will be
worthy of Juno's hatred? I have made safe
my fame, no land is silent about me:
40 the freezing race of the Scythian bear has seen me,[6]
the Indus beneath the Sun, Libya beneath the Crab.
I call you, bright Titan,[7] as witness: I have met up with you
wherever you shine, but your light has not been able
to track my triumphs. I have outrun the courses of the sun
and daylight halted well before my boundary posts.[8]
Nature yielded, the earth was not up to my pace—

it tired first! Night and furthest chaos
dashed against me. To this world I returned from where
no one makes it back. I faced down threats of Ocean,
no storm availed to shatter any raft that I 50
weighed down. How small a range has Perseus next to me?
The empty ether replenishes no more
your wife's hatred, and the earth fears to bear
beasts for me to conquer, finds no more monsters.
Beasts are denied me! Hercules now begins to take
the place of monster! How many evils have I smashed,
barehanded—how many crimes? Whatever horror stood in my
way,
my bare hands laid flat. As a youth I feared no beasts,
not even as a baby.[9] Whatever I'm commanded is light,
no lazy day has ever dawned for me. 60
How many monsters have I laid low, though no king
ordered me![10] My courage drove me—
harder than did Juno. But what good is it to have made
mankind unafraid? The gods still have no peace.
The entire earth, now purged, sees all it feared
in the heavens: Juno has relocated the beasts.
The Crab, slain, now circles the torrid zone,
is called Libya's constellation, nurtures her harvests.[11]
The lion hands on the fleeting year to Astraea,[12]
while he, tossing on his neck his fiery mane 70
dries the damp South Wind and plucks the clouds away.
Look! Every beast has now invaded the sky's vault
ahead of me! I, the victor, gaze up from earth
at my own labors, the constellations Juno gave
to beasts and monsters first, to make the skies
frightening to me. But even if she spatters the universe
and in her fury renders heaven worse than earth
and worse than Styx, Alcides will be given his place.[13]
If after beasts and wars and after the Stygian dog[14]
I've still not earned the stars, may Sicily's Cape Pelorus 80
touch the flank of Italy, to be one land henceforth:[15]

I'll chase the seas from there. If you decree its waters joined,
Jove, may the Isthmus merge its waves, and on the now
joined sea
let Attic vessels race on a new route.
Let the world mutate, the Ister rush along
new valleys, the Tanais receive new passages.
Give, Jupiter—at least give me gods to guard:
you'll be free to pull your lightning from
the part that I'll protect. Whether you bid me guard
90 the icy pole or else the torrid zone,
in this part know the gods themselves are safe.
Paean Apollo earned temples in Cirrha and a heavenly home
for one serpent slain.[16] —O how many a Python
died in Hydra! Bacchus and Perseus have now
joined the gods: but what a tiny region of the world
the conquered East, of beasts how small a part the Gorgon!
What son of yours and my stepmother's has earned
the stars by his own merits? I claim the heavens I bore.[17]
But you, Lichas, comrade of the toils of Hercules,
100 announce my triumphs, the vanquished house of Eurytus,[18]
his kingdom crushed. And you men, quickly drive the flock
to where the shore lifts up the temple of Cenean Jove[19]
and looks upon the Euboean sea, fearful for its tide.

CHORUS[20]

He is equal to the gods whose life
has matched his fortune. Deathlike is the lot of one
whose life is slowly measured out in groans.
Whoever has thrust the plundering fates
and that last river's ship beneath his feet,[21]
will never yield imprisoned arms to chains,
110 nor march, a famous float, in another man's parade.
The man for whom death's easy is never wretched.
If his boat betrays him in mid-Ocean
when the Southwest Wind has driven out the North
or the East Wind the West, and they split the sea,

he does not gather fragments of his shattered ship
hoping for shore in midexpanse of sea.
He who can yield up his life up on the spot,
he alone can never suffer shipwreck.
We waste away disgracefully, we weep,
our hair is filthy with our country's soil. 120
No plundering fire, no crashing down crushed us:
you, death, chase the blessed and flee the abject—
we abide. No area will be granted for our nation's crops,
only for forests, alas![22] Tumbled temples will become
squalid shelters. Some cold Dolopian now[23]
will drive his herds where the strewn ash
that's left of shattered Oechalia is still warm:
in that town a herdsman of Thessaly
will play his songs on his unskilled pipe,
and sing our days in tearful strains. 130
When god has gathered some few centuries,
they'll wonder where our nation's site had been.
Blessed, I dwelled then at not barren hearths
in the not infertile acres of Thessalian soil:
Now I'm called to Trachis, the harsh rocks
and bristling brambles on its arid crags,
woods unwelcome even to mountain-ranging herds.
But if a better fortune beckons some slave girls,
swift Inachus will ferry them across[24]
or they will live by Dirce's walls, where Ismenus 140
flows slowly with its slender stream.
But that's where puffed-up Hercules' mother wed.
What Scythian cliffs, or what stone gave you birth?
Did Mount Rhodope bear you like a wild Titan,[25]
or sheer Mount Athos, or the wild Caspian range?[26]
What striped tiger offered you its teats?
False is the story of that doubled night
when the heavens held back the stars too long,
the Morning Star gave up its turn to Evening,
and the Moon, too sluggish, barred the Sun.[27] 150

Impervious are his limbs to any wounds,
he feels iron to be dull, steel is too supple,
the sword breaks on his naked body
and stones bounce off it: he makes light of fate
and challenges death with his untamed physique.
Spear points could not pierce him,
nor a bow drawn with a Scythian shaft,
not the missiles the cold Sarmatian wields,[28]
nor, near the rising sun, the Parthian
160 who aims wounds at his Nabataean neighbor,
more accurate than Cretan bowmen's hits.
Oechalia's walls he pushed down with his body;
nothing can stand up to him: what he seeks to conquer
has already lost. How few have fallen to
wounds—his hostile face is good as fate,
it suffices to have seen the threats of Hercules.
What massive Briareus,[29] what swollen giant,[30]
when standing on the piled-up mound of Thessaly[31]
and laying viperish hands upon the sky,
170 has been so grim of face? Great benefits are granted
to great massacres: no further evil is left,
for we poor girls have seen the angered Hercules.

IOLE

But I, who am doomed—oh, it is not the temples, toppled
with their gods, the scattered hearths,
the fathers burnt together with their sons,
gods with men, temples with tombs—
—it is no shared wrong I lament.
Destiny calls my tears
to somewhere else, my fate commands me
180 weep for other ruins.
What shall I first lament? What last bemoan?
I want to weep in concert for them all.[32]
Too few breasts did Earth bestow on me
for the blows to ring out as my fate deserves.

Make me Niobe, the weeping stone of Sipylus,[33] O gods,
or put me on the banks of the Eridanus,
where sadly sound the trees that were the
sisters of Phaethon,
or attach me to the rocks of Sicily,
where I, a Thessalian Siren, can bemoan my fate, 190
or whisk me to the Edonian woods,
where the bird of Daulis ever weeps[34]
for her son in the shadow of Mount Ismarus.
Adjust my beauty to my tears,
and let rough Trachis ring out with my sufferings.[35]
Myrrha of Cyprus[36] preserves her own tears,
and Ceyx' wife bewails her stolen spouse,
Tantalus' daughter is her own survivor,
Philomela has escaped her shape
and the weepy Athenian maid cries out,[37] "my son": 200
why have *my* arms not yet assumed winged feathers?
I shall be happy, happy,
when a forest is called my home,
and alighting, a bird in my native fields,
I rehearse my miseries in a plaintive hum,
and legend will speak of winged Iole.
I saw, I saw, the miserable fate of my father,
when he was stricken by that fatal club
and he lay spattered through the whole royal hall:
if fate, Father, had granted you a tomb, 210
how many times would I have had to seek you!
And was I able to gaze upon your death,
Toxeus,[38] your tender cheeks not yet adorned
with beard, your blood not toughened yet?
But why, my parents, do I lament your fate,
since an even-handed death has guided you
to safety? My destiny asks tears of me.
Soon, so soon, I'll pick up wool and spindle,
my mistress' prisoner.
Cruel beauty, loveliness that will give birth to death for me, 220

for you alone my whole house fell,
when father denied me to Alcides
and feared to be the father-in-law of Hercules.
But let me now approach my mistress' house.

CHORUS

Why look back madly at your father's
bright realms and your forefathers?[39]
Your earlier prosperity must vanish from your looks.
Those who can suffer the state of slave and king alike are happy,
230 and are able to adjust their look.
Whoever has borne misfortune with a tranquil mind
has robbed the evil of its weight and power.

ACT 2

NURSE

What savage rage goads women when one home
lies open to both bride and concubine!
Scylla and Charybdis roiling the straits of Sicily
are less frightening, any beast is better.
When the beauty of the captive concubine blazed forth
and Iole glowed like a cloudless day
or as a bright star sparkles in the clear night,
240 the wife of Hercules stopped still and grimly stared
like one possessed. Just so, an Armenian tiger, having given
birth,
lies beneath a cliff and spies an enemy and leaps,
or a Maenad made to wield the thyrsus bears
Bacchus caught inside her, and, doubting where to turn her
steps,
halts momentarily. Then through the home of Hercules
she races, crazed; the whole house hardly holds her.
She runs, wavers, stops, all her pains march
through her face, in her inmost bosom scarce
anything remains, tears follow upon threats,

no attitude endures, nor is her rage content 250
with but one visage: now her cheeks burn,
now pallor drives away the blush, her pain
goes through all forms: she whines, she begs, she groans.
The door has creaked. Look—at a headlong pace
she bares the secrets of her mind in a muddled voice.

DEIANIRA

Whatever portion of the ethereal realm you tread,
wife of the Thunderer, against Alcides send
a beast enough for me! If some dragon
vaster than a whole swamp stirs its copious heads,
unknowing of defeat; if some huge horrid 260
dreadful thing is more than beast, a sight for Hercules
to turn away his eyes, let it emerge from its
deep cave; or if no beast's allowed, convert my very soul,
I pray, to something—anything that's evil
I can become in this mood: grant me a likeness
equal to my pain: my breast can't hold my threats.
Why search the caverns at the ends of earth
and stir up the world? Why ask hell for evils?
In this same breast you'll find all beasts that he
might fear: take up this weapon for your hates— 270
for I'm a stepmother.[40] I can ruin Alcides:
drive these hands anywhere. Juno, why hang back?
Use me while I'm raving! What horror do you bid me
to become? Find it![41] Why stall? —You may now hang back,
my wrath's enough.

NURSE

Control the protests of
this crazy breast of yours, my child, subdue the fires,
rein in your pain, and show yourself the spouse of Hercules.

DEIANIRA

Will captive Iole give brothers to my sons
and from a slave become Jove's daughter-in-law?

280 A fire will not run its course beside a flood,[42]
nor will the thirsty Bear drink the blue sea:[43]
I won't go unavenged. You may have borne the sky
and all the world is in your debt for peace—
there's something worse than Hydra: it is the pain
of an enraged bride. What fire in burning Aetna seethes
so high into the sky? Whatever you have beaten,
my spirit will beat that. A captive will steal my bed?
Till now I was afraid of fiends, now there's no such evil.
The scourges have withdrawn, in place of a beast has come
290 a hated concubine. O highest governor of the gods,
and you, bright Titan, I was wife of Hercules
only when he feared. The promises I made the gods
have worked to help a prisoner, and I was blessed
for a concubine's sake: for her you heard my prayers, O gods.
He comes back safe for her. My pain, that no
mere punishment can please—seek horrid agonies,
unspeakable, undreamed of. Go teach Juno
what hate can do! She doesn't know how to rage enough.
For me you used to wage your wars, for me
300 Achelous stained his wandering waters with his blood,[44]
when he became a pliant snake, then dropped the snake
and changed his menace into a fierce bull,
and in one enemy you beat a thousand beasts.
Now I displease you, a captive's been preferred to me—
but she'll not be! The last day of our marriage
will also be the last one of your life.
What's this? My mind draws back and lays aside its threats,
my wrath's retreated. Wretched pain, why do you wilt?
You're losing rage, you give me back again
310 a chaste wife's faithfulness. Why stop the flames from feeding?
Why enervate the fires? Keep up my momentum.
Let's proceed as equals: there'll be no need for vows.
His stepmother will come to guide my hands
unbidden.

NURSE

What's the crime you plan in your insanity?
Will you destroy your husband, whose acclaim 315
the setting and the rising day have known, whose fame,
raised up to heaven, holds the lands beneath?
Mother Earth will rise against those pyres,[45]
and first your father's house, then all Aetolians
will be crushed, soon stones and torches 320
will be hurled against you, and the whole world
will stand up for its champion: though one, how many
penalties you'll pay! Go think you can escape the earth,
the human race—Alcides' father wields a thunderbolt.
Behold the menacing fires even now cross the heavens,
the sky thundering now that the bolt is loosed.
Dread death itself, which you might deem safe! For there
the uncle of your Alcides holds sway.
Wherever you run, poor woman, there you'll see
gods-in-law!

DEIANIRA

That it will be the utmost crime 330
I do myself confess; but my pain commands it.

NURSE

You will die.

DEIANIRA

I'll die the wife of famous Hercules,
nor will any day, when night's been shaken off, mark me
as widowed, nor will some captive concubine capture
my marriage bed. Sooner will the day be brought forth from
the west,
sooner will the icy pole color the Indians
and Phoebus color Scythians with his warm chariot,
than will the girls of Thessaly see me cast off.
I'll quench the wedding torches with my own blood.
Let him die or kill me: to the beasts he's battered 340

he can add his wife, and count me too
among the toils of Hercules. If I'm to die,
at least I'll wrap my body round Alcides' bed:
Yes, I'm pleased to go to Hades as Hercules' bride—
but not without revenge. If Iole has conceived something
by my Hercules, I'll rip it out with my own hands
and midst the very wedding torches attack the concubine.
He can slay me as a sacrifice on his wedding day
in hatred, provided that I fall on lifeless Iole:
350 To trample those one hates is a lucky way to die.

NURSE

Why feed the flames yourself and willingly
foment your massive pain? Poor thing, why fear in vain?
He liked Iole: sure, while her father was alive
and it was the daughter of a king that he pursued. That queen
has fallen to a slave's estate. His love's lost energy
and her unhappy station has drained much from that one.
Illicit things are loved, but all that's licit lapses.

DEIANIRA

Worse fortune fans the flames of love the more.
He loves her just because she's lost her father's home,
360 because her hair lies stripped of gold and jewels:
for pity he may well love her very sufferings.
This is habitual with Hercules: he loves his captive women.

NURSE

The sister of Priam,[46] Dardanus' heir, was dear to him, sure—
he gave her as a slave. To this add all the wives,
the girls he liked before: he wandered everywhere.
The girl from Arcady, while she danced weavingly
for Pallas, Auge, bore the violence of rape, and then
was dropped: she keeps no token of the love of Hercules.
Why mention others? Thespius' daughters are unoccupied:
370 Alcides burnt for them—with a brief flame.
He favored, as Timolus' guest, the Lydian girl
and sat at the light distaff as love's captive,

twisting the tender thread with that fierce hand.
Those shoulders laid aside the trophy of the beast,
he tamped his hair down with a bonnet, stood like a slave,
his shaggy locks limp with Sabaean myrrh.[47]
He was afire everywhere, but with a fickle fire.

DEIANIRA

After roving passions, lovers usually stay put.

NURSE

Will he prefer a slave, an enemy's child, to you?

DEIANIRA

The way deep beauty sits upon the woods in spring, 380
when the first warmth dresses them, the grove still bare,
but when the North Wind's driven out the slackened South
and cruel winter has shaken off the entire foliage,
you see the unsightly grove with trunks all bare—
that's how my beauty's run its lengthy course,
forever shedding bits and shining less:
that former grace is gone: whatever it was in me
that was once pursued has toppled and now totters;[48]
so too maternity snatched much of it from me,
and old age will rip it out, with hurried strides. 390
See how the slave does not lose her deep dignity?
Her finery's all gone and filth has settled,
but through her very afflictions shines her charm,
and harsh fate and fortune have stolen nothing from her,
save sovereignty. This fear, my nurse, assails
my breast, this terror snatches sleep away.
I was a wife renowned in all the nations,
and every girl wished for my marriage bed
with jealous prayers—all who begged any gods
too much for anything. For Argive girls I was 400
the standard for their prayers. Will I ever have a
father-in-law like Jupiter, O nurse? Who in this world
will be given me for husband? Even if Eurystheus, who
commands

Alcides, would wed me with his wedding torches,
it's less. To lack a monarch's bed is easy,
but she's fallen far who's lost a man like Hercules.

NURSE

Children often reconcile a couple's hearts.

DEIANIRA

So too those very children may split their bed apart.

NURSE

That slave meanwhile is brought you as a gift.

DEIANIRA

410 The man you see go in renown through cities,
wearing the lifelike trophy of a beast upon his back,
who gives realms to wretches and steals them from the great,
his horrid hand weighed down with that huge club,
whose triumphs men of farthest China sing
and all who lie within the fenced-round globe—
he's frivolous. It's not glory's charm that drives him:
he does not roam the earth to be Jove's equal,
nor to walk great among the Argive towns—
he seeks something to love, he chases after virgin's beds.
420 If one's denied to him, she's raped. He rages against nations,
looks for brides among the ruins: unbridled vice
is called heroic virtue. Famed Oechalia fell
and a single Sun and single day beheld
it stand and fall: the cause of war was love.
A father will fear each time that he denies
Hercules his daughter, is an enemy if he declines
to be his father-in-law. If he's not son-in-law, he slays.
After this, why do I harmlessly hold back these hands—
until he should feign madness and with that cruel hand
430 direct his bow and murder his own son and me?
That's how Alcides drives out his own wives,
that's his divorce. He can't be guilty, either:
to the world he's made his crimes' cause seem

his stepmother. Why be stunned and sluggish, madness?
My crime must precede his. Strike while your hand is hot.

NURSE
You'll kill your husband?

DEIANIRA
The concubine's, for sure.

NURSE
The child of Jove?

DEIANIRA
Alcmena's son as well.

NURSE
With sword?

DEIANIRA
With sword.

NURSE
And if you can't?

DEIANIRA
I'll kill by guile.

NURSE
What madness is this?

DEIANIRA
It's what my husband teaches.

NURSE
You'll kill a man even his stepmother could not kill? 440

DEIANIRA
Celestial wrath makes wretched whom it crushes;
man's wrath makes them null.

NURSE
Spare him, poor woman—and fear him.

DEIANIRA
Whoever's disdained death disdains all else.
I'm pleased to march upon the sword.

NURSE

Your pain,
child, is greater than the wrong. Let blame provoke hate fairly.
Why answer middling with cruel? As you've been hurt, be
pained.

DEIANIRA

You think a concubine slight evil for a wife?
Count as too much whatever fosters pain.

NURSE

Has your love for celebrated Hercules left you?

DEIANIRA

450 It has not left me, nurse; it stays and sits fixed deep
within my marrow, trust me. But the pain
of love enraged is huge.

NURSE

With magic arts
and admixed prayers wives often bind their spouses.
I've ordered woods to grow green in winter's midst,
the thunderbolt already thrown to stop; I've roused
the deep when winds are stilled, and smoothed the roiling sea,
dry earth has opened itself up to fresh springs.
Stones have gained mobility. I've dashed the gates
and shades of Dis: commanded by my prayer
460 ghosts speak, the infernal dog keeps still.[49]
462 Sea, earth, hell, and the heavens serve me,
461 midnight has seen the sun and day the night.
463 Laws have no force against my incantations.[50]
I'll bend him: my spells will find the path.

DEIANIRA

The herbs that Pontus grows or the ones that Pindus[51]
feeds beneath the cliffs of Thessaly, or somewhere else:
where will I find the bane to which he'll yield? The moon may
drop
to earth by magic chants, abandoning the stars,
and winter may see harvests, the swift thunderbolt

stall, intercepted by a spell, conversely 470
midday boil under coerced stars—it will not
bend him.

NURSE

Love has conquered even gods above.

DEIANIRA

Perhaps Love will be conquered and will yield his arms
to one alone, and Love will be the final toil of Hercules.
But by every power of the heavenly gods, I beg you,
by this fear of mine: whatever secret thing I plan,
hide deep within and suppress with silent trust.

NURSE

What is it that you wish to be concealed?

DEIANIRA

Not spears, armor, or the threat of fire.

NURSE 480

I'll avow that I can keep a silent trust,
if it is free of sin; but sometimes trust is criminal.

DEIANIRA

Come then, look round, so no one takes our secret by surprise.
Your gaze must go exploring everywhere.

NURSE

Look! This place is safe and free of witnesses.

DEIANIRA

In a secluded place within the royal house
there is a silent recess that guards my secret.
That place receives no morning sun, nor evening
sun, when Titan carries off the day
and sinks his weary wheels into the reddening sea.
There lies concealed the guarantee of Hercules' love. 490
Nurse, I'll confess: the author of this evil was Nessus[52]
whom Nephele conceived and bore to Thessaly's lord,
where lofty Pindus pokes its head among the stars
and Othrys,[53] rising over the clouds, is frozen.

For when, subdued by savage Hercules' club,
Achelous, readily rendered into every shape,
with every beast used up, at last was bared
and bowed his ugly head that has one horn,
when conquering Alcides took for wife—
500 he was going back to Argos, but by chance the stream
Evenus, meandering through fields and hauling its deep torrent
to the sea, was roiling now almost above its banks.
Used to crossing eddies at the fords, Nessus
asked a fee, and now bearing me on his back
where dwindling spine joins man to horse,
was breaking through the menace of the swollen river.
Wild Nessus now had wholly exited the waves,
with Alcides still advancing in midford,
cutting the rapacious current with huge strides.
510 —But when he saw Alcides was still far,
he said, "You'll be my booty and my wife.
He's blocked by waves," and holding me he bore me off,
quickening his pace. But waves don't hold back Hercules:
"Faithless ferryman," he says, "the Ganges and
the Ister could run mixed, with joined riverbeds,
I'd beat both, and with an arrow overtake your flight."
His bow anticipates his words: delivering
a distant wound the reed-shaft halts his flight fast
and drives home death. Nessus, seeking daylight now,
520 catches the wound's flowing gore in his right hand
and gives it to me, inserted in his hoof
which he ripped off and split with his brute hand,
and dying adds these words: "By this bane," said he,
"witches have said that love can be spellbound;
skilled Mycale taught this to the girls of Thessaly,
the one among all witches whom the Moon escorts,
abandoning the stars. You'll give him clothes smeared
with this very gore," he said, "in case some hateful
concubine wins your marriage bed, and your fickle spouse
530 gives his deep-thundering father another daughter-

in-law. Let no light see it, let banished gloom alone
conceal it: thus will the potent blood retain
its power." A stupor interrupts his words
and sleep instills his languid limbs with death.
You, to whom my trust gives access to my secret,
see to it that the potion dousing his sleek clothes
runs through limbs to brain and silently
invades his inmost marrow.

NURSE

Child, I'll execute
your orders instantly. You must address with prayers
the unconquered god who shoots sure shafts from tender hand. 540

DEIANIRA

I pray you, you whom world and gods above and sea
and he who wields Etna's thunderbolt[54] all fear,
frightening to your cruel mother, bow-wielding boy,
direct a swift barb with your surefire hand,
not from your light arrows—take one, I pray,
from the heavier batch, which never yet your hands
have loosed on anyone; no light arrow's needed
so that Hercules can love. Stretch your hands out tautly
and ready your bow so both tips meet.
Now, produce that arrow with which you once 550
attacked rough Jove,[55] when the god laid down his
thunderbolt and, his brow bulging suddenly,[56]
cut through the raging sea, a bull bearing the Assyrian girl.[57]
Loose love on him, let him surpass all precedents:
may he learn to love his wife! If Iole's charms
have lit torches in that Herculean breast,
quench them all, and let him drink my beauty.
Often you've tamed thundering Jupiter,
and him who wields the dark staff of the lightless world,
leader of a larger throng, lord of the Styx, 560
god harsher than an irate step-mother:
win this trophy, be the only one to conquer Hercules.

NURSE

The brew's brought out, and the garment that wore out
every slave girl's hand at Pallas' spindle.
Pour on the potion and let Hercules' clothes
drink in the blight, and I'll increase the bane with prayers.
But here comes busy Lichas, just in time:
let's hide the dire brew lest our plot be bared.

DEIANIRA

O Lichas, you ever-loyal name to kings,
570 a thing which tyrants' houses never have,
take this cloak that my hand wove while he
went wandering through the world and held,
undone by wine, the Lydian girl in his fierce embrace,
while he asked for Iole. Perhaps I'll bend that bestial heart
by deserving it: good deeds have beaten wicked men.
Bid my husband not to wear these clothes
till he's fed flames with incense and appeased the gods,
binding his stiff locks with a laurel of white poplar.
I'll make my way unto the royal home
580 and tend with prayers the mother of horrid Love.
You women of Calydon,[58] whom I brought as friends
from your fathers' hearths, lament my sorrowful fate.

CHORUS

We, your throng of friends in your first years,
weep for your fortunes, daughter of Oeneus,
weep for your doubtful marriage bed, poor girl.
We used to splash our way through Achelous' ford
with you, when spring was wholly ended and
he had slackened now his swollen waves
and lightly, with an even pace, Lycormas snaked[59]
590 his tawny way, and did not roll
his stream headlong from bursting fountainheads.
We would proceed through Pallas' altars
and perform our virgin dances,
with you we used to bear the relics

hidden in Cadmaean baskets,[60]
when with winter's star now banished
the third season summons sunshine
and lands granted by the grain-bearing goddess,
and Attic Eleusis confines the initiates.
Now too, whatever lot you fear, 600
take us as your fate's faithful friends:
for faith is rare when better fortune
has collapsed.
Whoever you are who hold the scepter,
though all the public in your courtyard
may pound your hundred doors at once:[61]
though you walk amid so many people,
amid so many people there's no trust.
The Erinys grips your golden doorway,[62]
and when the great gate lies wide open, 610
swindles enter, cagey hoaxes,
the hidden sword. When you prepare
to walk among the people, envy attends you.
Each time Dawn replaces night,
believe a king is born anew.
Few serve kings instead of kingdoms,
palace splendor draws the masses.[63]
This one wants to walk in brilliance
beside the king through all the cities,
glory burns his wretched breast; 620
another wants with wealth to sate
his hunger, but none of gem-rich Hister's[64]
tract suffices,
not does all Lydia quench his thirst,
not the land which, exposed to Zephyr,[65]
is stunned that brilliant Tagus glows with golden waters.
Not even if entire Hebrus served him
and rich Hydaspes joined its fields
and he saw Ganges with all its waters
running inside his own holdings: 630

Nature's little for the greedy.
This one waits on kings and kings' halls,
not like a plowman, always bent over
the plow he presses, may not cease;
not like the thousand farmers furrowing the fields:
he only wants wealth so he can hoard it.
That one waits on kings so he can trample
all, ruin some, and raise up no one:
he wants power just to harm.
640 How few die at the destined time!
Those whom Cynthia sees happy,[66]
those same the newborn day sees wretched.
Rare is the man both old and happy.
Turf, softer than Tyrian purple,
always brings sleep free of fear;
golden ceilings rupture slumber,[67]
purple brings on wakeful nights.
If only rich men's hearts lay open!
How great the fears their towering fortune
650 stirs within them!
Though the North Wind pound the straits, the Bruttian surf is
gentler.[68]
A poor man has a carefree heart:
he grips a cup of broad-branched beechwood,
but grips it with unshaking hand,
picks out food that's cheap and easy,
but casts no glances for drawn swords.
In golden goblets blood is mixed.
A wife wed to a humble husband
doesn't sport the Red Sea's brilliant
660 gifts displayed in fancy necklace,
choice gems from eastern waters
do not hang on jewel-laden ears,
soft wool in bronze bowls of Sidon
doesn't drink red dyes repeatedly,

what the Chinese pick from trees where suns rise,
exposed to Phoebus' eastern winds,
she doesn't stitch with Lydian needle:
any old plants have tinged the wool
her untrained hands have woven.
But the bed she warms is not at risk. 670
With dire torch the Erinys chases
girls whose day the throngs attend.
A poor man does not think he's blessed
until he's seen the blessed fall.
Whoever shuns the middle path
never runs a course that's stable:
when Phaethon asked for one day only
and a son stood on his father's chariot
and did not follow the normal path
but sought out stars unknown to Phoebus' 680
flames on wheels that wandered widely,
he ruined the world and himself with it.
While Daedalus ploughed heaven's middle pathway,
he kept to placid regions[69]
and did not give a sea his name;
but when Icarus dared surpass
real birds
and son despised his father's wings
and flew too near to Phoebus himself,
he gave an unknown sea his name: 690
what's great is repaid hurtfully with ruin.
Let others be called blessed and great,
but let no crowd hail me as mighty,
may my light vessel hug the shore
and no great wind bid my small boat
to cleave the middle of the sea.
Fortune bypasses safe inlets
and seeks ships in the midmost deep
whose topsails dash against the clouds.

ACT 3

(*Deianira rushes out of the palace in fear.*)

CHORUS

700 But why does the queen, with fearful looks,
like a maenad struck by Bacchus,
rush out scared with headlong stride?
What fortune spins you yet again,
poor woman, tell us:
though you deny it, your looks declare what you are hiding.

DEIANIRA

A wandering tremor haunts my shaken limbs,
my hair's on end, and terror dwells
in my still stricken mind, my frenzied heart
beats wildly, my liver, frightened, throbs in trembling veins.
710 The way the South Wind rumpled sea still swells,
although the day is calm, with wearied winds,
my mind is harried still, though fear is shaken out.
When once the god's begun to oppress the blessed,
he pushes on: great things have this finale.

CHORUS

What wild mischance, poor girl, spins you round?

DEIANIRA

When the cloak was sent, stained with Nessus' gore,
and I'd made my way in grief to my boudoir,
my mind formed a sort of fear, contrived a trick.[70]
I chose to make a test. Nessus forbade
720 that the wild potion be exposed to sun, the blood to flames:
this very guile forewarned that there'd be tricks.
By chance, the fiery Titan, his light speckled
by no cloud, was letting loose the seething day
—my fear even now scarce lets my lips unclench.
Amid the fires of the sun and his bright torch,
where the cloak was stained and the clothes smeared,
the shed blood curdles,[71] and warmed by Phoebus' plumes
it ignites (I can hardly tell the horror).

The way the East or tepid South Wind melts the snows
that at spring's start gleaming Mount Mimas melts,[72] 730
and as Point Leucas blocks the Ionian Sea
and breaks the rolling waves, the wearied swell
foaming on the shore, or incense sprinkled
for the gods dissolves on tepid altars,
so the whole wilts, loses its pile.
As I'm amazed by this, what I'm amazed by
disappears, the very earth stirs up
a foamy quake, everything touched by
the gore reels, silently swelling. . . .[73] He's shaking his
head—
my son, I see him, frightened, making his way 740
at a feverish pace. Out with the news you're bearing!

HYLLUS

Go! Flee! Search out whatever lies beyond
earth and sea and stars, ocean and hell!
Fly, Mother, further than Alcides' labors!

DEIANIRA

My mind anticipates some vast disaster!

HYLLUS

Seek Juno's temple, as the spoil of her triumph:
it's open to you, all other shrines are shut.

DEIANIRA

I'm guiltless: say what fortune crushes me.

HYLLUS

That glory of the world, its one defense,
whom fate had given the earth in lieu of Jove, 750
is gone, O Mother. Some unknown scourge is burning
the Herculean limbs and muscles; he, who tamed beasts,
he, the victor vanquished, mourns and feels pain.
What more do you want?

DEIANIRA

The wretched rush to hear
their wretchedness. Speak: in what state

is our house now? O Lares,[74] wretched Lares:
now widowed, now expelled, now crushed, I'll go.

HYLLUS

Not you alone mourn Hercules. He lies
bemoaned by the whole world: don't think it's your
760 fate only, Mother: all mankind's clamoring now.
See! All bemoan whom you bemoan in grief:[75]
the harm you suffer is shared by every land.
You've a head start on grief: poor woman, you're the first
to mourn for Hercules, not the only.

DEIANIRA

Tell me, tell,
I beg you, how near death does my Alcides lie?

HYLLUS

Death, conquered once in its own realm, avoids him
and fate dares not commit so great a sin.
Clotho herself,[76] perhaps, has thrown her distaff down,
with trembling hand, and fears to bring about
770 the doom of Hercules. O day unspeakable!
Is this the last day great Alcides lives?

DEIANIRA

You say he's beating me to fate and ghosts
and to the nether world? Or can I reach
death sooner? Tell me if he's not yet dead.

HYLLUS

The Euboean land, which swells to a high peak,
is pounded on every side. Cape Caphereus splits[77]
the sea of Phrixus: this flank's subject to South Winds.
But where it suffers the snowy North Wind's threats,
the erratic Euripus bends its wandering waves
780 and turns its course seven times and back again,
till the weary Titan sinks his steeds in Ocean.
Here on a lofty cliff which no cloud hits,
glistens the ancient temple of Cenaean Jove.
As at the altar stood all the votive herd,

and the woods all bellowed with the gilded bulls,
he doffed his lion's spoil, filthy with grime,
and dropped his heavy club and eased his shoulders
of the quiver's weight.[78] Then gleaming in your garment,
his bristling hair bound with white poplar,
he lit the altar: "receive," he said, "these harvests 790
on your hearth, true father, and may the holy fire
sparkle with plentiful myrrh which the rich Arab,
revering Phoebus, culls from Sabaean trees.
Earth has been pacified, also sky and sea,
all beasts are subdued, I've returned as conqueror.
Lay down your thunderbolt"—amidst his prayers
a groan sounds; he himself is stunned. Then he fills
the sky with ghastly screams. As a runaway bull,
the ax sunk in, lugs wound and weapon and fills
to trembling the temple with its loud lowing, 800
or as a loosed thunderbolt resounds throughout
the world, he smites with groans the stars and sea.
Vast Chalcis echoed and all the Cyclades
took in his cries. The crags of Caphereus here,
there the whole wood re-echoed Hercules' cries.
We see him weep, the crowd believes his former
madness has returned, the slaves take flight.
But he, his face distorted by the flaming heat,
seeks and hunts just Lichas amid them all.
He, clutching the altar with a trembling hand, 810
pre-empted death with fear, left little of
himself for vengeance. The other grasped the trembling
corpse by the hand: "Is this the hand, this, O fates,"
he said, "by which I'll be deemed defeated? Has Lichas beaten
Hercules? Look, more bloodshed, as Hercules slays Lichas.
He'll soil my deeds: be this my final labor."
He soars, thrown starward, sprays clouds with his roving
blood. Thus springs an arrow heavenward,
dispatched at the command of a Getic hand,[79]
or one a Cretan's launched: yet lower still 820

will their shafts fly. His trunk falls in the sea,
his neck on rocks—one man lies in both places.
"Halt!" says Hercules; "madness hasn't stolen my wits.
This evil is more grim than frenzy or fury.
It's me I want to rage against!" He barely names
the bane and rages, lacerates his limbs
and plucks and tears his huge limbs with his hands.
He tries to shed the cloak: at this one thing
have I seen Hercules fail. But as he tried to pull
830 it off, pulled off his limbs despite himself: the cloak's
part of his brutish body, garment mixed with skin.
The cause of his dire death's not in the open,
but cause there is. Scarce equal to the evil, faint,
he presses now the earth with face cast down,
now begs for water—but water does not beat the evil;
he seeks the wave-resounding shores, he gains the sea—
a band of slaves restrains him as he strays.
O bitter Fate! We were Alcides' equals!
A ship now brings him from the Euboean shore,
840 the gentle South Wind hauls Hercules' weight.
His soul has left his limbs, night presses on his eyes.

DEIANIRA

Why wait, my soul? Why stunned? The crime is done.
Jove summons back his son, Juno her foe.[80]
He must be restored to the world—what can be, grant!—
but let the driven sword run through my limbs;
thus must it be done, thus. Can a hand so slight pay back
so great a penalty? Slay with your bolts, O Father-in-law,
your wicked daughter-in-law; nor with some slight shaft
let your hand be armed: let that bolt spring from the sky
850 with which, had you not fathered Alcides, you would
have seared the Hydra. Strike me like a rare scourge,
an evil worse than the enraged stepmother.
Send forth a bolt like that sent formerly

at errant Phaethon. By killing Hercules I, myself,
have ruined the people too: why ask the gods for bolts?
Spare your father-in-law: let Alcides' wife
be ashamed to pray for death. This hand will do
for vows—I can answer my own prayer! Quick, seize
a sword. Why sword? Whatever weapon leads
to death is enough. I'll leap from a lofty cliff— 860
let this one be chosen, this Oeta, which summons first
the newborn day: I want my body flung from here.
Let the sheer crag rip and every rock
catch part of me, let my slashed hands hang there
and the rough mountain's side grow wholly red.
One death is slight—slight, but it can be lengthened.
My soul, you don't know how to choose which blade
to fall on: would that Hercules' sword were planted
in my bed: on this sword it is right to die.
Is it enough for me to die by just one hand? 870
Gather, nations, let the world hurl stones
and burning torches, let no hand tarry now,
snatch arms: it's your avenger I have slain.
With impunity cruel kings will now wield scepters,
unbridled evil with impunity will now be born.
Altars that saw worshippers as offerings
will be restored: I've made a road for crimes.
To tyrants, kings, monsters, beasts, and savage gods
I have exposed you, the avenger snatched away.
Partner of the Thunderer, you wait? You don't strew 880
and hurl a fire snatched from Jove, aping your brother,
and slay me yourself? Famous praise is snatched from you,
a huge triumph: I beat you to the death of
your own foe.

NURSE

Why drag down a stricken house?
Whatever's impious in the deed is due to error;
Whoever's guilty without intent is not guilty.

DEIANIRA

Whoever pardons fate and spares himself
deserved to do wrong. I want death as my sentence.

NURSE

One who seeks to die desires to look guilty.

DEIANIRA

890 Death alone makes innocent the deceived.

NURSE

You'll flee the Sun?

DEIANIRA

The Sun himself fled me!

NURSE

You'll leave this life?

DEIANIRA

This wretched life, to follow Alcides.

NURSE

He lives on and breathes the airs above.

DEIANIRA

When Hercules could be conquered, he began to die.

NURSE

You will forsake your son, cut short your fate?

DEIANIRA

She whom her son has buried has lived long.

NURSE

You'll follow your husband?

DEIANIRA

Chaste wives usually go first.

NURSE

Condemning yourself, poor woman, you convict yourself of crime.

DEIANIRA

No one who's guilty cancels his own penalty.[81]

NURSE

To many life's been granted when their error, 900
not their hand, was guilty. Who passes sentence on his fate?

DEIANIRA

Whoever's been dealt a fate that is unfair.

NURSE

But he himself struck Megara down,[82] transfixed
with his own arrows, and his pride of sons,
firing Hydra-poisoned arrows with a maddened hand.[83]
Thrice made murderer of kin, he still pardoned
himself, if not his madness. In Cinyps' stream,[84] under Libya's sky,
he wiped away the crime, cleansed his right hand.
Poor woman, how far will you go? Why damn your hands?

DEIANIRA

Alcides, conquered by them, damns my hands. 910
I want to avenge the crime.

NURSE

If I know Hercules,
perhaps he'll come as victor over that bloody garment;
pain, defeated, will yield to your Alcides.

DEIANIRA

Rumor is the Hydra's potion has consumed his joints,
a boundless plague has ruined my husband's limbs.

NURSE

You claim the poison of the serpent slain by him
cannot be conquered, though he withstood that monster when
it lived?
He crushed the Hydra, when he stood as victor in
midswamp, teeth fixed in him and his limbs smeared with
oozing poison. Will Nessus' blood curb him, 920
who conquered the very hands of hideous Nessus?

DEIANIRA

It's pointless to hold back one resolved to die.
I have decided thus to flee the light:
Whoever dies with Alcides has lived enough.

NURSE

By these old hairs, a suppliant—look!—and by
these all but mother's breasts, I beg of you:
lay down these puffed up threats of an injured heart,
cast out your stern resolve on dire death.

DEIANIRA

Who convinces someone miserable not to die
930 is cruel. Though death's indeed a punishment,
it's often been a gift, to many a mercy.

NURSE

At least acquit, unhappy woman, your own hand:
let him know the deed arose from guile, not from his wife.

DEIANIRA

I'll be defended there: the ones below will clear me;
I am condemned by me! Let Pluto purge these hands.
I'll stand beside your banks, forgetful Lethe,
and as a sad shade I'll receive my husband.
But you, who torture the dominions of the gloomy sky,[85]
get ready for your task—my error will surpass
940 crimes anyone has dared: Juno did not dare snatch
Hercules from the earth. Prepare a ghastly punishment.
Let Sisyphus' neck relax and let the rock
press on my shoulders. Let the fickle water flee
me and the deceitful liquid mock my thirst.[86]
I deserve to offer my hands to your whirls,
O wheel that tortures the Thessalian king.
Let the greedy vulture gouge my liver on both sides.
One Danaid is missing; I'll complete her turn.
Make room, ghosts: admit me as your fellow,
950 wife from Phasis:[87] this hand is worse, worse
than either crime of yours, as guilty mother
or as dreadful sister. Add me as fellow to
your crimes, O Thracian wife.[88] Receive your daughter,
Althaea, Mother, and now acknowledge your true
progeny; yet what thing so great was it that

your hands slew? Close off Elysium to me,
you faithful wives who occupy the groves
in the sacred wood. If any has spattered her hands
with her husband's blood, nor mindful of the chaste torch
has stood with drawn sword like some savage Danaid,[89] 960
let her recognize her hands in me—and praise them.
I'm eager to go over to this crowd of wives—
but even this crowd will flee such dreadful hands.
Unconquerable spouse, my soul is innocent,
my hand wicked. O my too credulous mind,
deceitful Nessus and your semibestial guile!
Desirous to snatch him from his concubine, I ripped him
from myself. Back, Sun! Back, Life, who keep the wretched
in the alluring light! To me, since I'll lose Hercules,
this light is worthless. I'll exact the punishment 970
for you, pay with my life—or should I prolong
my fate, O spouse, and save my death for your own hands?
Is any of your valor left, and can your armed hands[90]
draw the bow and shoot its shafts?
Or do your weapons hesitate, does your bow ignore you,
now your hand is slack? If you can deliver death,
O spouse, I wait for your hand bravely.
Let death be deferred: break me like guiltless Lichas,
spatter me on other towns and hurl me to some world
unknown to you. Kill me like the bane of Arcady,[91] 980
or whatever else opposed you; at least from those,
my spouse, you did return.

HYLLUS

I beg you, mother,
spare yourself, pardon your fate: error's without guilt.

DEIANIRA

If you would seek true piety, Hyllus,
then kill your mother now. Why did your timid hand just
tremble? Why turn away your eyes? This crime is piety.
You hesitate, coward? I snatched Hercules from you.

This hand, this one, slew your father, thanks to whom
the Thunderer's your grandfather. I snatched from you an honor
990 greater than I granted you with life.[92] If crime's
unknown to you, learn from your mother. If you wish
to sink your sword into my throat or you prefer
to assault the maternal womb, your mother will show you
a fearless soul. So great a crime will not
be carried out by you alone: I'll be laid low
by your hand, but the will is mine. Are you afraid, Alcides' son?
This way, you'll carry out no orders, nor roam
the world destroying evils, should some beast be born.[93]
Recall your father: ready a right hand that's fearless.
1000 Look! my breast, so full of cares, lies open. Strike!
I waive the crime. The Eumenides themselves[94]
will spare your hand. The lashes' sound has cracked.
Who's this who braids her hair with a poisonous snake
and flaps black feathers on her filthy temples?
Why pursue me, dread Megaera, with your flaming torch?
Demanding satisfaction for Alcides? I'll pay.
Are the judges of those below already seated, dread one?
Behold, I see the prison's dreaded doors.[95]
Who's this old man who bears the massive rock
1010 on his worn shoulders? Look, the all but conquered stone
seeks to roll back. Who gives up his limbs to the wheel?
Look, here dread Tisiphone stands ashen, demands
a trial. Megaera, I implore you, spare
the lashes, spare them, keep back the Stygian torches.
It was a crime of love! What's this? The earth
teeters, the palace creaks, the roof is shaken.
Whence this menacing mob? The whole world rushes
at my face, the nations roar on every side,
the whole cosmos is demanding its avenger.
1020 Cities, spare me. In my rush where can I flee?
Death only will be granted as haven for my cares.
Bear witness, blazing wheel of shining Phoebus,

bear witness, gods above: about to die I leave
Hercules still on earth.

HYLLUS

She's fled in frenzy.
Unhappy me, my mother's part is played: she has resolved
to die. Mine's left, to block her urge to death.
O wretched sense of duty: if you prevent your mother's
death, you're wicked to your father; if you suffer her to die,
you sin against your mother. Crime presses on both sides.
Yet she must be restrained; I'll go pluck her from death.[96] 1030

CHORUS

What the sacred Thracian sang
beneath the slopes of Rhodope,
tuning his Pierian lyre,
Orpheus, offspring of Calliope,[97]
is true: nothing's eternal.
The crash of raging torrent
stopped still before his measures,
its waters lost their impulse,
forgot to follow up their flow.
And while the rivers took a pause, 1040
the Bistones,[98] furthest of the Getae,
thought the Hebrus had run dry.
Woods came and brought their birds along,
sitting in the trees they came;
if any one flew through the air,
and heard his songs while flitting by,
it lost its strength and fell.
Mount Athos ruptured its own crags
and bore the centaurs right along
and stopped still by the Rhodope, 1050
its snows melted by songs.
The Dryad flees her own oak tree
and hastens to the bard.

Wild beasts together with their lairs
come to your incantations,
and the lion of Marmarica[99]
sits next to sheep who have no fear,
nor do deer tremble at the wolves,
and the serpent leaves its lair
1060 forgetful of its poison now.
Even when through Taenarus' door[100]
he approached the silent Manes,
striking up his grieving lyre,
he conquered with his tearful song
Tartarus and the sad gods
of Erebus, nor feared the pools
of Styx, where gods above swear oaths.
The never-stationary wheel
stuck, languid, its whirling conquered;
1070 while he held the vultures back with song
Tityos' liver grew.
The boatman too was listening:[101]
the ferry of the infernal lake
arrives without the stroke of oars.
First then the aged Phrygian,
shook off, forgetful, his wild thirst,
as the waters stood stock still,
nor stretched his hands out to the fruit.
So too when Orpheus was pouring out
1080 his charming songs among the ones below,
even the relentless stone was able
to be tamed and trail the bard.
Once more the goddesses replenished
the used-up distaffs of Eurydice.[102]
But when, forgetful, Orpheus did look back,
not trusting that Eurydice
was given back and following him,
he lost the trophy of his song:
restored to life she died again.

Then seeking solace in his songs, 1090
in tearful measures Orpheus sang
these words before the Getae:[103]
"Laws were given to the gods above:
even the god who allocates the times
and set four turning points
in the onrushing year;
for everyone the greedy Fates
weave their threads on distaffs.
Death follows birth for everything."
The overpowered Hercules 1100
bids us believe the Thracian bard.
Yet soon, soon, when laws are overthrown,
when that day will come upon the world,
the southern pole will overwhelm
whatever lies in Libya
and what the far-flung Garamantes retain.[104]
The northern pole will overwhelm
whatever lies beneath its vaults
and the arid North Wind strikes.
Fearful, once the poles are lost, 1110
the Sun will shake away the day.
The tumbling palace of the sky
will drag down both the east and west
and a kind of death and chaos
will destroy all gods alike,
and death will set up the final fates
for itself and to itself.
What space will contain the world?
Will the road to Tartarus part
and lie wide open to the fractured poles? 1120
Or is the space that separates
the upper air from earth enough
and more, for the downfall of the world?
What will contain so great a crime
of fate, what single place above

contain Tartarus, the sea,
and stars, three realms?
But what is this outlandish roaring
that reaches my stunned ears?
1130 It is a Herculean clamor!

ACT 4

(*Hercules is carried in on a litter by his slaves.*)

HERCULES

Turn back, bright Sun, your panting horses, and send forth
the night. May this day on which I die perish
from the earth, the sky grow grim with pitch-black cloud:
block my stepmother's view! Now, Father: it is right
that blind chaos return. Both poles should be
smashed, the world's frame ruptured on all sides.
Why spare the stars? Father, you're losing Hercules.
Jupiter, inspect now every part of heaven,
lest some giant hurl Thessalian cliffs
1140 and Othrys be a light weight for Enceladus.[105]
Now, now proud Pluto will be loosening the doors
of his dark prison, he'll shake off his father's bonds[106]
and give him heaven back. I, who was born
on earth to be your lightning and your fire,
return to Styx, and fierce Enceladus will arise
and hurl the mass that presses him at the upper gods.
Father, my death will render insecure
your whole airy realm. Before you are despoiled
of your heaven, Father, bury me
1150 in the world's utter ruin, and smash the sky you're losing.

CHORUS

Not vain your fears, O Thunderer's son,
Now Pelion will press Thessaly's
Mount Ossa;[107] Athos piled on Pindus
will thrust its woods midst heaven's stars.
Then Typhoeus will conquer the crags

and carry Tuscan Inarime.[108]
Enceladus, not yet conquered by lightning,
will carry Aetna's forges out,
splitting the flank of the gaping mountain.
Heaven's realm now follows you. 1160

HERCULES

I, who left death behind, disdained the Styx,
returned through Lethe's bayous with my spoils[109]
—when the Sun near fell from his skidding horses—
I, whom the three realms of the gods have known,
I die. There's no sword thrust through my side
that hisses, nor is some rock the weapon of
my doom, nor stone that's like a shorn-off mountain[110]
nor all of Othrys; no giant with a vicious maw
has covered up my corpse with all of Pindus.
I'm conquered without foe, and what torments me 1170
more (O wretched valor), Alcides' last day
lays low no evil, nor do I expend my life, ah me,
on any deeds. You, overseer
of the world, you gods above, once witnesses
to my right hand, O entire Earth: have you decided
to waste the death of Hercules? O dreadful shame of mine,
O vile fate: a woman will be called the cause
of Hercules' doom! For whom do I, Alcides, die?
If the unconquerable fates wished me to fall
by woman's hand, and by so vile a thread 1180
my life has run its course[111]—ah me! I wish I'd fallen
to Juno's hate: I'd fall to a woman's threats,
but she at least holds heaven. Were that too much for the gods,
an Amazon born under Scythian skies might have
subdued my strength. By such a woman's hand
I, Juno's foe, am conquered! In this your shame's
more grievous, Stepmother. How can you call this day a
happy one?
When you raged, did earth bear you anything like this?

A mortal woman has outdone your hatred.
1190 Till now you raged at being Alcides' lesser:[112]
now you have *two* victors! The gods should be embarrassed by
their puny rages!
I wish the Nemean scourge had sated its maw
on my blood or, hemmed in by a hundred snakes,
I'd fed the Hydra with my gore.
I wish I'd been given to Centaurs as prey
or was sitting wretchedly bound to an eternal rock
amidst the shades, when I dragged up my final spoil
and Fate was stunned. Instead, from hellish Styx
I regained the light. I overcame the hindrances of Dis.
1200 Death fled me everywhere—all so that I'd lack
the glory of a famous death.[113] Beasts, O conquered beasts!
The triform dog, having seen the sun, did not
drag me back to Styx, nor under Western skies
did the wild herdsman's Spanish flock beat me,[114]
nor the twin snakes. Unhappy me, so often did I waste
a noble death. What final fame is this?

CHORUS

You see how valor, conscious of glory,
does not shudder at Lethe's river?
He's shamed by the cause, not pained by death.
1210 He wished to end his final day
via the vast bulk of a swollen giant,
to suffer a mountain-bearing Titan
and owe his death to a rabid beast.
But your hand is the reason, poor man,[115]
that it's no wild beast nor a giant.
And now what worthy source is left
of Hercules' death, save your right hand?

HERCULES

Unhappy me, what scorpion within, what Cancer[116]
plucked from torrid zones and riveted
1220 within burns up my marrow? Formerly

so full of blood, my liver bloats the parched lobes of
my swollen lungs[117]—my liver burns with dried up bile,
a sluggish heat has drawn off all my blood.
The curse consumed my outer skin, then made
an entry to my limbs; the plague undid my sides,
the evil ate away my inner joints and ribs,
drank up my marrow, sits in hollow bones.
The bones themselves don't hold, but liquefy,
dissolved, with ruptured joints, their mass collapsed.
My massive body's failed, my Herculean limbs 1230
can't match the plague. How great this evil which
I admit is huge, O dreadful curse!
Look, cities, see—see what's left now of that famous
Hercules! Do you, my father, recognize
Hercules? Did I with these arms squeeze
the crushed neck of the Nemean beast? Drawn with this hand
did my bow take Stymphalian birds down from the stars?
Did I with these feet outrace the speedy beast,
tossing its head bright with shining antlers?[118]
Did Calpe, broken by these hands, squeeze out the sea? 1240
By these hands, so many beasts, crimes, kings, lie fallen?
The world sat on these shoulders? Is this bulk mine,
is this that neck? Did I hold up these hands against
the crashing sky? What Stygian sentinel
will still be dragged forth by my hand? Where is
the strength that's buried in me? Why call Jove
father? Why, wretch,[119] claim heaven through the Thunderer?
Amphitryon will now be deemed my father.
Whatever plague is lurking in my gut,
come forth! Why attack me with a hidden wound? 1250
What sea beneath the frigid sky of Scythia,
what torpid Tethys bore you or Spanish Calpe[120]
pressing the Moorish coast? O dread monster,
whether serpent brandishing a bristly-crested head
or else some evil unknown even to me:
were you born from the blood of the Lernaean beast,

or did the Stygian dog leave you behind on earth?
You're every evil, and none—what kind of face do you have?
Let me at least know due to what evil I die,
1260 whatever plague, whatever beast you are,
be feared openly. Who gave you a place
inside my marrow? Look—my hand has torn
away the skin, exposed my guts; but a yet
deeper recess has been found: O Hercules-
like evil! Whence this weeping, whence these tears
upon my cheeks? This once unconquered face,
which never used to shed tears for its woes (for shame!),
has now learned to weep. What day, what land has seen
the sobs of Hercules? Dry-eyed I bore my toils.
1270 To you that valor that has crushed so many ills,
to you alone it's yielded. Before all others,
you first have torn tears from me. My face, harder than horrid
rock and steel and wandering Symplegades,[121]
has relaxed its grimace and shed a tear.[122]
By the highest governor of the sky!
The earth has seen me weeping, moaning, and what tortures me
still more, my stepmother has too. See! Again it burns
my guts, the fire's grown hot: where can I find a thunderbolt to
strike me now?

CHORUS

What can pain not overcome?
1280 Harder once than Getic Haemus,[123]
less pliant than the northern pole,[124]
he yielded his limbs to savage pain;
rolling his weary head on his neck
he shifts his weight from side to side.
His valor oft chokes back his tears.
Thus Titan, with his tepid star,
still dares not melt the arctic snows
and the icy light
subdues the flames of the risen sun.

HERCULES

My father, turn your eyes upon my ruin. 1290
Alcides never has sought refuge at your hands,
not when the Hydra unfurled its fertile heads around
my limbs; in the infernal lake I stood,
clutched by black night, along with Doom, but I
did not invoke you. So many bristling beasts
I conquered, kings and tyrants, yet did not turn
my gaze star-ward: this hand was ever surety
of my pledge. No thunderbolts flashed for me
in the sacred sky. This day has driven me
to wish something; now first—and last—you'll hear[125] 1300
my prayers: I beg you for a single thunderbolt.
Think me a giant: no less than they could I have claimed
the heavens for myself, but since I deemed you my
true father, I spared heaven. But cruel or pitying,
father, lend your son a hand with a hastening
death and seize this glory for yourself.
If this revolts you and your hand shrinks from the crime,
send blazing Titans from Etna's peak,
Father, to heave the Pindus with their hands
at me or fling Mount Ossa to crush me. 1310
Or let Bellona break the gates of Erebus[126]
and seek me with drawn sword; send brutal Mars,
let him be armed against me direly: true, he's my brother,
but by my stepmother. You too, Alcides' sister,
though only by my father, hurl your spear, Pallas,[127]
against your brother. I stretch suppliant hands
to you, stepmother, I pray, you at least must cast
a shaft. I'm up to dying by a woman's hand.
Now you're worn down and sated, why still nourish threats?
What more do you ask for? You see as suppliant 1320
Alcides: never land or beast has seen me
beg for your mercy. Now indeed I need an angry[128]
stepmother. Your pain ends now? Now you lay
aside your hate? You spare me when my prayer is to die.

O earth and towns, will no one lend a torch
or arms to Hercules? You take away
my shafts? May no land spawn fierce beasts when I'm
entombed, and never let the world entreat
my hands. If any evils will be born,
1330 let there be born another me:[129] on every side
bash in my wretched head with stones, overwhelm
my suffering. You wait, ungrateful world? Forgotten me?
You'd be prey still to ills and beasts had you
not borne me. Snatch your avenger from his ills,
O peoples: this chance is given you: repay
what's due: my death will be the fee for everything.

ALCMENA

What lands shall I, Alcides' wretched mother, seek?
Where, where's my son? If what my eyes see is true,
he's there! slumped back, tossing, with panting heart.
1340 He moans. It's over! Let me be the last, my son,
to embrace your limbs, let your escaping breath
be gathered by my lips. Receive my arms
in an embrace. Where are your limbs, that star-
supporting neck that bore the world? Who left you
that scant part of you?

HERCULES

Yes, you see Hercules,
Mother—a shadow and vile remnant of myself.
Acknowledge me, Mother: why turn away your eyes
and drop your gaze? You blush that Hercules
is called your child?

ALCMENA

What world, what land has borne
1350 some unknown beast? What direst evil triumphs over you?
Who is the conqueror of Hercules?

HERCULES

You see Alcides prostrate by a wife's guile.

ALCMENA

What guile is great enough to rout Alcides?

HERCULES

The kind that satisfies an angry woman.

ALCMENA

Whence did the plague alight upon your limbs or bones?

HERCULES

A cloak gave entry to a woman's poisons.

ALCMENA

Where is that cloak? I see but naked limbs.

HERCULES

Consumed along with me.

ALCMENA

So great a scourge has been devised?

HERCULES

Imagine the Hydra, Mother, and with her
a thousand beasts roaming deep in my entrails. 1360
What flame so great cuts through Sicilian clouds,
what Lemnos blazes so,[130] what region of the fiery sky
that doesn't let the sun run in its blistering zone?[131]
My comrades, throw me in the very sea,
and into rivers. What's the Danube that suffices me?
Not Ocean, greater than the earth, will quench
my fires. All liquids will fall short of my
distress, all water will dry up. Why did
you send me back to Jove, O governor of hell?
The right thing was to keep me! Return me to your gloom, 1370
and show this Hercules to those subdued below.
I'll haul up nothing: why fear Hercules once more?
Attack, death: do not tremble. Now I can die.

ALCMENA

At least repress your tears, control your grief,
present a Hercules unconquered by such ills,
and put off death: as often, conquer those below.

HERCULES

If the horrid Caucasus offered me, bound in
its chains, as feast to the greedy bird, if Scythia
groaned, no teary groan would have slipped out
1380 of me.[132] If the wandering Symplegades
squeezed me with both cliffs, I would endure
the threats of their recurring crash. Let Pindus
fall on me, and Haemus, and Athos which breaks up
the Thracian waves, and Mimas which shakes off[133]
the bolts of Jove. Not if this world itself
collapsed on me, Mother, and Phoebus' chariot
caught fired and blazed above my bed, would a base cry
subdue the mind of Hercules. A thousand beasts
might run at me and jointly rend me, the airy
1390 Stymphalian with wild shrieks strike here, the scary
bull with all its hump strike there, whatever
even alone was huge. Let a grove rise round
and harsh Sinis tear my joints:[134] though strewn about
I'll make no sound. Not beasts nor arms will shake from me
a groan, nothing I could attack.

ALCMENA

No woman's potion, Son, cooks up your limbs,
but a hard set of labors and long toil
have likely nurtured bloody diseases in you.

HERCULES

Where's the disease? Where? Is there any evil
1400 still in the world with me? Let it come here. Let someone
aim a bow at me: my bare hand will suffice.
Come! Let him advance!

ALCMENA

Ah me, that all too driving
pain has driven out his senses too.
Please, take away his bow and steal, I beg of you,
those hostile arrows. His eyes, the fire welling up,

portend a crime. What hideout can I seek, old as I am?
That pain is madness—that alone tames Hercules.
Why then should I in frenzy seek hideouts or flight?
Alcmene's earned the right to die by a strong
hand. Or let me perish in a crime, 1410
before some coward decree my death and a foul hand
triumph over me. Look! Pain binds up his veins
wearied by ills, worn out by sleep,[135] and rattles
his gasping chest with a heavy jolt. Be kind,
O gods: if you've denied poor me my famous
son, preserve at least, I pray, the avenger
for the earth. May his pain be shaken off and end,
and may this Herculean body regain its strength.

HYLLUS

O bitter light, O day, brimful of crimes!
The Thunderer's daughter-in-law is dead, his son 1420
lies fallen, I—grandson—survive; he dies by
my mother's crime, she by being tricked. Who in the rounds
of years, in a whole life, though old, will be
able to recount so many griefs? One day
has stolen both my parents. Not to mention other ills
and spare the Fates, I lose Hercules as father.

ALCMENA

Stifle your cries, Alcides' famous son,
grandson of wretched Alcmena, alike in fate.
Long sleep perhaps will overcome his pain.
But look, rest deserts his weary mind, 1430
returns his body to disease, and me to grief.

HERCULES

What's this? Is Trachis visible with its
icy ridge or, placed among the stars, have I
at last escaped the mortal race? Who readies heaven
for me? You, Father, I see you now, and spy
also my stepmother appeased. What celestial sound

strikes my ears? Juno calls me son-in-law.
I see a shining palace in the bright sky
and the track worn down by Phoebus' flaming wheel.

(*Hercules falls back in shock.*)

1440 I see Night's bed, the darkness summons me.
What's this? Who shuts the sky and drags me, Father,
down from the very stars? Phoebus' chariot just now
was breathing on my face, so near the sky was I.
I see Trachis: who gave earth back to me?
Oeta just now stood below and the whole world
was set beneath. O pain, you'd all but slipped away!
You force me to admit.—Spare me, forestall
these words. These, Hyllus, are your mother's gifts?
This present she prepares? Would that I could heave
1450 my club and crush her impious life as I subdued
the Amazonian blight round snowy Caucasus' flank.
Bright Megara, were *you* my wife when I was mad? [136]
Give me my club and bow. Let my right hand be
besmirched, I'll fix a blot on my own glories.
Let a woman be picked as Hercules' last labor.

HYLLUS

Stifle the dire threats, Father, of your rage.
She's dead, it's done; she's paid the penalty you seek.
My mother lies slain by her own right hand.

HERCULES

You're blind with grief.[137] She deserved to die
1460 at raging Hercules' hands. Lichas has lost
a mate. Both rage and impulse spur me on
to abuse her lifeless body. Why should her corpse
be exempted from my threats? Let beasts have her for food.

HYLLUS

She suffered more, poor woman, than the one she harmed.
You too might have wanted to subtract some of it. By her
right hand she died—and for your pain: she bore

more than you ask. You're laid low not by a cruel wife's
crimes or by my mother's guile. Nessus arranged this trick,
when stricken by your arrows he breathed out his life.
The cloak, Father, was dipped in the half-beast's blood; 1470
now Nessus exacts vengeance for himself.

HERCULES

I'm undone, it's all over: now my fate unfolds.
This is my last light. The oracular oak delivered once[138]
this prophecy to me, and the woods that shake up
Delphi's shrines with their murmurs on Parnassus:
"At the hand of a slain man, Alcides, you'll be brought low
one day, even though you won; this final end
you're granted, after you've traversed seas, lands, and shades."
I protest no more: it was fitting that this end be granted,
so that none one could conquer Hercules and survive. 1480
Let death be chosen now: bright, memorable, renowned—
and fully worthy of me. I'll make this day illustrious.
Let the whole forest be cut down and Oeta's woods
catch fire. The pyre may receive Hercules,
but prior to death. Young son of Poeas,[139]
you must perform this sad service for me.
May Hercules' flame make the whole day burn red.
To you now, Hyllus, I address my final prayers:
Among the captives one girl is dazzling, displays
her stock and royalty on her face, the daughter of Eurytus: 1490
Iole. Ready her for wedding torches and
your bed. Cruel conqueror, I took away her land,
her home, and gave her, wretched, naught but Alcides—
and he is snatched away. May she requite her suffering,
cherish Jove's grandson and the son of Hercules,
may she bear for you any child conceived by me.
You too, illustrious Mother, I beg, put aside
funereal keens: Alcides is alive for you.
I've made my stepmother seem a mere concubine,
thanks to my valor, whether that night when 1500

Hercules was born is true, or my father is a
mortal. Though my lineage be false, and
my mother's guilt and Jove's crime disappear, I earned
Jove as my parent: I conferred honor on heaven.
Nature conceived me for Jove's praise.
Why, he himself, though he's Jupiter, delights
to be believed my father. Now spare your tears,
my parent: you will be proud among the Argive mothers.
Has Juno borne the like, although she wields the
1510 sky's scepter and is the Thunderer's bride? She holds
the heavens but envied a mortal, and wished Alcides to
be called her own. Carry out now, Sun, your rounds,
alone, forsaken: I, who'd been your comrade
everywhere, now head for Tartarus and the ghosts.
But I'll bring this gloried fame to the underworld:
that no scourge overtly laid Alcides low,
and every scourge Alcides conquered overtly.

(*Exit Hercules.*)

CHORUS

O glory of the world, O radiant Sun,
at whose first warmness Hecate relieves[140]
1520 the weary jaws of her night chariot's steeds:
tell the Sabaeans placed beneath the Dawn,
tell the Hiberians placed beneath nightfall,
and those who are stricken by the sweltering sky,
and those who suffer beneath Ursa's Wain,
tell them that Hercules is hastening to
the eternal ghosts and the realm of the unwearying dog,
from which he never will return again.
Choose those rays that clouds pursue,
and pallidly behold the saddened lands,
1530 and let foul mists meander about your head.
When, Sun, and where, beneath what sky will you
track on this earth another Hercules?
What hands will this poor earth invoke

if near Lerna some multifarious scourge
will distribute its venom among a hundred snake-heads,
or if some boar riles up the forests
of that ancient people, the Arcadians,
or if some foster child of Thracian Rhodope,
harsher than the lands of snowy Helice,[141]
spatters its own stall with human gore?[142] 1540
Who will grant peace to fearful people if gods
above are angered and decree some thing
be born midst cities? Equal to them all
he lies, whom Earth bore equal to the Thunderer.
Let wails resound throughout the countless cities,
let women, with the knot that binds their hair
undone, beat their bared arms, let the gates
of all the gods be closed, let there gape wide
only the shrines of his unruffled stepmother.
You go to Lethe and the Stygian shore, 1550
from which no ships will bring you back again.
You go to the ghosts, piteous one, from which
you fetched a triumph, having conquered death.
A shade you will arrive, your arms exposed,
with languid features and wasted neck.
That boat will not bear you alone, yet you'll
not be contemptible among the shades.[143]
Between Aeacus and the pair of men from Crete[144]
you'll examine deeds and strike down tyrants.
Be merciful, rich kings, check your right hands. 1560
To keep your sword unsullied is cause for praise,
as is the fact that while you reigned, the bloody Fates
had least license to act against your cities.
But valor has its place among the stars.
Will you occupy a space in the arctic zone
or where the Sun brings out oppressive heat?
Or will you shine beneath the lukewarm west
where you'll hear Calpe resonate as its seas
clash round? What places in the cloudless sky

1570 will you weigh down? What place will be safe
once Alcides is received among the stars?
May your father bestow a place, at least,
far from the horrid lion and the seething crab,
lest the stars, set to trembling by your face
confuse their laws and even the Sun take fright.
As long as flowers will come in the warm spring,
and winters prune the forests' foliage,
or summer summon back the forests'
foliage, and fruit expire as autumn flees,
1580 no span of time will steal you from the lands.
As Phoebus' comrade, comrade of the stars
you'll go. Sooner in the deep will crops
be born, or the sea splash freshwater waves,
sooner will the constellation of the icy bear
plunge and taste the forbidden sea,
than nations will take respite from your praises.
We wretches beg you, father of all things:
let no beast be born, no scourge, and let
the piteous earth not shudder at cruel leaders,
1590 and in no palace let a man hold sway
who thinks that the sole glory of his rule
is to keep a sword forever aimed.
If anything in the lands again is feared,
we beg an avenger of the abandoned earth.
Oh no, what is this? The world booms.
Does his father mourn Alcides? Is it the cry
of gods or voice of frightened stepmother?
Is Juno fleeing the stars on seeing Hercules?
Did weary Atlas stagger at the weight?
1600 Or is it rather that the dire ghosts trembled
and the dog of those who dwell below
burst its chains and fled in fear when it saw Hercules?
We're wrong: here comes, with cheerful face,
Poeas' son, who on his shoulders wears

the bow and quiver known among the nations,
the heir of Hercules.

(*The chorus sees Philoctetes returning from Mt. Oeta.*)

ACT 5

CHORUS

Young man, I beg of you, announce Hercules' fate,
and with what attitude Alcides bore his death.

PHILOCTETES

As no one else his life.

CHORUS

So happy was he then
as he leapt on the final fires? 1610

PHILOCTETES

He showed that flames were
nothing anymore. What in this world did Hercules leave
exempt from being conquered? See: all's tamed.

CHORUS

What place for a brave man was there midst the blaze?

PHILOCTETES

The one evil in the world he'd not yet conquered—
even flame was conquered, it too joined the beasts.
Fire ended up among the toils of Hercules.

CHORUS

Come then, describe the way the flame was conquered?

PHILOCTETES

The whole sad company uprooted Oeta.
On this side a beech loses its shady leaves,
and sprawls with its whole trunk; another man bends a pine 1620
that menaces the stars and, fierce, recalls it
from midcloud; tottering, it shook the ridge and dragged
a lesser forest with it. The once-speaking Chaonian oak[145]

stands huge in width, blocks Phoebus, and extends
its every branch beyond the grove. With many
wounds hacked in, it menacingly moans
and breaks axes; the impacted steel rebounds
and iron suffers a wound and flees the trunk.[146]
At last it's shaken, then on falling caused ruin
1630 as wide as itself. At once the place
lets every sunbeam in, birds startled from
their perch fly through the air, their grove felled,
and chattering seek on weary wings a home.[147]
Now every tree resounded, even sacred
oaks felt hands bristling with steel,
primeval groves did not safeguard their thickets.[148]
A whole forest is piled up, crisscrossing trunks
raise to the stars a solemn pyre for Hercules:[149]
pine quick to catch the flame, and stubborn oak,
1640 and lowly holm-oak, but topmost a poplar[150]
forest caps the pyre, a copse of Herculean
foliage.[151] But he, like a huge sick lion,[152]
lying on its chest and roaring in the Libyan woods
is carried in—who'd think he was hurrying to flames?
His look was of one seeking stars, not fire,
as he weighed down Oeta and with his eyes scanned
the entire pyre; placed on it, he broke the logs.
He calls for his bow. "Receive this gift," he says,
"O Poeas' son, and take on the task of Hercules.
1650 The Hydra felt these arrows, through them Stymphalos' birds
lie dead
and every other evil I conquered at long range.
Boy destined to be happy, you'll never fire these
at your foe in vain: if you should wish
to pluck birds from midcloud, the fowl will drop,
unerring shafts will take their prey down from the sky.
Never will this bow fail your right hand:
it's learned to shoot the shaft and give sure flight
to arrows; the very arrows know their way,

fired from this string. I beg you, just arrange the fire and
the final torch for me. And let this club," he said, 1660
"that no other hand has held, burn in
the fire with me: let this one weapon follow
Hercules. You'd get this too," he said,
"if you could wield it. Let it help its master's
pyre." Then he demands the Nemean beast's
stiff hide to burn with him: the pyre is hidden
by this booty. The whole crowd moaned and grief
spared no one tears. His mother mad with sorrow
bared her eager bosom and beat her breasts,[153]
naked to the womb, with horrifying blows; 1670
assailing gods and Jove himself with cries
she filled all places with her womanish voice.
"Mother, you make foul the death of Hercules;
repress your tears," he said, "let womanish grief
retreat within. Why should Juno spend a glad
day thanks to your weeping? She delights
to see her rival's tears. Curb your weak heart,
Mother; it's a crime to lacerate the breasts
and womb that bore me." Roaring horribly,
as when he dragged the dog through Argive towns, 1680
and, Hades scorned, Fate quaking, he returned,
hell's victor—so he lay down on the pyre.
What victor in a triumph stood so happy
in his chariot? What tyrant's given laws
to nations with that face? Such peace shored up his
bearing! Tears ceased. Grief, thrust off, dropped from
us too, none groaned for him about to die.
It was shameful now to weep. She whose sex bids that
she mourn ceased, her cheeks dry—Alcmene: now
she stands a parent almost like her son. 1690

CHORUS

Did he send no prayers star-ward to the gods
or look, before he burned, to Jove with vows?

PHILOCTETES

He lay sure of himself and scanned the sky,
sought with his eyes to see if from some citadel
his father gazed down at him, then held out
his hands and said, "from whatsoever place you view your son,
Father, you, you, I beg, for whom one day stayed back[154]
when two nights merged, if both of Phoebus' shores
sing my praises and the Scythian race
1700 and the whole scorched region that the daylight bakes,
if earth is filled with peace, and if no cities
groan, if no impious one fouls altars,
if crimes are gone, receive this soul, I beg,
among the stars. Infernal death's abode
does not scare me nor do black Jove's sad realms:
but I feel shame to go as ghost to those gods whom
I conquered, Father. With clouds dispersed expose
the day so that the gaze of gods may see
Hercules burn. If you deny me stars and heaven,
1710 you'll be compelled, Father, against your will. If pain
extorts a cry, open up the Stygian lakes
and hand me to my fate. First test your son:
1716 let my stepmother see how I bear fire.[155]
this day will show I'm worthy of the stars.
What's done is slight: this day, Father, will prove
or condemn Hercules." When he'd said this,
1717 he called for fire. "Comrade of Alcides: do it!"
he said, "and seize not listlessly the Oetaean
torch! Why did your hand tremble? Does it shun
1720 in fear an impious crime? Give back my quiver,
you lazy, shiftless, clumsy—see what hand
would aim my bow! Why have your cheeks turned pale?
Take the torch up with the same attitude
you see in me. Look at me, wretch, about
to burn. See! Father calls me now, opens
the sky. Father, I come." His face was not
the same. With trembling hand I thrust in the burning

pine. The fire drew back, the torch resists,
and shuns his limbs—but Hercules pursues
the receding fire. You'd think Caucasus, 1730
Pindus, or Athos were burning. Not a sound
erupts, only the fire moans. O hard heart!
Placed on that pyre, huge Typho would have groaned
and fierce Enceladus himself, who set
upon his shoulders Ossa torn from the earth.
But he, rising midst the flames, half scorched and
lacerated, but looking fearless, said:
"*Now* you're a Herculean parent, this is how,
Mother, you should stand beside the pyre,
this is how Hercules should be wept."[156] Surrounded by the smoke 1740
and the fire's threat, unmoved, unshaken, not twisting his
ignited limbs to either side, he urges,
warns, takes action though he burns. He gave
firm heart to all his staff. You'd think he was on fire to burn.
The whole crowd's stunned, the flames lose credibility:
so calm his brow, such grandeur in the man.
He's in no rush to burn: when he'd assessed
enough was done for a brave death, he gathered
flaming trunks from all around: he threw the ones hardly on fire[157]
into the densest flames, and goes to look for 1750
where the greatest flames pour out—still fierce and undaunted.
With those flames he steeps his face; his thick beard lit up,
and though the threatening fire attacked his face,
and flames licked his head, he did not shut his eyes.
But what is this? I see her, sadly bearing
in her lap great Hercules' remains.
Flinging her ash-covered hair, Alcmene moans.

ALCMENE

Fear fate, O gods: so small are Hercules'
ashes. To this that giant's shrunk, to this!

1760 What massiveness, O Sun, has gone to naught.
This aged lap—it's awful!—has room for Alcides.
This is his grave. Look: Hercules scarce fills
the entire urn. How light his weight for me,
on whom the whole sky lay as a light weight.
You went, my son, to Tartarus once and to the farthest
realms, only to return—when will you come again
from hellish Styx? Not to drag up spoils[158]
or so that Theseus owe you daylight once again,
but when will *you* return, just you? Will the piled-on world
hold down
1770 your shade and Tartarus' dog be able to hold you
back? When will you pound the doors of Taenarus?
To what yawning gates can I, your mother, go
through which death is reached? You go to the ghosts—
a one-way trip.

(*To herself.*)

Why wear away the day
lamenting? Why, vile life, endure? Why hold on to
light? What Hercules can I bear to Jove again?
What son so great will call you mother,
Alcmene? Too too happy my Theban spouse,[159]
you entered Tartarus' domain in your son's prime;
1780 those below feared you, perhaps, as you arrived
because you came as great Hercules' father
even if falsely so. What lands can I, an aged
woman, seek, odious to cruel kings
(if any cruel king is left)? Unhappy me!
Every son who's groaned for parents slain
will seek recompense from me: they'll all crush me.
If some Busiris junior or junior
Antaeus terrifies the torrid region's towns,
I'll be led off as booty. If someone from Ismarus
1790 avenges the cruel Thracian's herds, his own
dire herds will tear my limbs. Perhaps an

angry Juno will seek revenge and all her pain
will flare; she's safe at last from conquered Alcides,
carefree—but I live on, her rival: what vengeance
she'll exact so I can't give birth! This son has made
my womb fearsome. What place can I, Alcmene,
seek? What place, tract, region of the world
will shield me, to what hideout should I go, a mother
who's known everywhere through you? If I seek
my land and my ill-fated home—Eurystheus holds Argos. 1800
Should I seek Thebes and the Ismenus, my husband's realm,
our bedroom where I once saw Jove
and was loved? Oh too too happy had I too felt
Jove as lightning![160] Would that as a babe
Alcides had been cut out from my guts.
As it is, time was granted me: granted
to see my son contend with Jove in glory,
so that it might be granted me to know
what fate can rip from me. What nation will
live mindful of you, son? The whole race is now 1810
ungrateful. Should I make for Cleonae[161] or
Arcadia's towns, find lands famous through your deeds?
Here a dire serpent fell, there a fierce bird,
here a bloodied king,[162] there broken by your hand
a lion that, though you're interred, inhabits
heaven. If earth is grateful, let every nation
shield Alcmene. Should I seek the Thracian
tribes and Hebrus' nations? This land too was
shielded by your deeds, the stables flattened
alongside the realm, cruel king laid low, peace granted— 1820
for where was peace denied? What tomb shall I, unhappy,
aged, find for you? Let the whole world vie
for your ashes. What nation, temples, tribes
ask for the remains of Hercules?
Who asks for, who demands, Alcmene's burden?
What tomb, what grave suffices, Son, for you?
The entire world! Your fame will be your epitaph.

Heart, why tremble? You have Hercules' ashes.
Hug his bones, his remnants will give help,
1830 they'll be defense enough. Even your shade will
frighten kings.

PHILOCTETES

Check your tears, though
they're due your son, renowned Alcides' mother.
Not to be mourned or weighted with a heavy death
is he whose valor's snatched his death from fate.
Eternal valor bans lamenting Hercules:
the brave ban mourning, baser folk demand it.

ALCMENE

Shall I, a mother, subdue my lament,
when the avenger of earth and sea is gone, and where the
red day on bright wheels views either Ocean?[163]
1840 So many sons did I, poor Mother, bury
in one: I lacked a realm but I could give a realm.
Of all the mothers the earth bears, I alone
refrained from vows, sought nothing from the gods,
while my son lived. What couldn't Herculean zeal
give me, what god could withhold anything[164]
from me? The answer to my vows was in his hands: whatever
Jove withheld, my Hercules would give.
Has any mortal mother borne one like him?
One mother turned to rock, stood fixed, severed from
1850 all her brood: that one bewailed two flocks of
seven.[165] For how many flocks was mine a match!
Up until now there lacked a towering model
for wretched mothers. I, Alcmene, will
provide it. Mothers, if persistent pain
still bids some of you to mourn, stop, or if deep grief
turns some to stone: yield all, of you, to my woes! Wretched
hands,
come beat this old breast. But is one ancient

feeble crone enough for such a corpse,
which all the world will soon desire? But still
prepare your arms for blows, though they be weary. 1860
To inspire indignation at the gods
by mourning, summon the whole race to lament.
Weep for great Jove's and Alcmene's
son and beat your breast for him,
at whose conception one day perished
and the Dawn combined two nights:
something more than a day has perished.
All you races, rain blows equally,
you whose savage tyrants he forced
to enter the houses of Styx 1870
and drop swords that dripped with people.
Pay back tears for such great merits,
let the whole whole world resound.
Let azure Crete weep for Alcides,
land dear to the great Thunderer,
the hundred towns must beat their arms.
Now you Curetes,[166] now you Corybants,
bang shields with Idaean hands:
armor is right as the means to mourn him.
Now, beat now for his real funeral: 1880
O Crete, Alcides lies dead, a man not lesser
than the Thunderer himself.
Weep for Hercules' death, Arcadians,
a tribe already before the Moon was born.[167]
Let Parthenius' and Nemea's
cliffs boom, grave blows strike Maenalus:
the bristling boar killed in your fields
demands a groan for great Alcides,
as do the birds who yielded to his arrows,
their wings stealing all the daylight.[168] 1890
Weep, Argive Cleonae, weep.
Here the right hand of my son smashed the lion

that once terrified your city walls.
Lash yourselves, Bistonian mothers,
let icy Hebrus echo the blows:
weep for Alcides, since no child
of yours any more feeds stables, and
herds don't rip your flesh and blood.
Weep, you land freed from Antaeus,
1900 the zone snatched from fierce Geryon.
Beat blows with me, O wretched nations:
may either Ocean hear your beats.
You too, you throng of hastening heaven,
weep, you gods, for Hercules' fate:
my Alcides on his shoulders
bore your heaven, gods, and sky,
when Atlas, carrier of star-bearing
Olympus, breathed free of its weight.
Jove, where are your citadels now,
1910 where is heaven's promised palace?
Alcides surely's died a mortal, is surely buried.
How many times he spared you the use
of lightning bolts, the times
you were supposed to spray your fire!
Hurl your torch at me at least,
pretend I'm Semele!
Do you have now an Elysian home,
my son, the shore
that nature calls all people to,
1920 or has black Styx, its dog stolen by you,
blocked the way and does fate detain
you at the first entry into hell?
What turbulence now grips the shades and ghosts, my son?
Does the ferryman take his boat and
flee, and centaurs, stirred up, strike
with their Thessalian hoofs shocked ghosts,
and has the frightened Hydra dipped

its snakes beneath the waves,
do your own labors fear you, son?
I'm wrong, wrong, I'm mad and raging, 1930
ghosts and shades do not fear you,
and the hide stripped from the Argive lion,
fearsome, covered with tawny mane,
does not lie on your left shoulder
nor do fierce teeth hem your temples.
You quiver has been made a gift,
a lesser hand will shoot its arrows.
You walk unarmed, my son, through shades
with whom you will forever stay.

HERCULES

(*Appearing overhead.*)

Why have me feel my doom by your lament, 1940
when I occupy the realms of starry sky,
at last restored to heaven? Stop! My valor's
made a path to the stars and gods themselves.

ALCMENE

Where does the sound that strikes my anxious
ears come from, the clamor that curbs my tears?
I understand it, I understand! Hell's been overcome.
Son, you return again from the Styx to me,
horrid death has been crippled twice!
Again you've overthrown the place of darkness,
the sad shoals of the infernal ship. 1950
Is Acheron now slow and passable?
Or are you alone allowed to return,
and fate does not detain you after death?
Or did Pluto shut your way ahead of time,
and frightened for his realm, feared for
himself? I surely saw you placed
on a blazing forest, when flames raged
to the sky, gigantic and fearsome.

You burned! Why did the final place
1960 not keep your shade? I beg you, what
part of you did the ghosts fear? Or is your shade
itself too horrible for hell?

HERCULES

Cocytus' groaning pools do not hold me[169]
nor did the dusky ship transport my shade.
Spare now your plaints, Mother: I saw the ghosts
and shades just once. The unconquered fire took
what mortal bit of you there was in me.
My father's part was given to heaven, yours to the flames.
So put aside the mourning that a mother
1970 prepares for an inactive son. Let grief be for the cowardly.
Valor makes for the stars, but fear makes for death.
Coming from the stars, Mother, I, Alcides, prophesy:
Bloodstained Eurystheus will soon pay you a penalty:
carried in a chariot, you'll ride over his proud head.
Now I must rise to the celestial zone;
Again I've conquered the realm of hell, I, Alcides.

ALCMENE

Remain a while—he's gone, he's left my sight,
fetched to the stars. Am I wrong? Do my eyes
think they saw my son? My poor mind's in doubt.
1980 You are a god, the sky has you forever:
I trust in your triumphs. I will seek Thebes' kingdom
and sing the new god added to the shrines.

CHORUS

Famed valor's never carried off to
Stygian shades. Live bravely and the
savage fates won't drag you over Lethe's stream,
but when your days, used up,
fill out their final hours,
glory will open the way to the gods.
But you, great tamer of wild beasts,
1990 subduer of the world, come near!

Now too watch over our lands, and if
some monster of new mien should shake
the nations with grave fear, smash it
with your three-pronged thunderbolt.
Send thunderbolts more forcefully
than your own father.

Thyestes

The *Thyestes* opens with the Fury Megaera, who forces the ghost of Tantalus to infect the family's house with his sins of murder and cannibalism. The chorus of men of Mycenae, unaware of this development, pray meanwhile that the hideous deeds of Tantalus and his son Pelops are over for good. Atreus comes on stage and vents his rage on himself for not having punished his brother Thyestes enough. He had exiled Thyestes after a struggle for the throne (and after Thyestes had committed adultery with his wife). Now he plans something worse. Despite the careful counsel of his attendant, Atreus decides he will kill his nephews and serve them to their father. He sends his own children to lure Thyestes back to the royal palace by pretending all is forgiven.

Thyestes returns to Argos but pauses outside the city walls in doubt. He praises the simple life he had been leading and does not believe his brother's change of heart. But his son persuades him that a share of the kingdom would be in both their interests, and he enters the city to be embraced by Atreus. The oblivious chorus sings of the strength of blood ties and the coming peace.

A messenger suddenly turns up to tell of what has been going on inside the palace. Atreus ritually sacrificed Thyestes' children, dismembered them, and cooked a stew with their flesh. The messenger reports that Atreus is serving this stew to a drunken Thyestes. The chorus, aghast, sings of the darkness that has fallen over the city; the sun has turned back on its path in horror.

Atreus comes out to gloat over his triumph. As Thyestes eats and drinks, he calls out for his kids and becomes suspicious when Atreus makes double entendres. Atreus then shows him the heads of the children on a platter. Thyestes assumes they have been murdered, and begs to bury their bodies, but now Atreus reveals the second horror: their father had eaten them. Thyestes calls out to the gods in horror and predicts vengeance, but the gods are silent.

Introduction

SHADI BARTSCH

The story of Thyestes and the house of Atreus is a horrific one even in the violent world of ancient mythology. The Atreids alone among the subjects of Greek tragedy are cursed by the occurrence and *recurrence* of their dreadful crime, an act matchless in its flouting of the laws of civilization and the structure of the family. This is cannibalism, but not just cannibalism: it is the consumption of one's own children's flesh and blood, an act that manages in this way to merge features of the two taboos of cannibalism and incest. This chain of horror is started by Atreus' and Thyestes' grandfather Tantalus, king of Lydia, who invited the Olympian gods to dinner but in his arrogance tried to defile them by serving them human flesh—the flesh of his own murdered son, Pelops. Only Demeter, distracted by her mourning for Persephone, absentmindedly took a bite. The other gods, wise to his ploy, restored the child to life, and the god Hephaestus crafted for him an ivory shoulder to replace the part he had lost. For his deed, Tantalus was condemned to live in Hades forever, in desperate thirst and hunger, surrounded by fruit trees just out of reach and standing in a stream whose water evaded his mouth. His terrible dinner marked the last time men ate together with gods.

Tantalus' son Pelops himself engaged in perfidy and murder (but not of his own children), finally becoming king of the entire Peloponnesus through his machinations. His sons Atreus and Thyestes, once adults, became rivals for the throne of Argos (or, alternatively, Mycenae), which Thyestes tried to make his own by suborning his brother's wife through sex. When Atreus discovered the adultery, he enlisted the gods' help in exiling Thyestes and Thyestes' children. This is the back story to our Senecan play: at the time of its opening, Thyestes and his three young sons have been wandering in the wild for an unspecified period of time. But the play does not begin by taking us straight to a view of this life in exile. Instead, it underlines the cyclical nature of the family crime by showing us the ghost of Tantalus first of all. Tantalus finds his hellish existence actually preferable to what a Fury commands him to do: to leave Hades and alight on his grandchildren's house in order to pollute it with the same atrocity he himself had tried to trick the gods into committing—namely, cannibalism. "Let them like *this* hate, and thirst in turn for kindred blood," the Fury orders, and it is done. Tantalus returns to his infernal caverns, and the audience shudders at this foretaste of what is to come. And then, at this very moment, for maximum dramatic irony, we switch scenes to the oblivious chorus of Argive men, who relive the horrors of their rulers' past but feel secure in their knowledge that the original perpetrator, Tantalus, has been punished. They hope and pray that the cycle of violence may end here as well. It is not to be so.

I will not summarize here the entire action of the drama: the story of how Atreus lured his brother and nephews back from exile, killed Thyestes' children in a perversion of sacrificial rite, cooked and fed them to their unsuspecting father, and then gloatingly revealed his crime—even wishing he could have caused still more suffering—is well known to us and was well known to antiquity as well. What is most interesting about this particular *Thyestes* are the nuances of how the playwright chooses to tell it. Unfortunately we have little to compare it with: the *Thyestes* of Varius Rufus, performed in 29 BCE to celebrate the victory of Octavian over the forces of Antony and Cleopatra, is lost, as are other dramas named *Thyestes* or *Atreus*; we know of versions on the Roman side by Ennius, Accius, Pomponius Secundus, the tragedian Gracchus, and Mamercus Aemilius Scaurus—leaving aside any lost Greek dramas (of which there were at least eight; see Tarrant 1985, 40–43). One line of Accius' drama struck a particular nerve and was quoted by both Cicero and Seneca (in *On Anger*) in describing the perverted psychology of the tyrant vis-à-vis his subjects: "Let them hate, so long as they fear." It is a viewpoint all of Seneca's dramatic tyrants seem to endorse.

A quick survey of the fragments suggest that in plot at least, Seneca did not innovate significantly from his predecessors. But the echoes of Seneca's own Stoic philosophizing in the language of the dramatis personae are impossible to miss, and these must be original.

It is not the action so much as the individual characters' rationale for their actions that, as always in Senecan drama, is the locus of interest to any interpreter. Indeed, despite its scenes of horror and the theme of generational pollution, it is the *Thyestes* of all of Seneca's dramas that lends itself most obviously to being read through the lens of Senecan Stoicism. Whether such a reading would provide a critique of Stoic thought, a vindication of it, or something else altogether remains an open question. But the centrality of Stoic thought is clear both in the chorus that precedes Thyestes' arrival at the gates of Argos, and in the crucial lines that Thyestes speaks in this, his first appearance on stage. The chorus's point of view could be taken out of any of Seneca's prose (344–51):

> A king is not made by his riches,
> the purple shade of his robe,
> a royal brow sporting a crown,
> or roof-beams shining with gold:
> a king can lay aside fear
> as well as the heart's ugly urges,
> can't be moved by maddened ambition,
> nor the favor of volatile mobs.

And later (388–89): "A king is a man who fears nothing / a king is a man who wants nothing." Following hard on these lines, Thyestes himself debates the choice of whether to return to Argos or not in the same Stoic terms. What this means is that the heart of the play (lines 404–90) is devoted to Thyestes' prolonged *philosophical* moment of hesitation about his prior decision (not shown on stage) to accept his brother Atreus' offer to share royal power in Argos and to return from his life in exile to a life (so he thinks) of power and wealth.

In focusing on this particular moment, Seneca was probably innovating. Certainly he is aiming at maximum dramatic impact: we are shown Thyestes in front of the very walls of Argos, at the last point when a change of heart is still possible. Since Seneca shows him so close to Argos, we must be meant to understand that Thyestes had early on decided to return; but almost as if the true predicative content of his earlier impulse is only now clear to him, he pauses now to analyze his decision for what it really is. Dramatic impact aside, then, why does Seneca place so much focus on the pivotal moment of Thyestes' change of mind? Why not just have him return and get on with the business of dramatizing the murder, cooking, and cannibalization of the children?

In fact, Thyestes' pause, in which he speaks in the Stoicizing idiom we have already heard from the chorus, is replete with meaning. He *at this moment* explicitly declares himself delighted with the poverty of his life in exile and also recognizes that his brother is too treacherous to trust (412, 473ff.). As he says of his poverty (449–64):

> It's a blessing
> to stand in no one's way, to eat your meal safely
> while sitting on the ground. Crimes don't enter hovels,
> the fare upon a humble table's safe to eat;
> poison comes in cups of gold. I speak of what I know:
> it's possible to choose bad fortune over good.
> I have no house set upon a mountain's peak
> to cast a shadow on the lowly, trembling plebs,
> pale ivory doesn't gleam upon my lofty ceiling,
> there's no man standing guard over my sleep.
> I don't use a fleet to fish, I don't drive back the sea
> by building massive piers, I don't stuff a sinful belly
> with the tribute of the world, no field is harvested for me
> from beyond the Getans and the Parthians,
> I'm not adored with incense, my altars are not decked
> in disregard of Jove.

Thyestes praises not only the simple life but also the principle of self-control as true kingship. "Father, you can be king," says his young son Tantalus, and Thyestes responds: "Yes, since I can control my death" (442)—that is, since I have complete control over my mind and body and do not fear death. In short, both Thyestes and the chorus have aligned themselves (as contemporaries of Seneca would know) with Seneca's own published sentiments about the dangers of ambition, wealth, and political power and the value of self-control. The idealized *sapiens* (wise man) of Seneca's philosophy treats money and comfort as indifferents—they are neither to be sought, nor to be disdained. They are certainly not to present a lure to pick one lifestyle over another. Why, then, does Thyestes both recognize these truths and, eventually, enter the city?

It is worth pointing out that Seneca himself was well aware that to many he seemed to contradict his own teachings: as Nero's quondam tutor and then advisor, he not only held an influential position at court but was also in a position to amass great wealth, which he did. This wealth was not put abstemiously to the side; we know that Seneca enjoyed a lifestyle very much like that of any exceedingly wealthy Roman, indulging in beautiful villas and the finest of everything money could buy. On the few occasions on which he tried to practice poverty to see if he could tolerate it (Marie Antoinette comes inevitably to mind) he openly admits that he found its difficulties to be substantial; likewise the exercise of mind over matter when he temporarily lives in cacophonous lodgings (cf. *Letters on Ethics* 56). Of course, we must always keep in mind that this is part of Seneca's self-presentation as an aspiring but flawed practitioner of Stoic ethical values. But Seneca's foibles—love of luxury, money, power—are those Thyestes has abjured. He was happy in exile, he claims, and true kingship does not require a kingdom (470). Given this, various explanations have been offered for his actual return, all of them possible—after all, we can only go off what the text divulges; there is no "inner life" except what is expressed. Thus Alessandro Schiesaro (2007, 106) for one, has suggested that Atreus all along has the superior psychological insight into Thyestes' character: "Atreus lures Thyestes back to Argos because he correctly assumes that Thyestes will not be able to resist the seductive prospect of a return home. The whole sequence of events bears out Atreus' initial claim that he understands full well the workings of Thyestes' mind: 'I know the untamable spirit of the man; bent it cannot be—but it can be broken' (199–200)."[1] And certainly *after* his return, when decked out in glorious robes and drinking wine, Thyestes has fully capitulated to such desires: "Let grief disappear, and terror, and grim / neediness, the mate of scared exile" (922–23).

But what about the very moment of doubt, so elongated in this play? Thyestes starts out Stoically enough. He emphasizes that he himself doesn't understand why he wrestles with such an easy decision (i.e., *not* to accept Atreus' offer of shared kingship); but when his young son Tantalus asks what he fears, instead of answering "nothing," as a Stoic would, he seems to be crumbling in his stance by saying he does not know. He sees nothing to fear ahead of him, but he fears nonetheless. This illogic represents a problem from the Stoic point of view: Thyestes is now describing his mindset in emotional terms, and, worse still, he does not understand those emotions and has not reached a place from to evaluate them properly. Yet even at this stage, he has not yet decided to proceed. He restates his view that "Not to need a kingdom is itself a massive kingdom" (470). And toward the end of his speech, even his fear is gone: "For me, I've long since ceased to fear" (485). Or rather, it is a different fear: fear for his sons.

This statement explains much, and allows us (if we wish) to offer an alternative reason for Thyestes' decision at the walls of Argos. Thyestes can uphold the mantle of Stoicism, but only so far: he continues to fear for his sons. And if he loves them enough to fear for them, he also loves them enough to want what (they think) is best for them and what young Tantalus wants very much indeed: to be once again the members of a royal family, to sit on the throne of kings, to rule: the things that Tantalus calls well-thought-out plans (490). The key line comes at 489, when, in capitulating, Thyestes says: "I follow you, [children]; I do not lead." This sentiment echoes, but perverts, the famous Stoic maxim about fate quoted by Seneca in *Letters on Ethics* 107.11: "Fate leads the willing, but drags the reluctant" (*ducunt volentem fata, nolentem trahunt*). Thyestes' reluctance to lead his children, either physically or in decision-making, suggests that he follows them with a degree of reluctance as well—even though he follows. Worse still, he has arrogated to them the role of Fate herself, the force that no human can resist. A Stoic Thyestes could perhaps resist them—but the parent Thyestes presents himself as without any choice of his own.

Young Tantalus is not dumb to the reversal of Stoic values, and indeed he characterizes Thyestes' *return*, not his staying away, as a triumph of will over emotion, thus using Stoic language to set Stoic values on their head (440–42):

> Whatever stands in the way and *blocks your will*—defeat it,
> and see what great rewards await on your return.
> Father, you can be king!

By engaging in mind over matter, Thyestes can be king. Unfortunately, this is now a real kingship, and it comes with a real brother. It seems Thyestes' final decision is motivated by his love for his children and his (philosophical and actual) error in believing a life as princes represents their best possible future. Fitch (2004, 219) remarks correctly that it is a play about desire: Thyestes' desire, these lines at least suggest, is that his children regain their heritage. Even near the very end, as Thyestes senses disaster looming, he prays: "Whatever thing this is, / I hope it spares my children and my brother" (995–96).

Here is why, *pace* many critics, the tragedy maintains a tragic element and does not descend to the level of staging merely a greedy weakling and a psychopathic tyrant, for neither of whom we can summon up any sympathy. Indeed, if Seneca had presented us with a Thyestes who grumbled about the life of poverty and was eager to return to the throne he had been driven from (as his punishment for adultery with Atreus' wife), it would be easy to dismiss him as a simple example of how humans cling to the wrong values and thereby make themselves wretched. It is hard to think of a more vivid example of bad decision-making leading to an unhappy outcome: it's one thing to weep over the loss of one's savings when the stock market crashes and quite another to realize you are belching up the remnants of your children. Not only would it be easier to judge Thyestes as a wretchedly deluded everyman, but the play itself would present a straightforward theatrical rendering of a "low" and uninteresting character: one who was not, in Aristotelian terms, *spoudaios* enough (of grand enough stature) to be the subject of a tragedy in the first place. As such, the drama would hardly present much by way of interpretative difficulty: greedy-guts gets his due in a vivid Stoic exemplum of one thousand lines of verse.

It is tempting to ask the question one can ask of all Seneca's drama (as opposed to his philosophically optimistic prose): Which has failed, Thyestes or the philosophical system he follows? The question is made particularly relevant by the drama's philosophical content. In the play, the exchange between Atreus and his servant, who pleads for good kingship, as well as the choral ode that follows, correlate almost perfectly with a comparison of good and bad kingship in Seneca's essay *On Clemency*, where of course it is good, not bad, leadership that Seneca endorses: the good king wins his people's loyalty through love, not hate. But Atreus triumphs here, and triumphs joyfully (885–88; later he will wish he had caused still more pain):

> My stride is equal to the stars, I tower over all,
> I touch the peak of heaven with my haughty head.
> Now the glory of the realm is mine, now my father's throne.
> The gods can quit their job: I've gained the purpose of my
> prayer.

We end with a happy Atreus and a devastated Thyestes. Was the latter simply a bad Stoic? Or is Seneca perhaps hinting that some bonds are too strong for even Stoicism to sever, some emotions too basic to be subjugated to conscious thought? We will never know.

Suggested Reading

Boyle, Anthony J. 1983. "Hic Epulis Locus: The Tragic Worlds of Seneca's Agamemnon and Thyestes." In *Seneca Tragicus: Ramus Essays on Senecan Drama*, edited by A. J. Boyle, 199–228. Victoria, Australia.

Fitch, John G., ed. and trans. 2004. *Seneca:* Oedipus, Agamemnon, Thyestes, Hercules on Oeta, Octavia. Loeb Classical Library 78. Cambridge, MA.

Leigh, Matthew. 1996. "Varius Rufus and the Appetites of Mark Antony." *PCPS* 42: 171–97.

Littlewood, Cedric A. J. 2004. *Self-Representation and Illusion in Senecan Tragedy*. Oxford.

Schiesaro, Alessandro. 2007. *The Passions in Play: Thyestes and the Dynamics of Senecan Drama*. Cambridge.

———. 2009. "Seneca and the Denial of Self." In *Seneca and the Self*, edited by Shadi Bartsch and David Wray, 221–36. Cambridge.

Tarrant, Richard J. 1985. *Seneca's Thyestes, with Introduction and Commentary*. American Philological Association Textbook Series 11. Atlanta.

Thyestes

LUCIUS ANNAEUS SENECA
TRANSLATED BY SHADI BARTSCH

DRAMATIS PERSONAE

GHOST OF TANTALUS, the grandfather of Atreus and Thyestes
FURY
ATREUS, king of Argos
SERVANT of Atreus
THYESTES, Atreus' brother
TANTALUS, son of Thyestes
MESSENGER
CHORUS of Argives

The action takes place outside Atreus' palace in Argos/Mycenae and, in act 5, inside the palace.

ACT 1

GHOST OF TANTALUS

Who drags me from my hateful home among the dead
as I lunge at food that flees my snapping mouth?
Which ill-intentioned god shows Tantalus again
the home he knows?[1] Has something worse been found
than burning thirst amid the waves, than gaping hunger
with no respite? Has the slippery stone which Sisyphus bore
come to be a burden for *my* shoulders now?[2]
Or the rapid-whirling wheel that tears one limb from limb,[3]
or the punishment of Tityus,[4] splayed in a yawning cave,
who feeds black birds of prey with excavations of his gut,[5] 10
and then refills by night the flesh he lost by day,
and as he lies, provides fresh food for new-arriving vultures?

I am reassigned—to what ordeal? Whoever you are,
harsh judge of shades below, who deals new tortures
to the dead: if my punishment can be made worse,
find a fate to scare the sentry of my sunless cell[6]
and awe bleak Acheron, a fate for fear of which
even *I* would tremble. Look, from my family line
a brood is born to overreach the race of Tantalus,
20 to make *me* seem innocent, to dare what is undared!
If any spot lies open in this wicked place of death,
with them I'll fill it up. While Pelops' house still stands
Minos will have no time to rest.[7]

FURY[8]

Go on, you hated shade,
and spur the wicked house-gods with your rage.
Let all compete in every crime, let each side
unsheathe the sword in turn: no limit to this anger,
no shame. Let heedless fury goad their minds,
let the parents' frenzy and their ceaseless sin[9]
devolve upon the sons; let none have leisure
to loathe atrocities gone by. Let more crime come,
30 and many crimes in one! While vengeance takes its toll,
let evil grow. Let haughty brothers lose their power,
then seek it back from exile; let the shaky fortune
of this bestial house revert from king to king,
let wretch be rendered ruler and ruler be made wretch,
let chance carry the kingdom on ever-changing tides.
These men banished for their crimes—when restored
their home by god, into crimes let them relapse, be hated
as they hate themselves. Let anger find no act taboo.
40 Let brother fear his brother, father fear his son,
and son his father.[10] O let the children die a dreadful end,
but let their birth be worse, let the wife-abomination
be a menace to her mate;[11] let war sail across the seas,
floods of gore bathe every land,
and lust be champion over mighty heads of state,

exultant. In this godless house, let incest be—
like any crime![12] Let right, and trust, and every law lie dead
for brothers. Let the heavens win no amnesty
from your fraternal evil—why do the stars still shine on high,
and their fires preserve the beauty due the world? 50
Let deepest night descend, let light pass from the sky.

(*Addressing Tantalus.*)

You! Confuse the house-gods, summon hatred, death, and
slaughter,
and fill all the house with Tantalus.
Yes, deck the hallway pillars, let the doors be festive green
with laurel, let the torch's flame glow worthy
of your coming: we'll have Procne's meal for the king of
Thrace—
but let there be more victims.[13] Why is the uncle's right hand
idle?
Why is Thyestes not yet sobbing for his sons?[14]
When will he raise his hand? Let cauldrons bubble,
their fires lit, and let the limbs be hacked away, 60
partitioned, and put in. Let blood discolor the family hearth,
let the dinner plates be set. Tantalus, you'll be a guest
at a crime you know too well. This day's my gift to you.
I loose your hunger for this meal. Sate
your starvation. Mix blood and wine, and let the blend
be drunk before your eyes. I have found a feast
which even you would flee—but stop! Where do you rush in
haste?

GHOST OF TANTALUS

Back to the pools and streams and hiding waters,
to the tree of fruit that shuns my lips.
Let me regain the filthy pallet of my jail, 70
or if I seem not miserable enough,
transplant me to another stream. Let me
be ringed by the river-fires of Phlegethon.[15]

You who have to pay the price set by the law
of fate, you who lie afraid within,
a crumbling cave and fear the peak that's soon
to fall, you in bonds who dread the savage jaws
of hungry lions and the dire procession of the Furies,
you who, already charred, ward off the torches
80 that they hurl, hear the voice of Tantalus
as he hurries near, believe me in my expertise.
Be glad to be merely in hell! O when will it be mine
to escape the world *above*?

FURY

First convulse your home
and carry warfare with you, and a lust to use the sword,
that curse of kings, and incite their fierce hearts
with maddened pandemonium.

GHOST OF TANTALUS

It is right that I be punished,
not be the punishment. Am I sent to be a deadly vapor
from the ruptured earth? A plague to spread death's onus
through the land? A grandfather to lead his children's sons
90 to ghastly sin? Great father of the gods—and of *me*,
shameful though you find it—even if my telltale tongue
should be sentenced to the greatest penance, torture,
I will not be hushed.[16]

(*To his descendants*)

I warn you! Do not pollute
your hands with death—it is taboo—or Fury-like
spill blood upon the altars. I will stand up and stop this crime!

(*To the Fury*)

You fiend! Why shake your lash before my eyes? Why the
threat
of slithering snakes? What stabbing hunger do you foment,
deep inside my flesh? My heart's inflamed,

it burns with thirst, and fires play within my desiccated flesh.
—I follow your command. 100

FURY

This delirium—deal *this* throughout your house,
let them rave like *this*, and like *this* hate and thirst in turn
for kindred blood. Your home can sense that you are home,
it shrinks in every part from hell's contagion.
And now—it's done in full! Go back to your infernal cave
and to the stream you know: the saddened earth already
suffers at your step. Do you see how the waters, driven
backward,
leave their springs, how river banks lie bare, how
a fiery wind drives the scattered clouds?
Every tree is stripped of hue, every branch 110
lies bare of fruit. The Isthmus,[17] whose ribbon strip
of land parts the nearby seas, once roared with waves
that broke close by; broader now, it hears afar
the water's sound upon its shores.[18]
Lerna's waters now have ebbed,[19] Phoroneus'
liquid veins cannot be seen. Divine Alpheus
holds back his stream, the ridges of Cithaeron
have lost their coat of snow, noble Argos
fears the drought it felt once long before.
Look! The Sun himself cannot decide to bid the daylight 120
follow;
he tries to force it with his reins—but it won't last.

CHORUS[20]

If any god loves Argos' land in Greece
and Pisa's homes, renowned for racing chariots;
if any god loves Corinth on the Isthmus,
its double harbors and divided sea;
if any god loves Taygetus' gleaming snows,[21]
which winter winds in winter's chill
deposit on the mountain's lofty peaks
(the summer melts them with boat-propelling breezes);

130 if clear Apheus with his icy stream
moves any god with his Olympian fame—
let him direct his gentle presence here, let him
forbid recurrent crimes, forbid a grandson
worse than Tantalus to take the throne,
forbid the younger to choose the greater guilt.
Worn out at last, may that godless clan cast off
the bestial passions of its parched progenitor.
Enough of sin: right has accomplished nothing,
nor evil shared by all. Myrtilus the chariot-driver
140 once betrayed his lord,[22] and died betrayed in turn;
the ride that he provided, he experienced himself,
and named the sea he fell in: the notorious Myrtoan.
No tale is better known to the Ionian ships.
Next, the little boy who ran to daddy's kiss:[23]
he won his father's welcome on a godless blade,
and died before his time, a victim at the hearth.
Tantalus! You yourself chopped up his corpse
to make a meal for the gods, your guests.
Endless hunger followed upon such food,
150 and endless thirst. For such a feral feast
there could have been be no fate more just.
Tantalus stands weak with empty throat:
above his guilty head there hangs a rich reward,
harder than the Harpies for a man to catch.
Beside him overhangs a tree with weighted boughs.
Bent and quivering with its fruit, it taunts the man
above the open straining of his jaws.
He starves and is impatient of delay, and yet
so often tricked before refuses to reach up;
160 he looks away, he bites his lips, and traps
all appetite within his gritted teeth.
But now the whole grove drops its treasure
closer still, and the luscious fruits above
make sport of him with dangling leaves.
They hone his pangs; his hunger bids him

lunge again, to no avail. He stretches out a hand—
to almost win is pleasing—but all in vain: the crop
and pliant trees spring up on high.
Then thirst comes on, no better than the belly,
it brings his blood to boil and burns him up 170
with blazing fire. The wretch stands and tries
to drink the water as it comes; the stream
evades and turns away, leaves behind a barren bed,
outpaces him who seeks it. He drinks—
from quickly ebbing water—a hearty drink of dust.

ACT 2

ATREUS

(*To himself.*)

You coward! Slug! You have no spine! But worst of all
—I think this is the greatest fault in tyranny—
you're unavenged! So many crimes committed, betrayal by your
brother,
all justice torn apart, and you *play* at being angry, Atreus,
and utter stagy plaints? The whole world should long since roar 180
with clash of arms, your fleets should roil on either side
Corinth's divided sea. By now the fields and towns
should be lit up with flame, on all sides should flash
drawn swords. Let all the land of Argos resound
under our cavalry, let no forest conceal our foe,
no fortress built along the ridges of our hills.
Let people sound the sign of war and leave behind
Mycenae. If any should hide my sibling's hated head
and shield the man from harm, let him die a dismal death.
This very palace, famous Pelops' home, can crash upon my head; 190
I only ask it crash upon my brother too.
Come, my soul, perform an act which every age will damn—
and speak of without cease. I have to dare a crime
that's heinous, bloody, just the kind my brother
would wish he'd thought of first. Vengeance can't be dealt

unless the stakes are raised. But what is vile enough
to overtop his crime? Is he humbled and dejected? Has he
learned
to keep a limit while life goes well, or be at peace
when it does not? I know the nature of the man:
200 he can't be taught, nor bent: and yet he can be broken.
And so, before he steels himself or summons strength,
we must attack, or be attacked ourselves off guard.
He will be killed or be the killer: between us lies the crime.
It awaits the first to seize it.

SERVANT

Your subjects' disapproval
deters you not at all?

ATREUS

The greatest good of power is this:
my subjects must both praise and bear
their ruler's acts.

SERVANT

If fear forces men to praise,
fear drives those men to hate as well.
But if you would be known for true support
210 you'll look for praise in hearts, not words.

ATREUS

The lowly man can often win praise from the heart,
only kings win lies. Let them want what they *don't* want.

SERVANT

Let a king want what's right: everyone will want the same.

ATREUS

Whenever "right" alone is granted to a master, he rules
on sufferance alone.

SERVANT

When neither self-control
nor care for law exists, nor human feeling, trust, and sanctity,
the kingdom can't stand firm.

ATREUS

Human feeling, trust, and sanctity
are private goods. Let kings go where they please.

SERVANT

Believe it wrong to hurt a brother, even if he's evil.

ATREUS

What's wrong against a brother is right against that man. 220
What crime has he not touched, what evil act
abjured? By seduction and by theft he stole
my kingdom and my wife; by fraud he seized
the ancient token of our rule, by fraud he wrecked our home.
There is a magic ram, bellwether to a battened flock,
the famous herd of Pelops in its highland folds.
Across his body thick-spun gold flows rich.
This is its fleece, and from the wool upon his back
scepters are gilt for new-throned Tantalids to bear.
The man who owns the ram is he who rules. The fate 230
of all the house relies on it. It grazes, sacred, in safe meadows,
a place apart enclosed by stones that gird
the fateful pastureland with rocky walls.
This very ram Thyestes took, the traitor—stupendous deed
of daring!—and the partner of my bed abetted in the crime.
From this came all our mutual slaughter, every evil started then.
I've wandered my own land, an exile and afraid,
no member of my family can rest for fear of ambush,
a harlot-wife is mine, and my brother's promise void.
Our home is tainted, my sons might not be mine,[24] all that I 240
know
is that my brother is my foe.

(*To himself.*)

You're stalling: why? Call up
some strength of mind, begin at last, and look at Tantalus, at
Pelops:
these are the archetypes my hands are called to match.
Tell me how to crush his loathsome life.

SERVANT

Stab him with your sword, let him gasp out his hateful breath.

ATREUS

You've come up with the final stage: I want the punishment in full.

Only a gentle ruler *kills*. In my realm,
death's a fate that people beg for.

SERVANT

No shred of human feeling moves you?

ATREUS

If human feeling ever visited my house,
250 it must depart. Let the foul band of Furies come,
the Erinys of strife and Megaera with twin torches
brandished high. My heart is still not blazing up
with frenzy fierce enough. I am a glutton
for some more monstrous horror.

SERVANT

What strange plan are you brewing in your rage?

ATREUS

Something beyond the limit of accustomed rage:
I'll leave no crime undone, though none's enough.

SERVANT

The sword?

ATREUS

—is not enough.

SERVANT

Then fire?

ATREUS

Still not enough.

SERVANT

What weapon will so great a grudge employ?

ATREUS

Thyestes.

SERVANT

This crime is beyond rage!

ATREUS

It is. An inner turmoil shakes and stuns me, 260
a whirlwind in my soul: I am swept I don't know where,
but I am swept. The earth bellows from deep below,
there's thunder in the cloudless sky, the whole house shrieks
as if its walls were toppling, the household gods can feel it
and turn aside their faces. —*Yes*, this is what must happen, this
atrocity
that makes you, O gods, take fright.

SERVANT

Tell me your plan: what is it?

ATREUS

Something swells within me, beyond the limits of my mind,
beyond what's rote, beyond the bounds of human habit,
it urges on my lagging hands. What is it? I don't know,
but it's gigantic. So be it. Here's work for you, my soul. 270
A crime that matches Atreus and fits Thyestes too:
let each of us commit it. A Thracian home once saw[25]
a meal to hush all tongues—yes, that crime was shocking,
but it's been done before. My anger needs to find
a greater horror still. Procne! You were a parent; inspire me,
and Philomela, do the same: our case is much alike. Give help,
propel my hand. Let the salivating father cut his sons
in pieces and with a smile consume his flesh and blood.
I like it, this is abundant crime. *This* modus operandi fits the
bill,
at least for now. Where is he? Why is Atreus still innocent 280
for all this length of time? My mind's eye sees the image of the
slaughter,
the whole of it, his childlessness served up before the father's
face.[26] My soul, do you revert once more to fear,
do you shrink before the deed? It must be dared, so do it!

The foulest outrage in this act of crime, the father
will take care of.

SERVANT

But what tricks are there to trap the man,
to snare him, make him put his foot within our noose?
He sees danger all around.

ATREUS

There's no way we could trap the man
unless he aimed to trap us first. He still wants to be the ruler.
290 This hope will make him brave the thunderbolt Jove shakes,
this hope will make him face the swollen whirlpool's threats,
and test the quicksand straits of the Libyan shore.[27]
Yes, this hope will make him confront the evil he thinks worst:
his brother.

SERVANT

Who will inspire his trust in peace?
Whose word will foster so great a trust?

ATREUS

Base ambitions are gullible.
I'll tell my sons to take a message to their uncle now:
"Leave strangers' homes, you exiled wanderer, and swap
your poverty for power: you'll rule Argos as lord with me!"
But if Thyestes prove too stern and spurns
300 this invitation, it'll still persuade his artless sons.
They're sick of their hard life and can easily be tricked.
On this side is the age-old frenzy to be king; on that,
grim poverty, hard labor. These will force the man
to yield, though steeled by many hardships.

SERVANT

The time gone by has made his troubles light by now.

ATREUS

Not so. His sense of hardship grows from day to day.
Misfortune is an easy load, unless it never leaves.

SERVANT

Find other agents for your inauspicious plan.

ATREUS

Children like to hear advice that's not the best.[28]

SERVANT

How you teach them treat their uncle will rebound upon your head: 310

A teacher's wicked acts have often come to haunt him.

ATREUS

Suppose no man should teach them fraud and crime:

Being king will give instruction. You're afraid they'll turn out bad?

They were at birth. What you call cruel and savage,

what you believe a ruthless act and excessively impious,

perhaps Thyestes plans as well.

SERVANT

Will your sons know

this trap is being prepared?

ATREUS

You cannot count on silence

in such tender years: they might reveal my snare.

Silence is learned through life's many adversities.

SERVANT

You're deceiving the very ones through whom you plan 320

to deceive another?

ATREUS

To make sure they are innocent of blame.

What need is there to link my children to my crime?

My hate should be revealed by me alone.

(*To himself.*)

—This isn't right, you're falling short: these sons you spare

could be *his* sons instead. Let Agamemnon know the truth

and help my plan, let Menelaus know the truth and help

his brother. The true proof of their doubtful birth

let's find out in this crime. If they refuse to fight my war,

if they don't wish to wage this hate, and if they call him uncle,

330 then he's their father. Let's start. —But often frightened faces
reveal too much, and great plans betray the planner
against his will. Let them not know they're agents
of so great a plot.

(*To the servant.*)

And you! silence about my plan.

SERVANT

There's no need to remind me: both loyalty and fear,
though chiefly loyalty, lock it deep within my chest.

CHORUS

At last this stock of nobility,
the race of ancient Inachus,[29]
has settled the quarrels of brothers.
What madness is it that drives you
340 to donate your lifeblood in turn
and sinfully grab at the scepter?
You seekers of strongholds don't know
where true kingship is to be found.
A king is not made by his riches,
the purple shade of his robe,
a royal brow sporting a crown,
or roof-beams shining with gold:
a king can lay aside fear
as well as the heart's ugly urges,
350 can't be moved by maddened ambition,
nor the favor of volatile mobs
(a favor not stable for long);
not whatever the West can dig up,
nor the golden waves of the Tagus,[30]
coursing their clarified bed,
not whatever the threshing-ground grinds
at the time of the hot Libyan harvest.
He's not scared at the crash of a fire-bolt
as it follows its zigzagging path,
360 at the East Wind whipping the sea

or the swell of the storm-swept Adriatic,
rabid with murderous waves.
He's a man untamed by the lance,
untamed by the point of the steel;
and he stands in a place always safe
and sees everything from above,
and happily goes to his fate
and never laments his own death.
Let's suppose all the kings should convene:
the ones who rouse Scythian nomads, 370
who hold the Red Sea and its coasts,
waters stained red far and wide
by rubies that shine in the depths,
or the race which unlocks the high Caspians,
ridges exposed to strong Slavs,[31]
or he who attacks those who dare
to cross the Danube on foot,[32]
or the Serians famed for their silks,[33]
wherever these people reside—
a good mind still makes a king. 380
He has no need for a cavalry;
no need for arms or the fainthearted
arrows which the Parthian shoots from afar
when pretending to flee;
he has no need to raze cities
with machines hurling rocks
from afar through the air.
A king is a man who fears nothing,[34]
a king is a man who wants nothing.
This kingdom one gives to oneself. 390
Let the ruler who wants take his stance
on the slippery rooftop of rule:
I'd like to loll in sweet calm.
Obscurity grants me safe footing.
Let me relish my easy repose,
and, known to none of my peers,

let my life flow by silently.
And when my days have all passed
without any hullabaloo,
400 let me die both old and a commoner.
Death only weighs heavy on him
whom everyone knows far too well
but who dies unknown to himself.

ACT 3

THYESTES

Oh roofs of my fatherland, riches of Argos! I've longed
to see you, best and greatest good for wretched exiles.
I see a stretch of native soil and my ancestral gods[35]
(if gods indeed exist), the Cyclops' sacred towers,
sublime beyond what human hands could do,
the racecourse where the young men throng, in which
410 I drove my father's chariot, and often won first prize.
Argos will come to meet me, a bustling crowd will come:
but Atreus too, no doubt! Go back! Back to your forest den,
the close-set groves, the life you shared with beasts,
beastly itself. The sheen of power, its éclat,
should not mislead you with its meretricious gleam.
When you inspect the gift you get, look at the giver too.
Just now I counted myself happy, resolute, among conditions
which all men judge as bitter; but at this moment I've regressed
to fear. My mind sticks fast, it wants to turn my body back,
420 but still I shuffle forward an unconsenting step.

TANTALUS

My father's struck aghast, his pace is slow, he turns his face
this way and that, and stays in uncertainty.[36]

THYESTES

Why, my soul, this waiting, why twist round and round
a simple plan so long? Do you trust in fallibilities,
your brother and the throne? Do you fear the hardships

you've tamed and learned to bear? Do you shun the toils
you put to use? Being miserable now pleases you.
Turn back your step, escape while still you can.

TANTALUS

Father, what cause compels you turn away, your homeland
now in view? Why hide your empty purse from so much wealth? 430
Your brother's anger's tossed aside, he's here to reunite,
he returns to you a portion of his realm, conjoins
our lacerated house's limbs, and gives you back to you.

THYESTES

You press me for an answer I myself don't know: why I'm afraid.
I don't see anything to fear, and yet I fear.
Although I want to go, my legs are weak, my knees won't budge,
I'm borne in a direction that's not the way I strive,
just like a boat whose oars and sail drive it on,
but which the tide drives back, opposing oars and sail.

TANTALUS

Whatever stands in the way and blocks your will—defeat it, 440
and see what great rewards await on your return.
Father, you can be king!

THYESTES

Yes, since I control my death.[37]

TANTALUS

Absolute power is—

THYESTES

—having nothing, if nothing is your desire.

TANTALUS

You will bequeath it to your sons!

THYESTES

The throne seats only one.

TANTALUS

Happiness is in your grasp, and you prefer your misery?

THYESTES

Trust me: power pleases under false pretenses,
what's hard is feared wrongly. When I stood atop the world,
I never ceased to fear, to shiver at the very sword
strapped to my side. It's a blessing
450 to stand in no one's way, to eat your meal safely
while sitting on the ground. Crimes don't enter hovels,
the fare upon a humble table's safe to eat;
poison comes in cups of gold. I speak of what I know:
it's possible to choose bad fortune over good.
I have no house set upon a mountain's peak
to cast a shadow on the lowly, trembling plebs,
pale ivory doesn't gleam upon my lofty ceiling,
there's no man standing guard over my sleep.
I don't use a fleet to fish, I don't drive back the sea
460 by building massive piers, I don't stuff a sinful belly
with the tribute of the world, no field is harvested for me
from beyond the Getans and the Parthians,[38]
I'm not adored with incense, my altars are not decked
in disregard of Jove. No rooftop garden bows
its treetops down to me, no pools heated by many hands
exhale their steam, I don't concede the day to sleep
and, wide awake till dawn, wine away the night.
No one fears me, my house is safe without a sword,
a great tranquility pervades my humble home.
470 Not to need a kingdom is itself a massive kingdom.

TANTALUS

But if a god is granting it, you shouldn't reject power.
You don't need to pursue it: your brother *asks* you to be king.

THYESTES

He asks? Then be afraid. Some treachery's to hand.

TANTALUS

A sense of family can return to one who spurned it,
true love can find the strength that it once lost.

THYESTES

His brother loves Thyestes? Ha-ha! Sooner the sea
will drench the constellations in the sky, the Sicilian tide
and its rapacious waves will freeze, ripe crops will rise
from the Ionian depths, black night will bathe the land 480
in light. Sooner water mix with flame, life
with death, the wind make treaties with the sea
and give it pledges.

TANTALUS

But what trick do you fear?

THYESTES

I fear them all: why set a limit to my qualms?
His power is as unbounded as his hate.

TANTALUS

But what can he inflict on you?

THYESTES

For me I've long since ceased to fear: it's you, my sons,
who render Atreus a source of fear for me.

TANTALUS

But you're on guard—why fear deception?

THYESTES

Once disaster strikes, it's too late to be cautious. But fine:
let's go. Your father testifies to this alone: I follow you,
I do not lead.

TANTALUS

God will protect
our well-laid plans. Go on, proceed with confidence. 490

ATREUS

My prey is caught and held inside the snare I laid.
I see the man himself, and next to him I see his sons,
the offspring of a hated line. Now I can loathe
without contingency. At last Thyestes is in my hands,
at last, and not just him, but all of him!
I can hardly curb my mind, my anger hardly yields to reins.

Just like a hunting dog who, held back by his long leash,
tracks the wild beasts and sniffs the path with snout
to ground: while still the boar whose lingering scent
500 he smells is far away, the hound obeys and roams around
without a bark. But when the prey is closer,
he fights against the leash, calls on his tardy master
with his howls, breaks loose from what restrains him.
When anger hopes for blood, it can't conceal itself.
But let it be concealed. See how his hair, weighed down by
coats
of dirt, hides a haggard face, how filthy
is his beard. But let me display my affection.

(*To Thyestes.*)

Brother, I'm pleased to see you! Give me the hug
I've waited for. Whatever gave us cause for rage,
510 let it have passed. From this day on let's cultivate
our blood ties and our love. Let hate be damned and disappear.

THYESTES

I can't excuse the things I've done, when I find you so kind.
I confess it, Atreus, I confess to all the things
you thought of me. Your love for me today has made
my case the worst on earth. The man who wronged
so good a brother is wrong indeed. My tears
must be my advocate: you are the first to see me beg.
These hands which never have clutched feet beseech you.
Let all our anger fall aside, let us expunge
520 the rage that swelled our minds. Brother, take my sons
to be the blameless pledges of my faith.

ATREUS

Don't hold my knees; let us embrace instead.
You too, children, all of you, helpmates of old age,
come to my arms. Strip off your squalid clothing,
Brother, which pains my eyes, and put on finery
equal to mine, and hold in common happily

a brother's realm. The greater grounds for praise are mine:
to return our father's crown to his unharmed son.
It's luck to have a kingdom, but goodness to bestow it.

THYESTES

I hope the gods repay you with rewards to match 530
your merits. But my filthy state must spurn the crown
you'd set upon my head. My unpropitious hand
will not take up the scepter. Let me hide myself
among the throng.

ATREUS

This throne has room for two.

THYESTES

What you hold I count as mine, my brother.

ATREUS

Who snubs the gifts of Fortune, when her currents come his way?

THYESTES

A man who knows how easily such currents ebb and flow.

ATREUS

Do you forbid your brother to win himself some glory?

THYESTES

Your glory's won already, mine is left to win:
repudiation of the throne is my steadfast aim. 540

ATREUS

I will give up my share of rule, if you refuse to take up yours.

THYESTES

Very well. I'll bear the name of king which you bestow,
but the army and the laws will serve you, as will I.

ATREUS

Wear this binding crown upon your august head:
I'll proceed to sacrifice the victims owed the gods.

CHORUS

Who could believe this? Ill-tempered Atreus,
bestial, unbridled, half-insane,

stood dumbstruck at his brother's sight.
There's no force to beat true love of kin.
550 Strangers' quarrels last forever,
those whom real love held once, it'll hold again.
When anger roused by great events
rends good will and sounds the call to arms,
when swift horsemen make a racket with their reins,
and on both sides the brandished sword gleams bright,
the sword that raving Mars, who craves fresh blood,
whose blows rain thick and fast, has drawn,
then love will stay the sword and lead
unwilling enemies, hands clasped, to peace.
560 What god has brought this quick accord
from so much strife? Just now through all Mycenae,
the arms of civil war resounded,
ashen mothers held their babies,
wives feared for their armored men
who took their swords up joylessly,
arms rusty with the ravages of peace.
One man tried to bolster weakened walls,
one to strengthen towers hobbled
by neglect, one to lock the gates with iron
570 bolts. Along the heights the trembling sentry,
guardian of the anxious night, kept watch.
The fear of war is worse than actual war.
But now the danger of the brutish sword has passed,
now silent is the baneful blare of trumpets,
now the clarion's shrill call is hushed:
deep peace returns to the rejoicing city.
Thus, when the northwest wind pounds Italian seas[39]
and swells surge from the depths,
Scylla howls inside her battered lair
580 and sailors still in port are fearful of the deep,
which greedy Charybdis gulps down and vomits up,
and savage Cyclops, on seething Etna's peak,
quakes at father Neptune's rage and fears

that overflowing waves might douse
the fire that crackles in eternal forges,
and poor Laertes in his shaken Ithaca
believes his kingdom could be drowned.[40]
But if the winds have fallen in their strength,
and the sea sinks down more placid than a pool,
and the main, which boats once feared to cleave, 590
on all sides unrolls for party boats
a surface decked with billowed sails:
then at your leisure you could count the fish below
where recently beneath the gale-force winds
the tossed Cyclades trembled at the sea.[41]
No fate remains for long. Joy and suffering
yield in turn; joy is the shorter-lived.
Time's whimsy swaps the highest for the low.
One who sets a crown upon his brow,
at whom the kneeling nations cower, 600
whose nod makes Medes lay down their arms,
and Indians, to whom the sun is closer,
and Scythians, whose horsemen menace Parthia,
—*this* man's scepter-holding hand is nervous,
and he fears and foretells elusive chance
that moves all things, and fears fickle time.
All you to whom the king of land and sea
has granted jurisdiction over life and death,
wipe off that haughty and inflated look.
The very thing a subject fears from you, 610
a greater king can hold above your head.
Every reign is but a rung upon a ladder.
The rising sun might see a man exalted,
the setting sun might see the same laid low.
No one should trust too much in happy times,
no man despair of better times in bad.
Clotho mixes this with that and prevents[42]
fortune's stability, but spins fate on her wheel.
No god will favor you so far that you can trust tomorrow;

620 god keeps our lives in constant motion
and spins them in the whirlwind of fate.

ACT 4

(*The messenger rushes in, aghast at what he has seen.*)

MESSENGER

What wind will hoist me, send me headlong through the air
and wrap me in black clouds, to banish from my eyes
such enormous sacrilege? This house would even shame Pelops
and Tantalus!

CHORUS

What is this news do you bring?

MESSENGER

What kind of place is this? Argos? Sparta, where once resided
loving brothers, Castor and Pollux? Corinth, which guards
a gate between two seas? Is it the Danube granting flight
630 to the fierce Alani,[43] or the Caspian under its eternal snows,
or home to Scythians who wander wide afield?
What is this place that knows such monstrous horror?

CHORUS

Speak out, lay before us what this horror is.

MESSENGER

I can't until my mind has calmed, until my rigid frame
lets loose my limbs from fear. The vision of the gruesome act
still stands before my sight! Take me far away from here,
you maddened winds, take me where the stolen day
is borne.

CHORUS

Still grimmer now's your grip upon our doubting minds!
Reveal the thing that haunts you, make the perpetrator known.
640 I don't ask who it is, but which of two. Tell us at once!

MESSENGER

Atop the citadel, a part of Pelops' house
looks to the south. The farthest side is mountain-high

and guards the town, and keeps in thrall
a throng impudent to their kings.
Here a giant hall gleams bright, and ample
for a crowd. Its golden architraves repose
on columns marked by marbled hues.
Beyond this well-known part, where nations meet,
the wealthy house extends to many rooms.
Far in the back, there is a secret spot. 650
In deep embrace it holds an ancient grove,
a sanctuary of the realm, where no tree spreads
fertile branches, or feels the pruning knife.
Only the yew, the cypress, and the darkling ilex
nod in the dusky wood, and over all a lofty oak
looks down, and far outstrips the grove.
Here the sons of Tantalus are sworn in on their thrones,
here they look for help in disaster and in doubt.
Here their fastened gifts are set: loud trumpets
and wrecked chariots, the booty of Myrtilus' sea, 660
the wheels destroyed by waxen axle-pins,
and the crimes of every race: in this place hangs
Pelops' Phrygian headdress,[44] here the spoils of war,
a cloak on which is shown barbarian defeat.
A sullen spring forms in the shade, and stagnates in
a dusky swamp. It's like the horrid water
of the dreaded Styx, by which the gods swear oaths.
They say here in the dark of night the gods of death
lament, and clanking chains resound within the grove,
and shades ululate. Whatever one might fear to hear 670
there can be seen; a ghoulish throng escapes
the ancient tombs and walks; monstrosities beyond our ken
trample the spot; the whole wood ever
glows with flame, and high trunks burn though fireless.
The grove often reverberates with barks from
triple throats, the house is often terrified by gigantic
phantoms. Nor does the coming of the day allay
one's fear. The grove has its own night, and still at noon

the dread owed to the underworld prevails. From here
680 unerring answers come to those who ask. With a colossal crash
the fates are set free from the shrine, the cavern roars,
the god unlocks his voice. It's here that raving Atreus
drags the children of his brother, to this place.
The altars are prepared—who could do justice to the tale?—
he ties behind their backs the children's royal hands,
he binds their grieving heads with purple ribbon.
There's incense here, there's Bacchus' sacred wine,
a knife next to the human sacrifice, and salted meal.
All due process is observed, so that this heinous crime
can be ritually correct.

CHORUS

690 Who takes the knife in hand?

MESSENGER

He does! He acts as priest, and with sepulchral prayer
chants fatal incantations in the tones of a fanatic.
It's he who at the altar stands, he who grasps the children
doomed to death, arranges them, takes up the blade,
and he who plays assistant—no segment of the rite is
overlooked.
The grove begins to shake, and all the building sways
with the movement of the earth, like the ocean's undulation,
uncertain where its mass should fall; and from the left part
of the sky a comet plunges, and drags along a sooty tail.
700 The wine poured on the fire is changed
and flows as blood; the kingly crown upon his head
slips twice and thrice, and ivory weeps within the shrines.
The omens trouble everyone—excepting Atreus, who stands
alone, unmoved, and terrifies (what's more) the gods
who threaten *him*. And now, no more delay!
He stands before the altars, looking grimly side to side.
Just as along the Ganges' brush a starving tigress waits
and wonders in her mind which of two bulls to kill,
lusting for her double prey but uncertain whom to maul

the first (she turns her gaping jaws now here, 710
now there, and keeps her hunger in suspense),
so too harsh Atreus surveys the lives now hostage
to his godless rage. Which one to slaughter first? This is
his quandary, and whom the second stroke should sacrifice.
It makes no difference, but he hesitates: to organize atrocity
is its own source of pleasure.

CHORUS

Who then's the first to feel the blow?

MESSENGER

He grants the prior place (don't think him scant in love of kin)
to the son named for his grandsire: Tantalus is first to fall.

CHORUS

How did the child face his death? What was his mindset, his
expression?

MESSENGER

He was completely self-composed and didn't waste his time 720
pleading for his life. That monster stabbed him, shoved the
sword
in to the hilt; and pushing on it all the way
he plunged his hand up to the throat. When the sword was
extricated, still the corpse was standing, and pausing long to see
if it should fall this way or that, it fell upon its uncle.
Next that savage hauls to the altar Plisthenes,
and puts him by his brother. He hacks his throat and severs it.
The neck once cut, the trunk falls prostrate on the ground,
the head, protesting, rolls away with incoherent mumbles.

CHORUS

What did he do when he'd dispatched this double death? 730
Did he spare the third-born son or heap crime onto crime?

MESSENGER

Just as a thick-maned lion in the forests of Armenia
may have conquered many kills yet stalks the herd no less
(his jaws are steeped in gore, and though his hunger's sated,
his rage to kill endures: he stalks the bulls from every side

and, sluggish, scares the calves with fangs themselves fatigued),
like him Atreus rages, and swells inside with anger,
and holds the sword that drips with double death; forgetful
of the object of his rage, he skewers the body of the boy
740 with hostile hand. The sword that enters in his chest
at once comes out the other side. He falls,
extinguishing the altar with his blood, and dies
a death that comes from both his wounds.

CHORUS

This crime is savagery!

MESSENGER

You shudder at the tale? If the nightmare only ended here,
we'd consider the man pious.

CHORUS

Is there room in nature for something
worse, more diabolical?

MESSENGER

You think this was the culmination of his crime?
It was a step.

CHORUS

But what more could he do? Did he toss the carcasses
to wild beasts to tear apart? Did he refuse the sacrament of fire?

MESSENGER

I wish he had refused! I don't ask that earth should cover,
750 or fire burn, the dead. Let him give the boys to birds to feed on,
let him expose the bodies as ghastly food for animals.
After what I saw, I pray for what we count as punishment—
let their father see them graveless! No human generation
will believe this crime. Posterity will call it lies.
He pulls the quivering guts out while still the boys have breath;
the arteries still pulse, still the heart pumps fearfully.
He handles their intestines, does a haruspicy,[45]
and notes the still-warm markings of their organs.
When he's sated with his victims, he's fancy-free to plan
760 his brother's feast. He himself carves up each corpse

into component pieces, amputates the shoulders
from the trunk, and then the arms that slow him down,
he strips the joints without a qualm and cuts apart the bones.
He keeps only the heads and the hands once pledged in faith.
Part of the guts he sticks on spits; set atop slow fires,
they drip. Other parts hot water heats. The pots in which they
bubble
glow white-hot. The fire jumps beyond the food it cooks,
and twice, three times, is forced back to the hearth
that shudders at its load, and though compelled to stay,
the fire burns against its will. The liver hisses on the spits. 770
It's hard to say whether the corpses or the fire
groans the more. The fire's reduced to pitchy smoke;
the smoke itself, a dark and ponderous veil, does not
rise straight nor climb high to the skies—
its ugly cloud sits on the household gods themselves.
O too tolerant Sun, although you fled from this,
and stopped the day while in midsky and made it dark,
still you were too late. The father rends his sons
and chews his flesh and blood with bloody mouth.
He's in full dress, his hair's a-drip with liniment, 780
he's rendered dull by wine. Often his stopped-up throat
jams on the food he eats. Thyestes, there's just one silver lining
to your calamity: you dine in ignorance.
But even this will pass. The Sun himself can turn his chariot
back
and take the path he came on, oppressive night
can rise at dawn, and at another's hour, and try
to cloak the crime in unaccustomed dark,
but still this deed will out. Every sin will be exposed.

CHORUS

O Father of earth and the gods, at whose rising
dark night and her glories turn tail, 790
why choose to rescind your journey,
and squander the day at high noon?

Why, Phoebus, re-veil your bright face?
It's too early for Vesper, night's herald,
to summon the nocturnal stars; too early as well
for your wheel, rounding its goal in the west,
to unyoke the hardworking team.
It's too early for day to decline into night,
for the third of the trumpets to sound out the twilight.
800 The farmer is stunned that dinnertime's come
while his oxen are far from being weary.
What's struck you aside from your course in the sky?
What is the cause of your horses' diversion
from their infallible path? Do the giants, losers in war,
the prison of hell now unlocked, once again
instigate war? Does Tityus, torn,
his chest all worn out, redouble
his ancient rage? Has Typhoeus dug himself up
from the mountainous mass that entombed him?[46]
810 Has a pass that's sky-high been constructed
to pass through the hostile Phlegraeans,[47]
does Ossa in Thrace weigh down Thessalian Pelion?
Earth's normal rotations are all lost to view,
the sun no more rises, no more will he set.
Dewy Eos,[48] mother of dawn, who is used
to hand to the Sun-god his reins, is aghast
at the bounds of her kingdom upturned.
She's inept at washing the tired-out horses,
she doesn't know how to plunge in the sea
820 manes that are steaming with sweat.
The Sun as he sets is himself unaccustomed
to see the dawn rise, their meeting is new;
he orders the darkness to fall, but he finds
that night is not ready. The stars don't appear,
the skies do not twinkle celestial fire,
the Moon cannot rout the tenebrous shades.
But whatever this is, let it only be night.
All of our hearts are a-tremble, we're struck

by grim trepidation.
What if the world collapses, shaken by 830
fated destruction, and again anarchical Chaos
should destroy both humans and gods,
and nature again shroud the earth,
the ambient seas and the lights
that wander the high-spangled sky?
No more will the Sun, the lord of the stars,
his deathless torch rising, give
signs of the summer and winter. No more
will the Moon, as she meets Phoebus' rays,[49]
banish the fears of night, and riding swift 840
on her orbital path, outrace the reins
of her brother. The throng of the gods all together
will fall piled in the selfsame abyss.
The Zodiac, bearer of signs, who weaves through
the sacrosanct stars and cuts through the zones
at an angle, who causes the long years to circle,
will see as he falls the planets fall too. The Ram,[50]
who lets us unfurl our sails to warm Zephyr
before the gentle spring comes, himself
will plunge headlong into the waves 850
over which he transported scared Helle.
The Bull,[51] who bears the Hyades, daughters of Atlas,
on his bright horns, will drag down together
the Twins and the curving embrace
of the Crab.[52] Hercules' Lion,[53]
burning with fiery heat, will fall once again from the sky.
The Virgin will fall to the earth she abandoned,[54]
the weights of the Scale, dispenser of justice,
will fall and drag down bad-tempered Scorpion.
Elderly Chiron, who sets feathered arrows 860
to the string of Thessalian bow,[55] will lose
all those arrows, the string having snapped.
The glacial Goat, who brings back winter's sloth,
will tumble and break Aquarius' urn,

whoever Aquarius is;[56] with him the Fish;
will depart, the last of the sky's constellations.
An engulfing whirlpool will swallow
the stars never bathed by the sea,[57]
and the slippery, riverlike Snake, who
870 bifurcates the Bears, will fall too;[58]
and cold Cynosura,[59] crackling with frost,
the smaller Bear joined to great Dragon;[60]
Arctophylax as well, tardy guard
of his wagon, no more a celestial fixture.[61]
Why us? Why were we the ones to deserve,
of the peoples of earth, that the world
with its overturned poles should destroy us?
Is it us for whom time's last day comes? Ghastly this fate we were born to, whether
880 we were the wretches who banished the sun
or we were the victims of loss.
But enough of our fear, we should end our laments.
That man would truly be frantic for life
who wanted to live while the world died around him.

ACT 5

ATREUS

My stride is equal to the stars, I tower over all,
I touch the peak of heaven with my haughty head.
Now the glory of the realm is mine, now my father's throne.
The gods can quit their job: I've gained the purpose of my prayer.
This is good, it's more than good, now even I am sated.
890 But why should I be sated? I'll go on and fill the father
with the death of those he loved. The day has set,
so shame cannot prevent me. Do it while the sky's still void!
I wish I could retain the fleeing gods, and force them all,
dragged back against their will, to see the feast,
my vengeance. But this will be enough, that the father see.

Even if the day forbid, I will dispel for you
the darkness under which your sorrows lurk.
For too long now you've sat a guest before your meal,
without a care and cheerfully. Enough of lavish
dining, enough of wine: for evils of this scale, 900
Thyestes must be sober.

(*To the servants.*)

You slavish throng!
Unlock the temple doors, let the festive hall lie open.
I want to see what color stains his face when he sees
his children's heads, what are the first words discharged
by his grief, and how his body gasps for air and stiffens
with the shock. Here's the fruit of all my work.
I want to see, not his final misery, but how it comes.
The dining room is open, and gleams with many torches.
The man himself sprawls on a couch of gold and purple;
he's drunk and props his heavy head on his left hand. 910
He belches. I am the greatest of the gods, I am
the king of kings! I've exceeded all my wishes.
He's full; he drinks the wine from a giant silver cup.
Don't be sparing! Even now some gore remains
from all those victims; the color of the ancient vintage
will conceal it. With this glass, this very one, let the meal end.
Let the father drink his children's blended blood:
he'd have drunk mine. Look, he's bursting into song
and cheerful cries; he's lost his self-control.

THYESTES

O heart of mine, dulled with long pain, 920
lay aside now your anxious concern.
Let grief disappear, and terror, and grim
neediness, companion of terrified exile,
and shame that weighs heavy
when life is hard. It matters much more
from where you fall, not where to.

When you've plunged from the loftiest
peak, it's a great thing to regain sure
footing. It's a great thing, when pressed in the crush
930 of disaster, to bear with unbending neck
the weight of a kingdom laid low, to suffer
encompassing ruins with a head
held up high, no coward undone by
misfortune. But now—banish the clouds
of affliction and dismiss the scars of the past.
Let a joyous expression return in good times,
dismiss old Thyestes from thought.
And yet—this is a trait of those who have suffered,
to never believe their good luck.
940 Though prosperity has been restored,
it's hard for the downcast to smile.
Why do you summon me back, why forbid me observe
this day's celebration, why do you bid me
to cry, you sadness that comes from no source?
Why stop me from decking my hair with beautiful
flowers? It forbids me, indeed it forbids!
The roses of springtime fall from my head,
my hair, though damp with rich balsam,
stands straight on end in sudden horror.
950 My face floods with tears despite its own wish,
groans interrupt me while I speak. Grief
is fond of the mourning it knows, and
a dark urge to sob overwhelms the unhappy.
I want to cry out ill-omened laments,
to rip at these clothes steeped in Tyrian
dye, and to howl in dismay.
My mind gives me sign of future distress,
it foretells its own grief. On the sea,
a powerful storm can be near
960 when still waters swell without wind.
You're crazy! What are these sorrows and troubles
except mere invention? Offer your brother

a heart full of trust. Whatever it is that upsets you,
you fear without cause—or too late.
I don't want to be sad, but a nebulous terror
wanders inside me, sudden streams dampen
my eyes, and yet there's no cause. Is this
terror or grief? Does great pleasure
have its own tears?

ATREUS

Brother, it's a happy day. Let's honor it with shared 970
consent. This day will reinforce my power
and bind our solid pact of stable peace.

THYESTES

I've had my fill of food, my fill of wine as well.
I'd reach my peak of happiness, if my sons
were only here to celebrate with me.

ATREUS

Believe it, they *are* here, in their father's warm embrace.
They're here and they will stay. No portion of your sons
will be held back from you. I'll offer you the faces you desire,
I'll fill the father fully with his young menagerie.
You'll be replete, no fear. Just now, mixed in with mine, 980
they tend the pleasant duties of the children's table—
but they'll be summoned. Take this brimming cup of wine,
an heirloom from our clan.[62]

THYESTES

I'll take it as a present from
my brother's feast. Let wine be poured to our ancestral gods,
then I will drink. But what is this? My hands will not
obey, the goblet's weight increases and pulls down my arm.
When I raise the wine, it shuns my very lips,
cheats my open mouth and eludes my sip.
The very table totters on the oscillating floor.
The torch is barely lit; the air itself is heavy; 990
it's stunned to be abandoned by both the night and day.
What's this? The sphere of heaven shakes,

and weakens more and more; a denser fog collects
with thick-set gloom, and night has found a hiding place
in night. The stars all disappear. Whatever thing this is,
I hope it spares my children and my brother. Let the tempest
spend itself on this base head. No more delay, give back my
sons!

ATREUS

I'll give them back. No future day will take them from you.

THYESTES

What is this agitation that roils my intestines?
1000 What quivers deep within? I feel a load that's out of place.
My chest emits a groan, but the groaning is not mine.
Come, my sons, your luckless father calls you:
come. This pain will leave me when I see you—
I hear their reproachful words—from where?

ATREUS

Father, open wide your arms:
they're here.

(*He takes the lid off the platter that holds the heads of Thyestes' children.*)

Do you recognize your sons at all?

THYESTES

I recognize my brother! O Earth! Can you endure such evil
on your soil? You ought to break apart, to plunge us both
down to the shades and hellish Styx, and by a yawning path
propel this kingdom and its king to vast Chaos!
1010 You should uproot Mycenae from its foundations
and overturn its homes. We ought long since to stand,
myself and Atreus, in Tantalus' company. Rend your limits
on all sides, and if there is a region lower still than hell,
than our progenitors, then sink your chasm
in a massive hole and heap the whole of Acheron
on our buried selves. Let guilty souls wander above
our heads, let Phlegethon, a river made of flames,
flow with full force above our place of exile, and with

its burning waters drive before it all its sands—but
the earth still lies unmoved, a sluggish weight. 1020
The gods above have fled.

ATREUS

Why not receive in happiness the sons
for whom you've so long waited? Your brother isn't stopping
you:
delight in them and kiss them, share embraces with the three.

THYESTES

This is our pact? This is the favor shown to me, this is a
brother's pledge?
This is the way you set aside your hate? I don't ask you
to give the father back his sons unharmed; I only ask what you
can give
with hate and crime uncompromised. I ask this as a brother to
one:
let me bury them. Just give me back what I will burn
at once. I'm their father but I beg you: let me lose them,
not regain them.

ATREUS

What's left over from your sons 1030
you have; what's not left over, you have as well.

THYESTES

Do their bodies lie outside as food for birds of prey?
Are they being saved for lions, are they nourishment for beasts?

ATREUS

It was you—you ate this foul feast, you ate your flesh and blood.

THYESTES

It was this that shamed the gods! This drove the day back
into dawn! What should I say? The agony! How to
lament? What words can possibly suffice? I see
their sawn-off heads, the hands he ripped away,
the feet he tore from broken shins—these parts were what
the greedy father was too full to eat. Their organs 1040
churn inside me. The pollution trapped inside my guts

strains and seeks an outlet but has no way to leave.
Brother, give me your sword: it's steeped already
in my blood. With this steel I'll cut a pathway for my sons.
The sword's refused? Then let my chest reverberate
bruised by my crushing blows—no, hold your hand, you
wretch,
we should be gentle to the dead! Who's ever seen such evil?
What Black Sea thief who lives on jagged cliffs[63]
in the hostile Caucasus, what Procrustes, terror to
1050 Attic lands?[64] Look: I, the father, was a burden
to my sons, and now they burden me.[65] Is there a limit to this
crime?

ATREUS

There ought to be a limit when you *do* the crime,
not when you avenge it. Even this is little by my lights.
Straight from the wound itself I should have poured
the still warm blood into your throat: you'd have drunk
your living children's gore. But my anger was defrauded
by my haste. In wounding them I drove too deep the sword,
I killed them at the altar, appeased the fires with votive
1060 carnage. Carving up the lifeless flesh, I cut the limbs
in morsel sizes and submerged some parts in boiling pots,
the rest I set to dripping on slow fires.
While still they lived, I sliced the legs and sinews off.
I saw their pierced livers moan on slender spits,
I fed the flames with my own hand.
In all of this the father of the boys
could have outdone me. My rage has borne no fruit.
He ripped apart his children with impious teeth,
but did not know them, nor they him.

THYESTES

O seas enclosed by wandering shores!
Hear me! And you, gods, hear me too, wherever
1070 you have fled, hear this atrocity! You in the underworld,
hear me, and hear me, lands! —O Night, heavy with

dark and hellish fog, take time to hear my cries!
To you I am abandoned, you are the only one to see
this wretch, you also have no stars. My prayers won't be wicked.
I'll plead for nothing for myself—what prayer now could be
on my behalf? My prayers will look to you.
You, highest ruler of the sky, lord with command
of the ethereal court: wrap the world entire
in threatening cloud, clash together armies of the winds
on every side, in every corner thunder with a crash. 1080
Don't use the hand with which, wielding a lesser bolt,
you strike our houses and our undeserving homes, but that
by which the triple-mountained mass collapsed, and
the giants who stood equal to those peaks.[66] With *that* hand
fetch your armaments and launch your fires. Avenge
the stolen day, let loose your flames, and with your lightning
resupply the light lost from the sky. Don't hesitate
too long: my case and his are evil both. Or let the evil all
be mine: aim at me, and with your triforked spear of flame
impale this chest. If I the father want to bury my sons 1090
or to consign them to the final fire, I myself
must be committed to the flames. But if the gods
cannot be moved and no force strikes the sinful with its bolts,
let endless night endure, let it conceal with far-reaching gloom
these vast atrocities. Sun, I offer no complaint if you persist
in absence.

ATREUS

Now at last I praise my work, now
the trophy's truly mine. My sin would have been squandered
if your suffering were less. Now I believe my sons were born
to me,
now I can trust once more my marriage-bed is pure.[67]

THYESTES

Why did my children do to earn this punishment?

ATREUS

They were your children. 1100

THYESTES

You gave the children to their father—

ATREUS

Yes I did, and best of all,
I knew that they were yours.

THYESTES

I call those gods to witness who preside over the pious.

ATREUS

Why not call the marriage gods instead?

THYESTES

Who repays crime with crime?

ATREUS

I know why you complain: you're angry that I beat you to the crime.
It's not the fact you gorged upon a ghastly meal, but that
you weren't the one who cooked! This had been your aim:
to make a matching meal for me, your unsuspecting brother,
assault my children with their mother's aid, and with the same death
strike them down. Only this stood in your way:
you thought my sons were yours.

THYESTES

1110 The avenging gods will come:
my prayers hand you to *them* for punishment.

ATREUS

And for *your* punishment, I hand you to—your sons.

Agamemnon

The play deals with the most famous vendetta in Greek mythology, that of the House of Atreus. The actual story starts several generations earlier, when Tantalus kills his son Pelops to serve at a banquet for the gods. For this act of impiety, Tantalus receives the punishment of eternal hunger and thirst. Pelops, restored to life by the gods, commits a crime of treachery which results in a curse upon his family. The curse emerges in the rivalry between his two sons Atreus and Thyestes, with its gruesome denouement in Thyestes' consumption of his own children. Atreus meanwhile produces two sons, Agamemnon and Menelaus. After Menelaus' wife Helen runs away with her Trojan lover Paris (son of Priam, king of Troy), Agamemnon leads the combined Greek expedition to retrieve her, after sacrificing his daughter Iphigenia so that the fleet can set sail for Troy.

Troy is finally sacked and the Greeks return home, but Agamemnon falls victim to his wife and her lover Aegisthus once he enters the palace. This is the subject matter of Seneca's play. It opens with the ghost of Thyestes who prophesies the death of Agamemnon. After the chorus sings of the vulnerability of power to fortune, Clytemnestra comes on stage to list her grievances against Agamemnon, including the fact that he has brought home a Trojan concubine, Cassandra, another child of Priam and a prophetess fated to never be believed.

After a subsequent choral odes in thanksgiving for Agamemnon's safety, the herald Eurybates announces Agamemnon's imminent arrival. As Agamemnon enters the house, Cassandra sees the event unfolding within: the murder of Agamemnon. Clytemnestra's daughter Electra leads her brother Orestes to safety, but is herself led away to prison while defying her mother. Cassandra is taken to be executed.

Introduction

SUSANNA BRAUND

Seneca's *Agamemnon* is a play seldom read, and when it is, it suffers from being compared to Aeschylus' *Agamemnon* and judged inferior. Such a comparison, cued by the titles of the two plays, is entirely inappropriate. If we consider that Agamemnon does not even appear until the end of act 4 of Seneca's play (782–807) and then is given only two short speeches framing a barbed dialogue with Cassandra, it is clear that this play is not really "about" Agamemnon. Rather, the play is episodic and centrifugal: it explores the perspectives of numerous characters. This phenomenon of multiple perspectives is not unique among Seneca's tragedies—the *Trojan Women* is perhaps the closest but *Agamemnon* is the most extreme case. We might ask ourselves what difference it would make to our expectations and judgements if the play were entitled *Cassandra* or *Clytemnestra*. Both these female characters have much larger roles than Agamemnon. Clytemnestra first appears at line 108 (the start of act 2) and is present for much of the play, including the final act. Cassandra enters as one of the captive Trojan women at line 586 and speaks around 130 lines throughout the rest of the play, before, during, and after her prophetic trance, and she in effect has the last word. And if there is any hero at all in the play, it is she.

Some of the earlier parts of the story of the house of Atreus are depicted powerfully in Seneca's play *Thyestes*, while the latter part of the story is depicted in several surviving Attic tragedies, including Aeschylus' *Oresteia* trilogy; Sophocles' *Electra*; and Euripides' *Electra*, *Iphigeneia at Aulis*, and *Orestes*. There were, besides, numerous other treatments of the story in earlier Greco-Roman tragedies that are not now extant but which may have furnished Seneca with ideas, including Ion of Chios' *Agamemnon*, Livius Andronicus' *Aegisthus* (third century BCE), and Accius' *Clytemestra*, which famously used 600 mules for the entry of Agamemnon when it was performed at the opening of Pompey's theatre in 55 BCE (Cicero, *Letters to His Friends* 7.12).

Despite being relatively short—just over a thousand lines—Seneca's *Agamemnon* has a generous scope, looking both backward and forward by alluding or referring to many elements in this multigenerational family feud. The ghost of Thyestes, a figure from the past, sets the play in motion, and the final act starts with Electra's preservation of the young Orestes for his future role as avenger. But the play has a wider scope still. It manages to incorporate two other major storylines from Greek mythology in its narratives of the sack of Troy and of the difficult homecomings (the *nostoi*) of the Greek heroes. In this way, it engages with vast tracts of Greco-Roman literature, in particular the Greek epic cycle (which included the Trojan War, the sack of Troy, and the *nostoi*), Athenian tragedy, early Latin tragedy, and Latin epic poetry. This is an impressive amount of material to navigate.[1]

The start of Seneca's play marks the vast difference from Aeschylus' treatment in his *Agamemnon*, which famously starts with the watchman complaining about the long wait for the beacon that will indicate that Troy has fallen. By contrast, Seneca begins with the ghost of Thyestes, a technique he will reprise in his later play *Thyestes*, which opens with the ghost of Tantalus. The speech of the ghost of Thyestes serves both as a prologue, recapping the salient elements in the story, and as a prophecy of the vengeance that will unfold during the play (44–49):

> Any moment now the house will swim with blood in
> retribution:
> I see swords and spears and axes, and the royal skull
> split by heavy blow of double-bladed axe;
> now crimes are near, now treachery, carnage, gore—
> the feast is being readied. The reason for your birth,
> Aegisthus, comes.

In this way Seneca immediately makes explicit Aegisthus' role as his father's avenger.

The main chorus in Seneca's play now enters—a chorus of Argive women. Their ode, highly characteristic of Seneca's Stoic sentiments in his lyrics, laments the instability of positions of power which are vulnerable to the whims of Fortune. Typical are lines 101–2:

> Whatever Fortune raises up high,
> she lifts it so she can hurl it down.

This is an ominous opening, especially when the chorus asks, "Is there a citadel that's not been toppled / by retributive crime?" (77–78). Clytemnestra, meanwhile, is in a turmoil of conflicting emotions. Initially she addresses herself and then she converses with her nurse, who tries to persuade her of the enormity and futility of her intended crime against Agamemnon and urges her to "suppress [her] fierce emotions" (224). A lengthy exchange between Clytemnestra and Aegisthus concludes with her quelling her doubts and reverting to her plan to kill Agamemnon. At this moment of tension, the chorus of Argive women express gratitude for Agamemnon's victory in an ode addressed to Phoebus Apollo, Juno, Pallas, Phoebe, and Jupiter.

When the herald Eurybates arrives to announce Agamemnon's imminent arrival. Clytemnestra makes a charade of welcoming him then asks for a narrative of the *nostos* which has, in Eurybates' words, rendered Agamemnon "the conqueror but like one conquered, / dragging homeward from his mighty fleet a few tattered ships" (412–13). Eurybates then delivers an enormous speech of more than 150 lines, by far the longest speech in any of Seneca's plays, in which he describes the storm (431–527), the death of Ajax (son of Oileus) at the hands of Pallas (528–556; there is a lacuna here), and the treachery of Nauplius, who lit beacons to lure the Greek fleet onto the rocks (557–78). All this material had been handled in earlier Greco-Roman literature, including the Greek epic *nostoi* and Virgil's *Aeneid*, where Ajax's death in the storm is mentioned at 1.39–45.

At this point, Clytemnestra catches sight of the enslaved women of Troy, including Cassandra, as they approach. This sets in motion the subsidiary chorus in the play (something also found in Euripides and the two probably non-Senecan plays transmitted with his tragedies, *Hercules on Oeta* and *Octavia*), the band of Trojan women who deplore the human instinct to cling to life even when life is not worth living (589–610). The women then deliver their first person narrative of the sack of Troy (611–58) to the death of Priam. This material clearly engages closely with the many earlier Greek and Roman plays on this theme (including Euripides' *Trojan Women*) and with Virgil's account of Troy's fall in the second book of the *Aeneid*; it also prefigures Seneca's own *Trojan Women*. This ode segues into the depiction of Cassandra's possession by the god, framed by the chorus and including Cassandra's long speech of prophetic frenzy. In the middle of her speech, Cassandra reports a "novel apparition" of a lion being killed by a lioness, which clearly prefigures Clytemnestra's murder of Agamemnon.

At the beginning of the final act (867–909), Cassandra's clairvoyant powers allow her to see what is happening inside the palace: she narrates the murder of Agamemnon as it happens, "the payback for ten long years" (867). As she watches she vaunts: "we conquered Phrygians are conquerors!" (869) The second part of act 5 takes a surprising turn by intimating some of the consequences of the murder. Electra and her young brother Orestes emerge running from the palace. Something like a *deus ex machina*, the family friend Strophius suddenly appears in his chariot, together with his young son, Pylades, who will later help Orestes when he returns to take revenge. Strophius has come to congratulate Agamemnon, but on learning of the situation he agrees without hesitation to Electra's request that he take Orestes away and keep him safe. The scene ends with a vituperative exchange between Clytemnestra and Electra in which Electra offers herself to her mother for slaughter but Aegisthus prefers to imprison her and torture her until she reveals where Orestes is. Last of all, Cassandra steps forward willingly to her execution (1005–9):

> I'm keen to be first to bring the message
> to my Phrygians: how the sea was filled with capsized ships,
> how Mycenae fell, how the chieftain of a thousand chiefs
> perished by a gift, by woman's lust, by treachery,
> to meet a fate that matched the Trojan sufferings.

In a comment on the cyclical nature of events, Cassandra earlier concludes (870–71):

Troy, it's good, you rise again. While falling, you've dragged
down
Mycenae too.

Thus Seneca introduces the ongoing vengeance within the House of Atreus and at the same time suggests payback for the sack of Troy lies in the downfall of Argos/Mycenae.

This insistence that the fall of Troy is a precursor of the fall of Argos is crucial to Seneca's handling of the story. The theme is introduced explicitly by Eurybates in his narrative of the terrible storm at sea, when he talks of the envy that the beleaguered Greeks had for those who died at Troy and makes the extraordinary claim that Agamemnon is envious of Priam's fate. The cyclical nature of events also manifests in the importance of banquets in Seneca's version of the story. He first makes the ghost of Thyestes refer to his grim feast as a precursor to the feast at which Agamemnon will be murdered, then he has Cassandra draw an analogy between final celebratory feast at Troy and the feast with which Clytemnestra welcomes her returning husband (875–80):

Let's watch! In the palace a thronging feast
is spread, like the Phrygians' final
banquet. The couch gleams with purple cloth from Ilium.
Their unmixed wine they drain from Assaracus' ancient gold.
He himself [Agamemnon] reclines on high in broidered robes,
wearing lordly trappings stripped from Priam's corpse.

This emphasis in the play on cyclical recurrence presents multiple characters contemplating revenge or retribution. Thyestes looks forward to retribution on his brother's son and Aegisthus understands that he is the agent of that retribution. Clytemnestra persists in her plan to take revenge for Agamemnon's sacrifice of her daughter Iphigenia ten years earlier. Electra makes possible the future revenge for the murder of her father, Agamemnon, by ensuring that Orestes is sent into safety. And for Cassandra, the murder of Agamemnon and the fall of Argos is retribution for the Greeks' sack of Troy and murder of her father Priam. These already multiple perspectives are increased by the presence of two different choruses: the bland ignorance of the chorus of Argive women contrasts starkly with the grim realities of slavery facing the chorus of Trojan women. Seneca's play offers no single authoritative version of events but opens up numerous perspectives in what appears to be a deliberate deheroization of the story of the House of Atreus.

Part of this deheroization is to make the murderous lovers, Aegisthus and Clytemnestra, the most complex characters in the play. Both experience inner conflict which must be resolved by talking things out, as we see when they address their *animus* ("spirit" or "mind," 108, 192, 228). Clytemnestra's words reveal that she experiences succeeding waves of emotion. This reflects Seneca's profound interest in the functioning of the passions (*affectus*), a topic he returns to repeatedly in the tragedies and in his philosophical writings. Clytemnestra, who is the most fascinating Clytemnestra in ancient literature, steps on the stage deeply engrossed in self-debate, a technique Seneca reprises in the speeches of internal conflict by Medea and Atreus in his *Medea* and *Thyestes*. She admits to feeling fear but, noting that "morality and law and honor, loyalty, devotion—all are gone, / and modesty which, once it's lost, cannot return" (112–13), and she goads herself to stay on the path of wickedness she has chosen. Her admission that she "lost all / self-control through blinding passion" (117–18) is cast in essentially Roman terms. She summarizes for the nurse her internal conflict (131–38):

> My agonies are too enormous to put up with waiting.
> My bones and heart are being scorched by flames.
> Fear combined with pain applies its goads.
> Jealousy pounds my breast, and then vile lust
> enslaves my spirit and refuses to be quelled.
> And then, among these blazes in my mind that's under siege,
> my shame fights back, though it's exhausted, abject,
> scuttled.

The stichomythia with the nurse reveals the seat of her resentment against Agamemnon: his treacherous sacrifice of Iphigenia (158–73).

A second cause for resentment is her jealousy of Agamemnon's relationships with slave girls, first Chryseis then Briseis and now Cassandra (174–91). She states (191): "home he comes as husband to a slave-girl, son-in-law to Priam." She goads herself to action by imagining herself displaced by Cassandra who she describes as a stepmother to her children (198–99).

In contrast with this complexity, Seneca's Agamemnon is a one-dimensional figure characterized by his stupid arrogance. This is clear as soon as he fails entirely to heed Cassandra's warning (798–99):

AGAMEMNON
No danger is awaiting you.

CASSANDRA
Great danger is awaiting *you.*

AGAMEMNON
What need a conqueror fear?

CASSANDRA
What he doesn't fear.

Agamemnon's weakness is developed in his behavior at the banquet when he first of all dons Priam's robes (879–80) and then docilely puts on the robe which Clytemnestra has woven for him, which fetters him with its "loose, impenetrable folds / [that] enclose his head and stop his hands emerging" (888–89). This makes a stark contrast with the worldly wise Agamemnon in Seneca's *Trojan Women* (see 255–91), who realizes full well that Greeks just as easily as Trojans can fall from greatness.

Two more of Seneca's characteristic interests emerge in his idiosyncratic treatment of the House of Atreus. He deploys his feisty Electra to produce a classic scene of resistance to tyrants that fits into his larger interest in the nature of good and bad kingship manifested in several other plays (e.g., *Thyestes*, *Hercules Mad*, *Trojan Women*) and above all in his treatise on clemency addressed to the young emperor Nero. The closing exchange between Electra and Aegisthus renders Aegisthus a classic tyrant, familiar to us from the pages of Roman declamation (994–1000):

ELECTRA

Grant me death!

AEGISTHUS

I'd grant it if you didn't want it.
Feeble is the tyrant who makes death a punishment.

ELECTRA

There's something worse than death?

AEGISTHUS

Yes, living, if you want to die.
House-slaves, take away this freak. Convey her far
beyond Mycenae; in the kingdom's furthest corner
keep her chained and penned inside a dark and unlit cave,
to make her prison crush this turbulent girl.

A final theme worth mentioning here is the Stoic idea of the freedom from suffering and slavery, literal and metaphorical, offered by death. Seneca deploys Cassandra and the chorus of Trojan women to articulate this. The language of the chorus evokes Seneca's Stoic perspective, according to which only the Stoic sage has the mental fortitude to face death willingly (e.g., 604–10):

Only the person who scorns the capricious gods
can break through all forms of enslavement.
He can look without grimness on the face
of dark Acheron, he can look on grim Styx.
He's brave enough to impose a limit on life.
He'll be a match for kings and for gods up above.
Oh, what suffering it is to not know how to die!

Similar is Cassandra's feisty exchange with Agamemnon (796–97):

AGAMEMNON

Do not fear your mistress, house-slave.

CASSANDRA

I do not: freedom is at hand.

AGAMEMNON

Live fear-free.

CASSANDRA

It's death makes me fear-free.

In conclusion, the play known as Seneca's *Agamemnon* turns out not to be about Agamemnon at all. Rather, the play explores the significance of the *death* of Agamemnon for multiple interested parties, both Argive and Trojan. In this way, Seneca expands the motif of revenge within the House of Atreus to encompass the payback that his death represents for the enslaved Trojan women. Seneca expresses this in typically Stoic terms of the inexorability of fate and the caprice of fortune. In the first ode the chorus sings that "the fates of rulers / are whirled by Fortune" (71–72); by the end of the play, Cassandra's words have clearly come true: "fate has moved into reverse" (*fata se vertunt retro*) (758).

Suggested Reading

Boyle, Anthony J. 1983. "*Hic Epulis Locus*: The Tragic Worlds of Seneca's *Agamemnon* and *Thyestes*." In *Seneca Tragicus: Ramus Essays on Senecan Drama*, edited by A. J. Boyle, 199–228. Berwick, Australia.

Henry, Denis, and B. Walker. 1963. "Seneca and the *Agamemnon*: Some Thoughts on Tragic Doom." *Classical Philology* 58: 1–10.

Fitch, John G. 1981. "Sense-Pauses and Relative Dating in Seneca, Sophocles, and Shakespeare." *American Journal of Philology* 102: 289–307.

Motto, Anna Lydia, and J. R. Clark. 1985. "Seneca's *Agamemnon*: Tragedy without a Hero." *Athenaeum* 63: 136–144.

Shelton, Jo-Ann. 1983. "Revenge or Resignation: Seneca's *Agamemnon*." In *Seneca Tragicus: Ramus Essays on Senecan Drama*, edited by A. J. Boyle, 159–183. Berwick, Australia.

Star, Christopher. 2012. *The Empire of the Self: Self-Command and Political Speech in Seneca and Petronius*. Baltimore.

Tarrant, Richard J. 1976. *Seneca's* Agamemnon. Cambridge

Agamemnon

LUCIUS ANNAEUS SENECA
TRANSLATED BY SUSANNA BRAUND

DRAMATIS PERSONAE

GHOST OF THYESTES, Agamemnon's uncle
CLYTEMNESTRA, queen of Argos and wife of Agamemnon
NURSE of Clytemnestra
AEGISTHUS, Agamemnon's nephew and Clytemnestra's lover
EURYBATES, herald
CASSANDRA, prophetic daughter of Priam and Hecuba
AGAMEMNON, king of Argos and son of Atreus
ELECTRA, daughter of Agamemnon and Cassandra
ORESTES (silent character), young son of Agamemnon and Cassandra
STROPHIUS of Phocis
CHORUS OF ARGIVE WOMEN
CHORUS OF CAPTIVE TROJAN WOMEN

ACT 1

The ghost of Thyestes appears just before dawn. Behind him is the royal palace of the Atreidae in Argos.

GHOST OF THYESTES

Here am I, departing hellish Dis' shady places,[1]
released from deepest cave of Tartarus,
unsure which world I loathe the more.
I, Thyestes, flee from those below, while those above flee me.
Look, my spirit shudders, terror shakes my body:
I'm looking at my father's—no, my brother's home.
This is the ancient threshold of the house of Pelops.[2]

Here it's custom for the Pelasgians to inaugurate[3]
the royal crown, and on this couch sit high
10 the kings whose proud hands wield the scepter,
here is where their councils happen—and here the feast.[4]
I want to turn back. Surely it is preferable to gaze upon[5]
the dismal lakes and guardian of the Styx[6]
as he shakes his threefold black-maned necks?
That's where, his body bound to turning wheel,[7] one shade
is carried back upon himself; where a fruitless, uphill
toil is each time cheated by the rock's descent;[8]
where an ever-growing liver's cropped by a greedy bird;[9]
and one parched by blazing thirst among the waves[10]
20 lunges at receding water, mouth deceived,
doomed to heavy punishment for his banquet for the gods.
But that old man—his guilt is naught compared with mine![11]
If we reckon up all those sentenced by the judge of Cnossos[12]
on account of their unspeakable acts,
with *my* crimes I, Thyestes, would outdo them all.
When filled up by my three sons buried deep inside me,
could I be outdone by my brother? I've consumed my *own* flesh.
Yet Fortune hasn't finished staining me, the father,
but, venturing another greater crime than that committed,
30 tells him seek outrageous couplings with his daughter.[13]
Fearlessly I drank her words and undertook the crime.[14]
So, to ensure that I as parent work through all my children,
my daughter, forced by fate, bears in her heavy womb[15]
a child deserving me as father. Nature's turned backward:
I have muddled father with grandfather—what monstrosity!—
husband with father, grandchildren with children, day with
night.[16]
But at long last, after death, the oracle's uncertain
promise finally responds to people wearied by calamity:
that king of kings, Agamemnon, chief of chiefs,
40 his banner followed by a thousand ships
that hid the seas of Ilium with their sails,

after ten of Phoebus' cycles, with Ilium defeated—
he is here—to give his throat to his own wife.
Any moment now the house will swim with blood in
retribution:
I see swords and spears and axes, and the royal skull
split by heavy blow of double-bladed axe;
now crimes are near, now treachery, carnage, gore—
the feast is being readied. The reason for your birth,
Aegisthus, comes. Why does shame weigh on your face?
Why's your hand, unsure of purpose, shaking, faltering? 50
Why torment yourself by pondering and asking
whether this is right for you? Just look at your mother: it is.
But why's the duration of a summer nighttime
abruptly stretched with long delay to equal winter's span?
What keeps the falling stars up in the sky?
I'm keeping Phoebus waiting! Give the world its daylight back
now!

CHORUS OF ARGIVE WOMEN

Fortune—deceptive in power's great blessings—
you set in precarious, unstable positions
the too-much exalted.
Never do scepters possess tranquil peace 60
or a day that is sure of itself.
Anxiety after anxiety harries them,
new storms always taxing their minds.
Not so violently does the tide at the Syrtes[17]
of Libya whip wave upon wave in its fury;
not so violently does churned-up water
swell from the depths of the Euxine,[18]
close to the land of the ice and the snow,
where Boötes turns his shimmering plough
clear of the waters of blue,[19] 70
as the fates of rulers
are whirled by Fortune.

They long to be feared and they dread to be feared.
They're offered no safe retreat by welcoming night.
Sleep the anxiety-tamer does not
soothe their hearts.
Is there a citadel that's not been toppled
by retributive crime?
Not been harried by fighting that breaks a taboo?
80 The halls are deserted by law, by respect,
and by marriage's sanctified loyalty.
They're replaced by Bellona,[20] grim with her hands
stained with blood, and Erinys who lashes the proud,
perpetual escort of hubristic homes,
homes which any moment can bring from the heights
to ground zero.
Though weapons be idle and treacheries cease,
still greatness sinks down through its very own weight
and fortune collapses beneath her own burden.
90 Sails filled by following southerlies
fear the excessively favoring winds.
The tower with its head sticking into the clouds
takes a beating from rainy South Wind.
The grove that spreads its shade so impenetrably
sees its venerable tree trunks shattered.
High hills feel the thunderbolts' strike.
Larger bodies are prone to diseases.
When the common herds
dash through their roaming pastures,
100 it's the largest neck that is chosen for sacrifice.
Whatever Fortune raises up high,
she lifts it so she can hurl it down.
Humility lasts for much longer:
blessed is the person, content with an ordinary lot,
who skirts close to shore where the breezes are safe
and, nervous to trust his skiff to the sea,
rows a course hugging the land.

ACT 2

CLYTEMNESTRA

My craven spirit, why seek out tactics that are safe?
Why waver? The better path's already closed now.
Once, with wifely loyalty you could have kept secure 110
the chaste bed of your husband and the widowed crown.[21]
Morality and law and honor, loyalty, devotion—all are gone,
and modesty which, once it's lost, cannot return.
Let go the reins and, headlong, goad on every wickedness:
for crimes the way ahead is always safe through crimes.
Think out to yourself now feminine deceptions,
something any wife might dare who's treacherous, who's lost all
self-control through blinding passion, something that would
suit
a stepmother's hands, or the girl ablaze with wicked lust
as she escaped from Phasis' kingdom on Thessalian ship:[22] 120
dare to use the steel, or poisons—or else, joined by your
partner,[23]
flee your Mycenaean home on stealthy ship.
But why this nervous talk of stealth and exile and escape?
That's what your sister did.[24] A greater outrage suits you.

NURSE

Queen of Greece, illustrious child of Leda,
why brood in silence? Why, when you have lost control,
keep fierce emotions in your swollen spirit?
Though you stay silent, all your pain is in your face.
So, whatever is the problem, grant yourself the time and space:
what reason cannot deal with, waiting often cures. 130

CLYTEMNESTRA

My agonies are too enormous to put up with waiting.
My bones and heart are being scorched by flames.
Fear combined with pain applies its goads.
Jealousy pounds my breast, and then vile lust
enslaves my spirit and refuses to be quelled.

And then, among these blazes in my mind that's under siege,
my shame fights back, though it's exhausted, abject,
scuttled. I'm driven by conflicting waves
just as when the ocean's whipped this way and that by wind and tide,
140 the water hesitates, unsure which power to yield to.
That's why I've dropped the rudder from my hands:
I'll go wherever anger, pain, or hope
conveys me. I've abandoned my vessel to the waves.
When the mind missteps, it's best to follow chance.

NURSE

It's blind recklessness that makes chance its guide.

CLYTEMNESTRA

When facing fortune at its worst, why fear its lack of certainty?

NURSE

Your guilt is safe and shielded from view, if you let it be.

CLYTEMNESTRA

In a royal household every fault is in the spotlight.

NURSE

You loathe your former crime and yet you plan another?

CLYTEMNESTRA

150 To limit wickedness is certainly a stupid thing.

NURSE

To heap up crime on crime exacerbates the cause for fear.

CLYTEMNESTRA

Both steel and fire have often served instead of remedy.

NURSE

No one at the outset tries the last resort.

CLYTEMNESTRA

In evil situations one must take the headlong path.

NURSE

But let the name of marriage restore you to your husband.

CLYTEMNESTRA

Give him a second glance after ten years' widowhood?

NURSE

You should be mindful of your progeny from him.

CLYTEMNESTRA

I am—and of my daughter's marriage torches
and my son-in-law Achilles.[25] That's the loyalty *he* showed her
mother.

NURSE

She paid for the delays of the fleet marooned 160
and galvanized the seas, immobile in their sluggish sloth.

CLYTEMNESTRA

That's my shame, my pain: to think that I, Tyndareus'
daughter,
of divine descent, birthed a sacrificial victim for the Doric fleet!
My mind relives my daughter's wedding,
which he made suitable for Pelops' house,[26]
when as father he stood before the altar with his sacrificial
words—
what an altar for a bride! Calchas shuddered at the answer
from the oracle, he shuddered at the flames as they recoiled.
O house, forever topping crimes with crimes:
with blood we bought the winds, with slaughter war! 170
But (you say) a thousand ships set sail together?
The fleet was not released with god's approval;
Aulis thrust the wicked ships out of its harbor.
His war, inaugurated thus, went on no better:
enslaved by passion for a slave, unmoved by prayer,
he held on to the Zminthean spoils of Phoebus' priest,[27]
frenzied even then with passion for a sacred virgin.[28]
He was not shifted by Achilles, who was unimpressed by
threats,
or by the only one to see the universe's destiny
(a prophet reliable for us but worthless in the case of 180
slave-girls),
or by his sickening people and the blazing pyres;
amidst the final slaughter of the fall of Greece,

without an enemy he's conquered and lethargic, finding time
for Love,
and he renews his love affairs; and so his bachelor
bed would never be without barbarian bedmate,
from Achilles he stole the girl from Lyrnesos to be his love,[29]
unabashed at tearing her from her man's embrace and seizing
her—
behold the enemy of Paris! Now, with his new wound
he is frenzied, fired by passion for the prophetess of Phrygia,
190 and, following his Trojan triumph and the overthrow of Ilium,
home he comes as husband to a slave-girl, son-in-law to Priam.
My mind, now arm yourself: not trivial are the wars ahead
of you.
In crime, action beats delay. Idle woman, what day are you
waiting for?
Until young Phrygian wives hold Pelops' crown?
Or are you slowed by your unmarried girls at home
and by Orestes, image his father? Their miseries to come
should goad you on—a whirlwind looms above them.
Why hesitate, you miserable woman? See, a crazy stepmother
to your children has arrived! If there's no other way, you have to
200 drive the sword into your own side and slaughter two at once:
mix your gore, destroy your husband by destroying yourself.
It's no miserable death to die beside your chosen victim.

NURSE

My queen, control yourself and halt your passions
and consider the enormity of your plan: he comes, the
conqueror
of savage Asia, the avenger of Europe, dragging
Pergamum enslaved along with slowly conquered Phrygians.
This is the man you now plan to attack by subterfuge?
He wasn't wounded by Achilles, with his savage sword,
although the surly warrior had equipped his reckless hand,
210 nor by crazy Ajax, better once he'd settled on his death,[30]
nor by Hector, solitary obstacle to the Greeks and to their war,

nor by Paris' unerring arrows, nor by swarthy Memnon,
nor by river Xanthus piling up the corpses mixed with weapons
or by Simois running red with gore,
nor by Cycnus, snow-white child of Ocean,
nor by warlike Rhesus with his Thracian phalanx,
nor by the Amazon with painted quiver, crescent-shield
and axe-wielding hand. *This* is the man you plan to slaughter
on his homecoming, staining altars with sacrilegious gore?
Will avenging Greece endure this crime unavenged?[31] 220
Picture cavalry, and weapons, and the sea bristling
with ships, and the soil overflowing deep with blood,
and the entire fate of the captive Dardanian house[32]
revisited upon the Greeks—suppress your fierce emotions.
Take it on yourself to calm your mind.

AEGISTHUS

The time I've always dreaded in my spirit and my mind
is here for sure, the crisis of my life.
Why turn to run, my spirit? Why shed your weapons
at the first attack? Be sure the savage gods
are engineering your destruction and a dreadful death: 230
present your worthless self to all the punishments,
receive the steel and fires in your breast,
Aegisthus. For one conceived as you were,[33] death's no
punishment.
You, companion in danger, born to Leda,
if you will only stand beside me, that craven leader,
such a *brave* father, will repay you with his blood.
But why this pallor all across your trembling cheeks?
Why this dazed and downcast gaze in listless face?

CLYTEMNESTRA

Married love prevails and turns me back.
I'm returning to the place I never should have 240
left. But now I must recover chastity and loyalty,
because the pathway to integrity is never too late.
Repentance of mistakes makes one virtually innocent.

AEGISTHUS

What crazy impulse has engulfed you? Do you believe or hope
to find a faithful spouse in Agamemnon? Even if
there was nothing lurking in the mind to rouse grave fears,
nonetheless his Fortune, arrogant and vastly
overblown, would foster swollen pride.
He was tough on his companions while Troy still stood:
250 what do you think's been added to a spirit naturally fierce
by the fall of Troy? He was Mycenae's king;
he'll return a tyrant. Success swells confidence.
A flood of mistresses crowds round him with
extraordinary pomp. But from the crowd, one stands out
and clasps the king: the servant of the god of prophecy.
Will you be conquered and endure a consort in your
marriage-bed?
That's not what *she* wants. The worst thing for a wife
is when a mistress openly controls a married home.
Tolerating partnership is alien to kingdoms and to marriages.

CLYTEMNESTRA

260 Aegisthus, why drive me to the edge of the abyss once more,
why fuel with flames my anger now subsiding?
The conqueror has allowed himself some freedom with a
captive girl:
it's better not to pay attention as wife, as mistress of the house.
There's one law for the throne, another for an ordinary bed.[34]
Then, too, my spirit, conscious of its vile offence,
doesn't let me pass strict judgment on my husband;
one in need of pardon must give pardon readily.

AEGISTHUS

Is that so? A deal for mutual pardon?
Are the rules of tyranny unknown, or new, to you?
270 To *us* they will be hostile judges, to themselves impartial,
thinking this the greatest proof of power,
if they alone can do what others can't.

CLYTEMNESTRA

. . .[35]

forgave Helen: she went home at Menelaus' side,
though she inflicted equal horrors on Europe and on Asia.

AEGISTHUS

No female swept that Atrides away in secret lust;[36]
his spirit, pledged to his own wife, was not bewitched.
The other is already pursuing the charge and readying his
arguments.
But just suppose that you'd done nothing vile:
what value is an honorable life, one free from scandal?
When the lord is full of hatred, you are guilty, no investigation. 280
Once discarded, will you return to Sparta, to Eurotas[37]
and your father's residence, an outcast? There's no way out
when kings divorce: with empty optimism you allay your fears.

CLYTEMNESTRA

None except the loyal knows my imperfections.

AEGISTHUS

Loyalty does not set foot across a royal threshold, ever.

CLYTEMNESTRA

With my resources, I'll ensure that loyalty's secured by money.

AEGISTHUS

Loyalty that's bought for money can be overcome by money.

CLYTEMNESTRA

Traces of my former sense of shame are rising up:
why are you disputing with me? Why are you seductively
prescribing plans that are immoral? I suppose that I, aristocrat, 290
should leave the kings of kings and marry you, an exile?

AEGISTHUS

And why do I, Thyestes' son, appear to you
inferior to Atrides?

CLYTEMNESTRA

You might as well say "grandson" too.[38]

AEGISTHUS

My birth has Phoebus' blessing: I am not embarrassed by my family.

CLYTEMNESTRA

How can you say that your outrageous family has Phoebus' blessing
when you drove him from the sky as he was pulling on his reins
in sudden night? Why involve the gods in our disgrace?
You're an expert robber of the blessed marriage-bed by guile;
it's only by illicit lust we know you are a man.
300 Get gone right now and take away from view the blot
upon our distinguished house: it's waiting for its king and husband.

AEGISTHUS

Exile's nothing new to me. I am used to misery.
If you command, my queen, I'll quit this palace, Argos too,
and even more: on your instructions I'm prepared
to use my sword to open up my trouble-laden breast.

CLYTEMNESTRA

As if Tyndareus' daughter would let this bloody deed take place![39]
A woman who goes astray with someone else owes loyalty even to her guilt.
Better slip inside with me, so our intellects together
can unravel this uncertain, threatening situation.

CHORUS

310 Sing of Phoebus, you famous lasses and lads!
For you, throngs in celebration garland their heads,
for you, the unmarried lasses of Argos
have let down their virginal hair
while shaking the laurel, as is the custom.
You too, our Thespian visitors, join in our dances;
and you who drink Erasinus' ice-cold springs,[40]
you who drink of Eurotas,[41]
and you who drink of Ismenus, silent in greening bank:

you were told by Manto, Tiresias' daughter,
foreknowing fate, 320
to pay ritual devotion to the deities born to Latona.
With peace now restored, Phoebus, victorious,
unbend your bow
and remove from your shoulder the quiver so weighty
with missiles so flimsy;
make the lyre of tortoiseshell sound out its voice when you
strike it
with quick-moving hand:
nothing fierce, nothing grand do I wish to be bellowed
in meters majestic,
but just such a song as you enjoy turning with daintier lyre, 330
when the erudite Muse reviews your playing,
a simple song.
You are also permitted to sound out with heavier string,
like your song
when the gods saw the Titans defeated by thunderbolt,
or when mountains stacked on towering mountains
built steps for hideous monsters,
when Pelion stood there with Ossa on top,
with pine-clad Olympus crushing them both.[42]
Come to us, queenly Juno, the sister, the wife, 340
and the sharer of powerful throne:
your throng in Mycenae, we worship you;
when Argos is troubled and calling for your divine assistance,
you are our only protection;
your hand's the dispenser of war and of peace:
victorious, receive now the laurels of Agamemnon.[43]
In your honor, the flute made of perforated boxwood performs
ceremonial song,
in your honor, the girls move their intricate strings
with a soothing sound; 350
in your honor, the mothers
of Greece brandish the worshipful torch:
at your glittering shrines, the bull's

consort will fall: of the plough
she's no knowledge,
her neck never marked by the yoke.
And you, the powerful Thunderer's daughter, illustrious Pallas,
who often directed your spear at Dardanian towers:
you're worshipped by mothers, both younger and older,
360 united in one single troupe;
and as you arrive, the priest unbolts the temple:
in your honor, the throng is approaching, their foreheads bound
with garlands entwined;
in your honor, the elderly men, long-lived and weary,
offer their thanks, their prayer now fulfilled,
and with wavering hands they pour wine in libation.
Trivia too we adore, remembering you with the well-known
words.
Lucina,[44] you order your mother's island of Delos
to stand quite still,
370 called "the Circler" before, when wandering wind-blown
here and there;
now it grasps the earth, with its roots fastened firmly,
rebuffing the breezes and anchoring the ships
that it formerly followed.
Victorious, you count up the dead of the
Tantalid mother:[45]
on Sipylus' highest peak she now stands,
a lamenting rock,
and still from the ancient marble the fresh tears gush.
380 Man and woman alike lavishly worship
your twin divinity.
And you above all, the father, the ruler,
thunderbolt-strong,
who with your nod makes the furthermost poles
tremble together,
our nations' creator, Jupiter, gladly accept our gifts
and smile on your own descendants four generations on,
undiminished.[46]

ACT 3

CHORUS

But look, a soldier, hastening with gigantic strides,
is rushing with explicit signs of joy—
his iron spear-tip bears the laurel. 390
Eurybates, ever loyal to the king, is here.

EURYBATES

Shrines and altars of the gods and native house-gods,
on my knees I worship you, hardly believing it,
exhausted after this long span.

(*To citizens.*)

Fulfill your pledges to the gods:
now at last returns the towering glory of the land of Argos
to his hearth-gods—Agamemnon, conqueror.

CLYTEMNESTRA

Blessed comes this message to my ears.
So where then is he dallying, my husband
ten years sought for? Is he traveling on land or sea?

EURYBATES

Safe, enhanced by glory, and illustrious with renown, 400
he has set his homeward footstep on the longed-for shore.

CLYTEMNESTRA

With sacrifices let us mark this finally successful day
and worship gods propitious, though so slow.
Please reveal where my husband's brother lives,[47]
and please reveal where my sister dwells.

EURYBATES

With prayers I ask for better outcomes and implore the gods:
the hazards of the sea prevent me speaking certainty.
Once the scattered fleet had broached the swollen sea,
no ship could see its sister ship.
Even Atrides himself, while roaming the immeasurable flood,[48] 410
took heavier losses from the sea than from the war.

He returns, the conqueror but like one conquered,
dragging homeward from his mighty fleet a few tattered ships.

CLYTEMNESTRA

Describe the mischance that engulfed our ships,[49]
the maritime disaster that dispersed the leaders.

EURYBATES

What you request is harsh to tell; you bid me mix
ill-fated news with joyous news. My sickened mind
refuses words and shudders at misfortunes so colossal.

CLYTEMNESTRA

Speak out: refusal to admit one's own calamities
420 increases fear. Misfortunes unconfirmed are greater torment.

EURYBATES

When Pergamum in its entirety fell by Doric torch,
they shared the loot and in a hurry head directly for the sea.
At last the soldiers lighten their exhausted flanks of swords;
their shields lie abandoned on the stern-decks.
The soldiers' hands grasp snug the oars;
their haste makes each delay too long.
When homebound signal blazes from the royal ship
and trumpet-call alerts the oarsmen in their joy,
the gilded prow marks out the path
430 and opens up the passage for a thousand ships to cut.
Then a breeze, at first just gentle, glides inside our sails
and moves the ships along; the tranquil waves,
with hardly any motion, ripple with the tender Zephyr's breath.
Owing to the fleet, the ocean gleams and lies concealed.
They rejoice to see the shores of Troy now empty,
they rejoice to see Sigeum lonely and deserted.[50]
All the army's keen to flex their oars
in synchronicity. They help the breezes with their toil
and move their sturdy arms in rhythmic strokes.
440 The furrowed waters quiver and the ships' sides hiss,
and white foam splits the blue-green sea.
Once a stronger breeze fills out the swelling canvas,

they downed their oars, entrusted ship to wind,
and, stretched out on the thwarts, the soldiers comment on
the land receding in the distance as the sails withdraw
or else they tell their stories of the war: brave Hector's threats,
the chariot and his body ransomed for cremation,
Hercean Jupiter splashed with royal blood.[51]
Then behold the Tyrrhene fish,[52] who, when sea lies calm,
gambol in and out, who leap across the sea-swells 450
with their arching backs. Throughout the strait they jump
for joy
and swim in circles, and they form an escort alongside,
happy to precede the ships and then again to follow;
now their dance-troupe touches playfully the front-most prow,
now it circles and surrounds the thousandth ship.
Now every shore is hid from view, the plains are out of sight,
and Ida's mountain ridges fade and disappear,
and now the smoke of Ilium—the only thing the most
determined
eye can see—is showing, thanks to its black trace.
Now Titan was unharnessing exhausted necks from yoke, 460
now light declining toward the deep, now day was diving down:
a wisp of cloud, increasing with a murky mass,
is staining setting Phoebus' shining beam:
discolored sunset made the waters suspect.[53]
Early night had strewn the sky with stars; the sails,
deserted by the wind, were slack. Then a muffled rumble,
threatening worse, tumbles from the hilltops,
and from shore and cliff-tops comes a long-drawn groan;
lashed by rising winds, the waters swell:
when suddenly the moon is hidden, stars obscured, 470
and night is doubled: dense fog overwhelms 472
the darkness; once all light's removed, the sea and sky
are indistinguishable. From every side at once the winds
swoop down and whip and churn the sea up from its lowest
depths:
Zephyr fighting Eurus, Notus fighting Boreas.[54]

Each wind hurls his missiles and in enmity they heave the
strait:
a whirlwind roils the sea: Aquilo swirls his deep Strymonian
snows,
480 Libyan Auster drives his sand-filled Syrtes
482 swelling the waves with rain; the east is struck by Eurus
as he shakes the Nabataean realms and gulfs of dawn.[55]
And what of frenzied Corus, lifting up his face from Ocean?
You'd think the world in its entirety was being
ripped up from its roots, the gods themselves were falling
from the shattered sky, dark chaos being overlaid.
Tide opposes wind and wind rolls back
the tide. The sea cannot contain itself:
491 the deep is lifted to the stars, the sky is gone,
490 and rain and waves combine their waters.
Their troubles are not even granted *this* relief,
at least to see and know the evil that destroys them.
Darkness overwhelms their eyes: the hellish night
of terrifying Styx. Yet fires do flare
as terrifying lightning flashes from compacted cloud.
The light, though evil,[56] holds such sweetness for the wretches:
even this they pray for. The fleet itself destroys itself:
prow wrecked prow and flank wrecked flank.
One ship is snatched abruptly by the yawning deep
500 which swallows it and spews it out, restored to different sea.[57]
Another founders under its own weight. Another offers to the
waves
its shattered flank. Another's buried by the tenth wave.
A tattered ship that's stripped of all its finery is drifting
lightly to and fro, with neither sails nor oars remaining,
nor upright mast with yardarms at the top:
the mutilated hull is floating over the entire Ionian Sea.
Experience and reason venture nothing: skill has yielded to
disaster.
Horror grips their limbs, the sailors all stand thunderstruck,
their tasks abandoned, oars slip out of hands.

Abject terror drives the wretched men to pray, 510
with Trojans and Danaans asking for the same thing from the
gods.
Ha, the power of fate! See their envy: Pyrrhus for his father,[58]
Ulysses for Ajax, the lesser Atrides for Hector,
Agamemnon for King Priam; those who lie at Troy
are called the fortunate—the ones who earned death standing
firm,
the ones preserved by fame, the ones concealed by conquered
earth.
"Will sea and waves convey men who've ventured nothing
glorious?
Will a coward's fate consume courageous heroes?
Must our deaths be wasted? Whichever of the gods you are,
not yet sated by our sufferings immense, at last 520
calm your power: our calamity would drive
even Troy to tears. But if your enmity endures
and you are set on the destruction of the Doric race,
why do you want these men to die along with us? 524
This fleet conveys Danaans—and it carries Trojans too."[59] 526
No more can be said: the sea usurps their words.
Here's one more calamity: Pallas Athena, armed
with thunderbolt of angry Jupiter. Whatever threats she can't
fulfill[60]
with spear or shield and Gorgon rage she tackles[61] 530
with her father's fire, and fresh storms
spiral from the sky.
. . .[62]
Ajax,[63] the only one unconquered by disaster,
fights back. While he's reducing canvas
with a tightened halyard, he's grazed by hurtling flame.
Another thunderbolt is poised: with all her force
Pallas, drawing back her hand, launches it unfailingly,
in imitation of her father. It pierces Ajax and his ship,
it carries with it Ajax and a portion of his ship.
Unperturbed, he stands up in the sea-salt like a towering crag,

540 scorched. He parts the maddened sea
and breasts the waves and as he grabs his ship
he catches fire: on the darkened sea
Ajax is alight. All the strait reflects the glow.
544 At last he climbs up on a rock and thunders furiously:[64]
547 "I was not deterred by terror of the war-god.
Phoebus' weapons did not stop me standing firm.
550 Besides the Phrygians, those were enemies that I defeated.
So why
should I quail at you, feebly wielding someone else's weapons?
Why not let him hurl them himself?" While he ventured more
in fury,
father Neptune, lifting up his head from deepest waves,
with his trident struck and undermined the rock,
destroying the crag. And as he fell, he took it with him,
and he now lies conquered by the earth and fire and sea.
Another greater ruin summons us to shipwreck.
There's a shallow stretch of water that's deceptive with its sharp
shoals
where treacherous Caphereus conceals his rocks beneath[65]
560 the swirling eddies; the strait is boiling on the reefs
and waves forever seethe in ebb and flow.
A sheer headland looms above, a vantage-point to both
twin seas: in one direction can be seen your Pelops' shores
and Isthmus which, bent back with narrow ground,
keeps separate Ionian Sea and Sea of Phrixus;[66]
the other way, there's Lemnos famous for its crime, and Chalcis
too,[67]
and Aulis which delayed the ships. This headland's occupied
by Palamedes' father, who wickedly
transmits a bright light from the summit's peak
570 and lures the fleet onto the reef with his deceptive beacon.[68]
The ships hang hooked on jagged rocks.
Lacking water, they are shattered by the shallows.
This ship's prow is swept away; the rest sits on the reef.
That ship is smashed by another traveling backward:

the wrecked ship wrecks. And now the ships, in fear of land,
prefer the sea. Toward the dawn the madness faded:
with atonement made for Ilium, Phoebus reappears;
the dismal light of day reveals the havoc of the night.

CLYTEMNESTRA

Should I lament or celebrate my husband's coming home?
I rejoice at his return but I must mourn our kingdom's 580
heavy loss. O Father, who vibrates high-resonating realms,
restore now to the Greeks the gods placated.
Now let every head be crowned with joyful garland,
sacred flute pour out its dulcet notes
and snowy sacrificial victim fall before the mighty altars.
But look! A dismal group, with hair unkempt,
the women of Troy are here, and over them with elevated step
comes Phoebus' priestess,[69] unrestrained and shaking the
divining laurels.

CHORUS OF TROJAN WOMEN

The terrible love of life—it's sad how sweet that misery is,
implanted in mortals, when escape from miseries 590
lies within reach and when death freely summons the miserable,
tranquil harbor of rest eternal.
It is a harbor untouched by terror,
by tempests of violent Fortune or fire
from the bigoted Thunderer.
Deep peace has no horror of citizens'
gatherings, or conqueror's threatening rage,
or seas maddened by bitter storm-winds,
or ferocious battle-lines, or dust-clouds
stirred by barbarian squadrons of horsemen, 600
or nations collapsing with cities entire,
the city-walls ravaged by enemy fire,
or untamed war.
Only the person who scorns the capricious gods
can break through all forms of enslavement.
He can look without grimness on the face

of dark Acheron, he can look on grim Styx.
He's brave enough to impose a limit on life.
He'll be a match for kings and for gods up above.
610 Oh, what suffering it is to not know how to die!
We witnessed our country's collapse
on the terrible night when Doric flames
swept through our Dardanian homes. Troy did not fall to war
or to weapons, as she once before fell to Hercules' arrows.[70]
She was not conquered by Peleus' and Thetis' son, nor by the
darling
of Peleus' son,[71] too ferocious, when,
agleam in his borrowed equipment,
he routed the Trojans, a pseudo-Achilles,
or when Peleus' son in his grief set aside
620 his ferocious resentment, when his rapid pursuit
made the women of Troy on their ramparts afraid.
In misery Troy lost her ultimate glory—courageous defeat.
She held out for twice five years,
only to fall by the subterfuge of one single night.
We witnessed the feigned gift—its gigantic hulk—
and trustingly, with our own hands,
we hauled along the deadly offering
of the Danaans. The charger stumbled several times
on the outermost threshold, pregnant
630 with kings and with warfare concealed in its hollows.
And we could have turned their treachery back
to make the Pelasgians victims of their own deceit.
Several times their jostled shields made a noise
and a quiet murmuring struck our ears,
as Pyrrhus, reluctantly following orders,
raged at ingenious Ulysses.
Neglecting anxiety, the Trojan youth
are delighted to touch the sacred ropes.
On one side Astyanax, on the other the virgin
640 betrothed to the pyre of Thessaly[72]
head up the groups consisting of age-peers,

she, the female, he, the male.
In celebration the mothers convey to the gods
their votive offerings,
in celebration the fathers advance to the altars.
Throughout the city there's just one expression
and, something never witnessed by us since Hector's
funeral fires, Hecuba happy.
Luckless sorrow, what is the start and what is the end
of the mourning you've set for us? 650
That walls built by the hands of the gods
be destroyed by our own?
That shrines with their own gods inside go up in flames?
There's not time to bewail those troubles:
the women of Troy weep for you, mighty father.
With my own eyes I witnessed the weapon of Pyrrhus
in the old man's throat, hardly stained
by his meager blood.

CASSANDRA

Hold back the tears that all of time to come will ask for,
Trojan women; make lament with melancholy keening 660
for your individual losses. My own sufferings
admit no partner. Take away your groans from
my calamities: alone I'll be enough for my own miseries.

CHORUS

It's helpful to mingle tears with tears:
when griefs that are hidden rip you apart
they burn all the more.
It's helpful to weep for our losses together.
And you, though you're tough and heroic, inured to misery,
you'll not be up to lamenting such massive tragedies.
Consider the desolate nightingale, 670
pouring her song from her springtime branch,
reprising "Itys" with shifting sounds;
consider the Bistonian bird, perched
on the rooftops, chirping her story

of her horrific husband's secret depravity;[73]
neither of them will be up to lamenting your family
with suitable sorrowing,
not even if Cycnus himself,[74] dazzling among
the snow-white swans, at home on the Hister
680 and on the Tanaïs,[75] desired to sing his last song;
not even if kingfishers sounded their "Ceyx"
with waves slapping lightly, when they,
imprudently counting on calm,
boldly put trust once again in the sea
and anxiously nurture their young in the nest as it bobs;
not even if the desolate horde, mimicking
unmanned men, were slashing their arms alongside of you,
stirred by deafening boxwood flute
to beat at their breasts for their Mother of Towers,
690 in mourning for Phrygian Attis.[76]
There's no limit, Cassandra, to our tears
because our sufferings have passed any limit.

ACT 4

CHORUS

But why do you rip the sacred garlands from your head?
Surely the unlucky, more than anyone, should revere the gods.

CASSANDRA

My miseries have now exceeded every fear.
I don't bother to appease the heavenly gods with prayer:
even if they want to be ferocious, they don't have the means to hurt me.
Fortune's used up all her strength!
What homeland's left to me? What father? Or what sister?
700 The burial mounds and altars have drunk my blood.
What about that thriving crowd of brothers?
All gone, of course: in the empty palace only
sad old men are left; in all the many marriage-chambers
all they see is widowed wives, except the Spartan one.

That famous mother of so many kings, the Phrygians' guiding-light,
Hecuba, prolific for the funeral-fires, discovered Fate's
new laws, and she assumed a bestial form:
rabidly she barked all round her ruined walls,
survivor of Troy, of Hector, of Priam, of herself.

CHORUS

Phoebus' priestess suddenly falls silent. Pallor overcomes 710
her cheeks and constant trembling seizes her entire body.
The holy garlands are thrust up, her soft hair bristles,
her panting heart whines with pent-up sound,
her roaming glance drops down, her eyes rove wildly,
rolling backward, then stare immobile.[77]
Now she lifts her head up higher than accustomed,
walking tall, and now she's ready to unlock
reluctant jaws, and now in vain she tries to keep the words inside
by closing tight her mouth: a maenad fighting with the god.

CASSANDRA

Why do you, the sacred peaks of Mount Parnassus, seize 720
and lash me with your goads of frenzy renewed and rob me
of my mind? Leave me, Phoebus, now I don't belong to you;
quench the flames you've planted in my breast.
I roam, demented, but now for whom? For whom am I a frenzied bacchante?
Troy's already fallen—what's my role as failed prophetess?
Where am I? Blessed light has disappeared, and deep night
blinds my face; the sky's obscured, concealed by darkness.
But look! the daylight flashes out with sun that's twinned
and Argos, twinned, lofts up doubled palaces.
Do I see the groves of Ida? The deadly shepherd sits 730
as judge between the potent goddesses.[78]
Kings, beware: be fearful of the covert breed:[79]
that rustic protégé will overthrow your home.
Why's that wild woman bearing unsheathed weapon

in her hand? And which man is her target,
Spartan in her dress but with an Amazon's steel?
What novel apparition now attracts my eyes?
The conqueror of wild beasts with towering neck,
the lion of Africa, abased beneath a base-born tooth
740 after suffering the bloody bite of brazen lioness.[80]
Why do you summon me, the sole survivor of my family,
my kindred ghosts? You I follow, Father, buried
under all of Troy. My brother, safeguard of the Phrygians
and terror of Danaans, I cannot see your former beauty
or your hands grown hot from burning ships;
instead, your mangled limbs, and shoulders wounded by
the heavy rope.[81] You I follow, Troilus: your meeting with
Achilles
was far too soon. Deiphobus, you have a face,
unrecognizable, the gift of your new wife.[82]
750 I rejoice to walk beside the Stygian lakes,
to see the savage dog of Tartarus
and greedy realms of Dis! Today this boat
of dire Phlegethon will carry royal souls,
conquering and conquered. Ghosts, I beg you;
water sworn by gods, I beg you too:
unseal a little the cover of the darkling world
to let the insubstantial crowd of Phrygians see Mycenae.
Take a look, you wretches: fate has moved into reverse.
The filthy sisters loom above
760 and brandish snaky lashes,[83]
holding half-burned torches,
pallid faces bloated.
Mourning garments
gird their withered flanks.
Night-time terrors hiss
and bones of a gigantic corpse
lie rotting, long decayed,
in slimy marsh.

And look: the tired old man[84]
isn't lunging for the water playing 770
at his lips: forgetful of his thirst
he grieves at death to come.
But Father Dardanus exults
and walks with elegance.[85]

CHORUS

Now the frenzy's finished roaming and has spent itself.
She collapses like a bull with bended knee
before the altar, wounded by a strike delivered to its neck.[86]
Let's lift her body up. —See, at last, he nears his household
gods,
Agamemnon, garlanded with victor's laurel,
and his wife in celebration went to meet him 780
and returns beside him, perfectly in step.

AGAMEMNON

At long last I return, safe and sound, to my father's
house-gods.
Greetings, my beloved land! To you, numerous barbaric tribes
have yielded booty, to you, Troy, queen
of mighty Asia, prosperous so long, has now surrendered.
Why's that prophetess collapsed and trembling,
swaying her failing neck? House-slaves, raise her up,
revive her with chill water. Now she sees the light again,
with wavering eyes.

(*To Cassandra.*)

Rouse your senses:
that longed-for harbor from your sufferings is here. 790
It's a day of celebration.

CASSANDRA

So it was at Troy, too.

AGAMEMNON

Let's worship at the altar.

CASSANDRA

My father died before the altar.

AGAMEMNON

Let's pray to Jupiter together.

CASSANDRA

Hercean Jupiter, you mean?

AGAMEMNON

Do you think it's Ilium you see?

CASSANDRA

Yes, and Priam too.

AGAMEMNON

This is not Troy.

CASSANDRA

(*Glancing at Clytemnestra.*)

Wherever there's a Helen must be Troy.

AGAMEMNON

Do not fear your mistress, house-slave.

CASSANDRA

I do not: freedom is at hand.

AGAMEMNON

Live fear-free.

CASSANDRA

It's death makes me fear-free.

AGAMEMNON

No danger is awaiting you.

CASSANDRA

Great danger is awaiting *you*.

AGAMEMNON

What need a conqueror fear?

CASSANDRA

What he doesn't fear.[87]

AGAMEMNON

My loyal band of house-slaves, hold her tight 800
till she's dislodged the god, so her violent frenzy does no harm.
But you, father, wielder of savage thunderbolts,
cloud-disperser, ruler of the stars and lands,
recipient of spoils of triumph from conquerors;[88]
and you, the sister of all-powerful husband,
Argive Juno: gladly shall I worship you with sacrificial flocks,
with offerings from Arabia and entrails given humbly.

CHORUS OF ARGIVE WOMEN

Argos, known for its noble citizens,
Argos, beloved of angered stepmother,[89]
always colossal are the sons that you rear. 810
You've brought to completion the number of gods:
your powerful Hercules won his election
to heaven with his labors, twice six in number.
For him, Jupiter broke the law of the cosmos
and doubled the hours of dewy night,[90]
ordering Phoebus
to drive his swift chariot more slowly
and, shining Phoebe, ordering
your two horses to return at a walk.
. . .
there came back the star that switches its name round, 820
amazed to be called Hesperus.[91] Aurora awoke
for the usual changeover, then sinking back
she rested her neck on her elderly husband.
Sunrise and sunset alike were aware of
Hercules' birth: that impetuous hero
could not have been sired in a single night.
For you, the hastening cosmos stood still,
you, the boy destined to scale the sky.
Your power was felt by the lightning-fast
lion of Nemea, when you crushed him tight in your arms,[92] 830

by the hind of Parrhasia,[93]
by the one who destroyed the Arcadian countryside,[94]
by the frightening bull, departing the fields of Dicte
bellowing.[95]
He conquered the snake, fertile in death,
stopping regeneration from its neck as it died.[96]
The multiple brothers,
threefold monstrosity born from a single breast,
he crushed with a blow from his club as he leapt,
840 and he led toward sunrise the herd of Hesperia,
stolen from triple-formed Geryon.[97]
He drove off the Thracian horses
not pastured on grassy banks of the Strymon
or Hebrus by the tyrant,
who cruelly offered the blood of his guests
to his savage stables.[98] The last drop of blood
to stain their pitiless jaws was that of their charioteer.
Ferocious Hippolyte witnessed
the booty as it was torn from her breast.[99] By his arrows
850 the bird of Stymphalus fell from high heaven,[100]
when the cloud split apart.
The tree so prolific with golden apples
recoiled from his hand, unused to plucking,
withdrawing upward, its branches lightened;[101]
its guardian, chill and unsleeping,
perceived the clinking of metal
only as Hercules left with his arms full,
the grove now empty of tawny metal.
The dog of the underworld, dragged up to daylight
860 by triple chain, fell silent and none of its mouths barked,
in its fear of the hues of the light unfamiliar.
With you in command, the duplicitous house
of the Dardanid crumpled,
feeling the bow that would later be feared for a second time;
with you in command, Troy fell in as many days
as later in years.[102]

ACT 5

CASSANDRA

Something gigantic is happening inside, the payback for ten
long years.
Good grief, what's this? Rise up, my spirit, take
your frenzy's prize: we conquered Phrygians are conquerors!
Troy, it's good, you rise again. While falling, you've dragged down 870
Mycenae too. Your conqueror's on the run!
The frenzy of my prophesying mind has never shown me
images so clear. I see, I'm there, I revel in it.
No erratic vision tricks my sight.
Let's watch! In the palace a thronging feast
is spread, like the Phrygians' final
banquet. The couch gleams with purple cloth from Ilium.
Their unmixed wine they drain from Assaracus' ancient gold.
He himself reclines on high in broidered robes,
wearing lordly trappings stripped from Priam's corpse. 880
His wife commands him to remove this enemy attire
and don instead a garment woven by his loyal
wife's own hand. I shudder and I'm quaking in my mind:
will king be killed by exile, husband by adulterer?
Fate has come: the banquet's final course will see
its master's blood, and gore will fall into the wine.
The fatal garment he's put on has fettered him, delivering him
to treacherous death: the loose, impenetrable folds
enclose his head and stop his hands emerging.
The half-man with his quaking hand inflicts a gash, 890
but he hasn't driven deep: midwound he freezes.
But the other, like a bristling boar in forest deep,
when, fettered in a net, he struggles to escape
yet tightens up his bonds by writhing, raging uselessly,
just so, longing to cut loose the blinding folds
encircling him, he searches for his enemy while tangled up.
Crazed, Tyndareus' daughter arms her hand with two-edged axe,

and, resembling the attendant at the altar when his eyes[103]
mark out the necks of bulls before he strikes with steel,
900 just so she weighs her wicked hand this way and that.
He's wounded! It's all over now! His not quite severed head
is hanging by a sliver, here the gore is pouring
from the torso, there his lips are roaring on the ground.
Not yet do they pull back: the man now strikes the lifeless victim,
hacking at his corpse, and as he stabs the woman helps him.
Both answer to their heritage with this colossal crime:
the man's Thyestes' son, the woman's Helen's sister.
See how Titan's at a standstill, hesitating at the zenith
whether he should run on his own course or on Thyestes'.[104]

ELECTRA

(*Addressing her brother Orestes.*)

910 Run away! You are the only remedy of father's death.
Run away, escape our enemies' evil hands!
Our house is utterly destroyed, our kingdom's falling.
Who's this, driving speedy chariot so fast?
Brother, I'll conceal your face behind my cloak.
Why flinch back, my crazy spirit? Is it outsiders that you fear?
Our own house is the one to fear. Now set aside your trembling dread,
Orestes: I see devotion and protection from a friend.

STROPHIUS

(*Entering in his chariot with his son Pylades.*)

I, Strophius, have left Phocis to come back, decorated
with the palm of Elis.[105] The reason that I've come is
920 to congratulate my friend for sacking Ilium
after it had been assailed by war for ten long years?
Who's this woman, drenching miserable face with tears,
fearful, grieving? I recognize her royal ancestry.
Electra, why this weeping in a joyful house?

ELECTRA

My father's lying murdered by my mother's crime.
His son is wanted, to accompany his father's death.
Aegisthus holds the citadel he's gained through lust.

STROPHIUS

No happiness lasts long!

ELECTRA

I implore you by my father's memory,
by his scepter, famed throughout the world, by fickle gods: 930
take this boy Orestes and conceal your honorable theft.

STROPHIUS

Though Agamemnon's murder counsels caution,
I'll set about it and, Orestes, I will gladly steal you away.[106] 933
Take this prize from the athletic contest
to adorn your brow and, holding victor's branch
in your left hand, let its greening foliage conceal your head:
let the palm of Jupiter of Pisa offer you a covering and an omen.[107]
And you, the close companion of your father's reins, 940
Pylades, receive a lesson in loyalty from your father's example.
You horses, all of Greece has already witnessed your swiftness:
gallop at breakneck speed from this place of disloyalty.

ELECTRA

He's departed, gone, his chariot racing recklessly,
he's disappeared from sight. In safety now I'll wait
for my enemies and put myself in harm's way voluntarily.
Here's the conqueror of her own husband, bloodied,
with marks of murder on her defiled clothing.
Even now her hands are dripping with the fresh-spilled
blood.
Defiant, her expression wears its crimes overtly. 950
I'll withdraw toward the altar. Cassandra, let me join you
as a suppliant,[108] since I share your trepidation.

CLYTEMNESTRA

You, your mother's enemy, unfilial, brazen creature,
how come *you*, a virgin, seek out public company?

ELECTRA

It's because I am a virgin that I've left the house of adulterers.

CLYTEMNESTRA

Who'd consider you a virgin—?

ELECTRA

Your own daughter?

CLYTEMNESTRA

Deal with your mother more respectfully!

ELECTRA

A lesson in devotion—from *you*?

CLYTEMNESTRA

You have the spirit of a man inside your swollen heart,
but once you're tamed by pain, you'll learn to act the woman.

ELECTRA

960 Unless I happen to be wrong, weapons well suit women.

CLYTEMNESTRA

And in your craziness, you reckon you're a match for us?

ELECTRA

The two of *you?* Who's that substitute Agamemnon of yours?
Talk like a widow: your husband's not alive.

CLYTEMNESTRA

I'm queen and I will break your untamed words,
the words of an unfilial virgin, later; meanwhile, quickly
tell me where my son, your brother, is.

ELECTRA

Beyond Mycenae.

CLYTEMNESTRA

Give me back my son, right now.

ELECTRA

And you, give back my father.

CLYTEMNESTRA

Where's he hiding?

ELECTRA

In peace and safety, not frightened of the new regime:
that should satisfy a *real* parent.

CLYTEMNESTRA

But not an angry one. 970
You'll die today.

ELECTRA

So long as it is by *your* hand I die.
I leave the altar. If your liking is to plunge
the sword into my throat, I offer you my throat.
But if you want my head severed like the animals,
I stretch it out: my neck awaits your blow.
The crime is ready: with this blood of mine, cleanse
the hand that's soiled and spattered with your husband's gore.

CLYTEMNESTRA

Aegisthus, equal partner in my danger and my power,
approach. My daughter is provoking her mother outrageously
with her insults, and she keeps her brother hidden and 980
concealed.

AEGISTHUS

Demented girl, suppress this shocking
talk and words not fit for any mother's ear.

ELECTRA

Am I to be instructed by the craftsman of this shocking crime,
a man conceived in crime, whose name is unclear even to his
own,
simultaneously his sister's son and father's grandson?

CLYTEMNESTRA

Aegisthus, do you hesitate to use your sword to sever
her unfilial head? She must give up her brother or her life at
once.

AEGISTHUS

She must complete her life concealed in an unlit rocky
dungeon. Once she's been tortured by every kind of punishment

990 perhaps she'll willingly return the boy she now conceals.
Helpless, starving, trapped, besmeared with filth,[109]
widowed prior to marriage, exiled, universally reviled,
denied the light of day, eventually she'll bow to pain.

ELECTRA

Grant me death!

AEGISTHUS

I'd grant it if you didn't want it.
Feeble is the tyrant who makes death a punishment.

ELECTRA

There's something worse than death?

AEGISTHUS

Yes, living, if you want to die.
House-slaves, take away this freak. Convey her far
beyond Mycenae; in the kingdom's furthest corner
keep her chained and penned inside a dark and unlit cave,
1000 to make her prison tame this turbulent girl.

CLYTEMNESTRA

But *her*, the prisoner-wife, companion of the royal bed,
with her life she'll pay the penalty.
Drag her off to follow the husband she stole from me.

CASSANDRA

No need to drag me: I will walk ahead of you.
I'm keen to be first to bring the message
to my Phrygians: how the sea was filled with capsized ships,
how Mycenae fell, how the chieftain of a thousand chiefs
perished by a gift, by woman's lust, by treachery,
to meet a fate that matched the Trojan sufferings.
1010 I do not hesitate: hurry me away; in fact, I'm grateful:
now I'm glad to have survived the fall of Troy, glad.

CLYTEMNESTRA

Die, you crazy girl!

CASSANDRA

Craziness awaits you too.[110]

Notes

Seneca and His World

1. See John G. Fitch, *Seneca's Anapaests: Metre, Colometry, Text and Artistry in the Anapaests of Seneca's Tragedies* (Atlanta, 1987). For Zwierlein's reviews of Fitch's method, *Gnomon* 60 (1988) 333–42; *Gnomon* 62 (1990) 692–96.

Oedipus

Introduction

1. Some sense of the range may be gauged from Lowell Edmunds, *Oedipus* (London, 2006).

Oedipus

For my translation I have consulted the following editions: J. G. Fitch, ed. and trans, *Seneca: Tragedies*. 2 vols. (Cambridge, MA, 2002–4) and O. Zwierlein, *L. Annaei Senecae Tragoediae* (Oxford, 1986), which remains the standard text. I have also consulted the commentaries by Bruno Häuptli, *Seneca:* Oedipus (Frauenfeld, 1983) and Karlheinz Töchterle, *Lucius Annaeus Seneca:* Oedipus (Heidelberg, 1994).

1. The Latin has *Titan*; the Sun-God was the son of one of the Titans, a race of gods earlier than the Olympian gods.
2. Polybus was the king of Corinth who with his queen, Merope, adopted the baby Oedipus.
3. A reference to the oracle of Phoebus Apollo at Delphi; the laurel tree was sacred to Apollo.
4. Phoebus is another name for Apollo.
5. Literally, "the race of Cadmus"; Cadmus was the founder of Thebes.
6. The Dog-Star is name for Sirius, associated with the heat of summer.
7. The Lion of Nemea is a name for the constellation of Leo; it is July.

8. Dirce was a spring; sometimes, by metonymy, Thebes.

9. Ismenos was a river in Boeotia, the region of Greece that included the city of Thebes.

10. Phoebus' sister was Diana, the Moon. Reading *die* with manuscript E.

11. The Latin personifies the wheat as Ceres, the goddess of agriculture.

12. That is, no one survives to mourn.

13. That is, many are only partly burned, not properly incinerated.

14. He means that he should have left long ago and that he should leave now even if that means returning to Corinth, where he believes he risks murdering his father and marrying his mother.

15. The Latin personifies war as the god of war, Mars.

16. The giants were huge warriors who rebelled against Jupiter and the Olympian gods.

17. The Sphinx; "prophetess" refers to the supernatural power of her riddles.

18. The riddle: What walks on four legs in the morning, on two at noon, and on three in the evening? Answer: A human, who crawls as a baby, walks as an adult, and in old age uses a stick.

19. The god Bacchus (in Greek, Dionysus) was the son of Jupiter and Semele, daughter of Cadmus, and therefore especially associated with Thebes.

20. The Parthians were famous for shooting their arrows over their shoulders as they fled the battlefield. Hence the expression "a Parthian shot."

21. Not what we call the Red Sea but the Persian Gulf and Indian Ocean.

22. The Latin names the god as Iacchus, a god sometimes identified with Bacchus, as here, personifying the vine or wine.

23. "The mob of sisters" refers to the Furies; Tartarus was the part of the underworld reserved for the punishment of the wicked.

24. "Erebus" refers to the underworld, named after the god of darkness.

25. "The Fire-River" refers to Phlegethon. Reading *suam mutat ripam* with manuscript E.

26. "Sidon" here denotes Thebes, which was founded by Cadmus, son of Agenor, king of Phoenicia; Sidon was a city in Phoenicia.

27. Most editors of the text print certain short lines in the choral passages as extra, supernumerary lines. Zwierlein marks extra lines after 166, 176, 185, 197, 407, 436, 466, 500, 718, 727, 731, and 991. I have dispensed with these in my translation, collapsing the lines as necessary.

28. "The Hound" refers to Cerberus, the three-headed dog that guarded the entrance to the underworld.

29. Literally, "Taenarean iron," referring to Taenarus, a place in Greece supposed to be an entrance to the underworld.

30. With supplement *uolitare sacros* proposed by Zwierlein.

31. The grove where the snake which Cadmus killed lived; see note on line 730.

32. Amphion was a son of Jupiter and built the walls of Thebes.

33. The hounds of Hecate, a goddess associated with black magic and the underworld; here an omen of death. With supplement *circa muros* proposed by Richter.

34. I have kept the sequence as transmitted in the text; Richter transposed 187b and 188a to follow 192

35. The only protest the dying can make against the cruelty of the gods is to die in the gods' shrines. Possibly the text should read *ipsis*, which would translate as "to glut the gods with themselves."

36. Oedipus' name contains the Greek root for "knowledge" or "understanding," which Seneca here alludes to through the Latin verb *noscere* (to know). For another etymology see note on line 813.

37. The previous king of Thebes, Jocasta's husband.

38. The mountain near Delphi, sacred to Apollo.

39. Castalia was the name of the spring that rose between the twin peaks of Parnassus.

40. Leto was the mother of Apollo and Diana; this reference is to Apollo's priestess at Delphi, the Pythia, the conduit of the oracle's responses. Lines 233–38 are in hexameters, the meter of oracular pronouncements.

41. Reading *spinx et* with manuscript E .

42. Apollo, here identified with the sun.

43. The twelve signs of the zodiac.

44. Neptune, god of the sea.

45. Dis, king of the underworld. See note on line 396.

46. The Latin specifies "the right hand," the hand associated with masculine action. I have omitted this in my translation throughout.

47. He refers to the isthmus of Corinth, which he believes to be his home.

48. Apollo.

49. Cirrha was a city near Delphi; "Cirrha's seer" is Apollo's priestess at Delphi. Cf. line 230.

50. Corinth again; Sisyphus was the founder of Corinth according to myth.

51. The Olenian fields were located in the hinterland of Corinth.

52. "Wandering waters" refers to Lake Copais in Boeotia, a large lake which changed water level and location from time to time; cf. Strabo, *Geography* 9.2.16–19, 40.

53. A brook that ran down from Mount Helicon into Lake Copais.

54. The Latin has "relying on peacetime."

55. The rainbow, personified.

56. The Latin has "Bacchus" as a personification of wine.

57. It was considered a bad omen if a sacrificial victim was reluctant to die.

58. Instead of spurting out toward the altar, as in a propitious sacrifice.

59. The two heads in one membrane represent Oedipus' sons, Eteocles and Polynices, who fulfil Oedipus' curse by contesting the rule of Thebes. The fact that the bulges are "cloven" evokes ancient Roman haruspicy which viewed a cloven head as a sign of civil war. Polynices brings an army from Argos—the sturdy "hostile side"—to assist him (363). Polynices and the Argives provide seven champions who fight at the seven gates of Thebes, hence the seven veins (364).

60. The Latin has "hostile side," a technical term in divination. The liver had two sides, the hostile and the friendly.

61. Seneca must mean either that the left portion of the lungs is missing or that the lungs are entirely located on the right side.

62. Augury, observation of the behavior of birds, and haruspicy, observation of the entrails of sacrificial animals.

63. One of the names of the god of the underworld. Other names are Pluto and Hades.

64. The thyrsus was a wand wreathed in ivy and vine-leaves and topped by a pine-cone, carried by worshippers of Bacchus. Nysa was a mountain in India, where Bacchus was said to have been born.

65. An oriental headdress; "Tyrian" denotes its purple color; Tyre, in Phoenicia, was the center of the purple-dye industry.

66. Juno; her hostility to Bacchus arises from his birth to Semele, one of Jupiter's many lovers.

67. The rivers Ganges (in India) and Araxes (in Armenia) represent eastern extremes. The Latin has "breaks the snowy Araxes"; Seneca may mean that people broke the ice to drink the water or that they sailed up the river or that a bridge had been built across it.

68. Silenus was a follower of Bacchus, in some sources his tutor; an old and wise satyr-like man who typically gets drunk and sings.

69. Thracian followers of Bacchus.

70. A mountain in Macedonia; the Edonians were a Thracian race.

71. A mountain actually located between Thessaly and Epirus; Seneca exploits poetic license here to call it "Thracian."

72. "Ogygian" here means "Theban," from Ogygus, an early king of Boeotia. For Iacchus see note on 158.

73. Line 441 transposed to follow 438 by Müller; lacuna after 441 proposed by Zwierlein.

74. A name given to maenads in Attica and Delphi.

75. Nereids, daughters of the sea god Nereus.

76. Ino's son Melicertes was named Palaemon when he became a god.

77. Addressed to Bacchus.

78. Ida was the name of a mountain range in Phrygia, with special associations with the goddess of Cybele.

79. A river in Lydia (in western Asia Minor) supposed to carry gold in its waters.

80. A nomadic Scythian tribe.

81. Getic is equivalent to Thracian.

82. A king of Thrace who persecuted the young Bacchus and was punished severely as a result.

83. An unknown race; the text may be corrupt.

84. The north wind.

85. Maeotis refers to the Sea of Azov.

86. Constellations: the Bear-Keeper (formed from Callisto's son Arcas) and the Great Bear and the Little Bear.

87. Bacchus tamed a Scythian race.

88. A river in Asia Minor associated with the Amazons.

89. Cithaeron refers to a mountain range which separated the regions of Boeotia and Attica; site of the murder of Pentheus as well as the abandonment of the baby Oedipus.

90. A complicated reference to the murder of Pentheus; *Ophion* derives from the Greek word for snake and seems to refer to the men who arose from the snake's teeth sown in the ground by Cadmus; Pentheus was Cadmus' grandson. However, Pentheus' father was called Echion, which might be a sound emendation of the transmitted text.

91. Proetus was a king of Argos; his daughters were driven mad by Bacchus when they resisted his rites.

92. On Juno's hostility to Bacchus see note on 418.

93. Ariadne, abandoned on Naxos by Theseus.

94. Wine; Bacchus was given the title *Nyctelian* in reference to his nighttime revels (from the Greek word for night).

95. Because Jupiter's thunderbolt had killed Semele, Bacchus' mother. Reading *oditque* with manuscript ω.

96. Lucifer is the morning star, personified.

97. The Bear refers to the constellation of the Great Bear or Little Bear or both (see note on 477), near the pole star, which never sets in the northern hemisphere; "Nereus" means "the sea," as at line 450.

98. A cult-title of Bacchus, meaning "the liberator."

99. Paphos was a city in Cyprus associated with Venus.

100. Charon; see note on line 166. Lethe was the river of forgetfulness (in Greek) in the underworld.

101. Chaos was the origin of Earth, Darkness and Night; here a figure for the underworld.

102. As at 770, I have substituted "hell" for "Dis," king of the underworld; see note on line 396.

103. On Dirce see note on line 42; the reference is to the warriors that sprang from the snake's teeth sown by Cadmus; cf. line 485 and note.

104. There follows a list of personifications. I translate *Erinys* as "Fury," an avenging spirit often identified with the Furies.

105. That is, the Theban people; on "Ogygian," see note on line 436.

106. Manto.

107. A mountain in Sicily.

108. Hybla was a town in Sicily rich in meadows.

109. Strymon was a river in Thrace.

110. Twin brothers, mythical rulers of Thebes; Amphion charmed the stones to form the city-walls with his music.

111. In the Latin Niobe is called *Tantalis*, the daughter of Tantalus, wife of Amphion; her boasts of her many children provoked Apollo and Artemis to kill them all. That is why she is "counting up her shades" in the underworld.

112. Agave, mother of Pentheus, king of Thebes, who with the other female followers of Bacchus (the Bacchants or maenads; see lines 435, 483) tore

her son to pieces in a Bacchic frenzy. This was Bacchus' way of punishing Pentheus for resisting his cult.

113. Ambiguous; most obviously the son's love for his mother; but also Jocasta's love for her baby that preserved him despite her husband's decision to have him killed.

114. The Latin has *Auster*, a personification of the south wind.

115. Lines 636–37 deleted by Zwierlein.

116. Oedipus is in his prime—maybe thirty years old—and by no means an old man.

117. Boeotia was the region of Greece that included Thebes.

118. Labdacus was a king of Thebes and the father of Laius, hence Oedipus' grandfather.

119. Cadmus is "the traveler from Sidon," son of Agenor, king of Sidon. His sister Europa has been abducted by Jupiter (716) and Cadmus has been sent to find her. He is afraid (717) to return home without her. He arrives at Delphi, here denoted as "the grove of Castalia," to ask Phoebus Apollo's oracle (719) how to find Europa. The oracle leads him to abandon his quest and settle in Boeotia, at "Dirce's spring," with his followers, here called "the Tyrian settlers" because the cities of Tyre and Sidon, both in Phoenicia, were often closely associated. The name Boeotia comes from Greek word for cow (*bous*, which is equivalent to the Latin *bos*. Seneca uses *bos* here to make the point, whereas he uses *vacca* at 719 to denote the heifer.

120. Reading *circa* with Reeve's emendation.

121. Oaks, named from the grove of oak-trees at the oracle of Jupiter in Chaonia, in Epirus.

122. Cadmus killed the serpent, sacred to Mars, and sowed its teeth in the ground, from which sprang fully armed warriors.

123. There is a lacuna in the Latin text here.

124. Seneca means that the first sound these newborn warriors ever made was the war-cry.

125. The evening star.

126. The newcomer refers to Cadmus.

127. Actaeon, who was punished for seeing the goddess Diana when she was bathing by being turned into a stag and torn to pieces by his own hounds.

128. That is, its antlers are large; stags' antlers increase every year.

129. The feathers and snares are methods used in antiquity to scare and trap the wild animals being hunted.

130. Diana, virgin goddess of hunting.

131. As at 573, I have substituted "hell" for "Dis," king of the underworld.

132. He refers to the oracle he received from Apollo at Delphi.

133. The name Oedipus—in Greek, *Oidi-pous*—appears to mean "swollen-foot." For a competing etymology see the note on line 216.

134. Some attribute the speeches at lines 825–27, 829–32, and 835–36 to the Old Corinthian.

135. Oedipus may be referring to the plague, the information that Polybus and Merope were not his real parents, or the indications that he was Laius' murderer.

136. He means himself.

137. Minos, king of Cnossus, a city in Crete. Minos imprisoned the inventor Daedalus and his son Icarus. To escape from this captivity, Daedalus devised wings of wax and feathers.

138. Icarus flew too close to the sun which melted his wings and he then plunged into the sea, which was thereafter known as the Icarian Sea.

139. Reading *compede* with F. Bücheler's emendation.

140. To tear him to pieces; see note on 616–18.

141. Ted Hughes' version makes the meaning clearer: "it's only death can keep a man innocent." Oedipus thinks that his innocence can be preserved by killing himself.

142. One of the three Fates, usually thought of as old women spinning; Lachesis drew the thread from Klotho's distaff and Atropos cut it.

143. The Latin has "while fearing fate"; the meaning is that it is impossible to escape one's fate and that any attempt to avoid it is likely to send you straight toward it.

144. Agave: see note on 616–18.

145. What I have translated as "That shames you?" might with different punctuation mean "That's why you feel shame"—that is, you feel shame because you are my son, your shame proves that you are my son (thus Gronovius).

146. An obscure and ambiguous phrase: the bond of blood (here translated "my blood's guarantee") may refer to the connection that Oedipus has with his mother or with his children, in either case well described as "ill-omened."

147. Literally, "in our names": their being mother and son is right; their being husband and wife is wrong.

148. Thunderbolts, the characteristic weapon of Jupiter.

149. Apollo, god of the Delphic oracle.

Hercules Mad

Introduction

1. R. E. Meagher, *Herakles Gone Mad: Rethinking Heroism in an Age of Endless War* (Northampton, MA: 2006), 48, 50.

2. K. Riley, *The Reception and Performance of Euripides' Herakles: Reasoning Madness* (Oxford, 2008), 37.

3. For Seneca's debt to mime and pantomime, see Hall 2008; Zanobi 2008; and Zimmermann 2008.

4. For discussion, see Graver 2007, 91–99.

5. This is the view vigorously defended by Zwierlein 1984.

6. Fitch 1987 provides a brief list of scholars on both sides of the question.

7. O. Zwierlein, ed., *L. Annaei Senecae tragoediae* (Oxford: Clarendon Press, 1986).

Hercules Furens

The main edition consulted for this translation is that of John G. Fitch, *Seneca's* Hercules Furens*: A Critical Text with Introduction and Commentary*

(Ithaca, 1987); the few instances where I depart from it are indicated in the notes.

1. "The Thunderer" refers to Jupiter or Jove, husband and brother to Juno.

2. Callisto, loved by Zeus and transformed into a bear then the constellation Ursa Major; Juno lists evidence in the heavens of Jove's infidelities.

3. Jupiter in the form of a bull carried off Europa.

4. Jupiter was said to have lain with three of the Pleiades (in the Latin called *Atlantides*, daughters of Atlas).

5. Seneca perhaps thinks of Orion, like Perseus and Castor and Pollux (whose mortal parent was Tyndarus, hence *Tyndarids*, "sons of Tyndarus"), as a son of Jupiter, though if so it represents an obscure version of the myth.

6. Apollo and Diana, at whose birth the floating island Delos became fixed.

7. Bacchus, son of Jupiter, was a god, and his mother Semele, in some versions, became a deity as well.

8. Ariadne was Bacchus' wife or mistress, and made a constellation in the form of a wreath; even apart from Jupiter's affairs, Juno sees the heavens as memorials to adultery.

9. Jupiter lengthened the night during which he slept with Alcmene and Hercules was conceived.

10. The Aethiopians were thought of as living both in the far east and far west, hence near the Sun's rising and setting (which explains their dark color).

11. The three-headed dog Cerberus.

12. Hercules briefly relieved Atlas of his burden.

13. The king who commanded the labors of Hercules.

14. The Doric land is Sicily, where Mount Aetna was believed to press down Typhoeus, slain by Jupiter's thunderbolt (hence Aetna's volcanic fires); Titans, Giants, and Typhoeus are here assimilated as rebels against Jupiter's reign.

15. The Moon was sometimes said to be the mother of the Nemean lion; in line 77 Juno discarded beasts as opponents of Hercules, but here

she presumably imagines the Moon producing a whole other class of monsters.

16. Patronymic derived from Alcaeus, Hercules' grandfather.

17. The Furies (among them Megaera, below).

18. Discord personified was sometimes regarded as one of the Furies.

19. Reading *manum* rather than *manu.*

20. The composition of the chorus is uncertain, but the sententious tone would suit a group of Theban elders.

21. The Big Dipper was seen as a wagon.

22. The Moon.

23. Philomela was raped by the Thracian king Tereus; she and her sister Procne, Tereus' wife, took revenge by killing Tereus' son Itys and feeding him to his father; subsequently all three were turned into birds, Philomela (in the Roman tradition) into a nightingale.

24. The Fates, thought of as spinning the threads of mortal lives.

25. A hind with golden horns, sacred to Diana; capturing it was one of the labors of Hercules, along with (in the order in which they are mentioned below) slaying the lion that terrorized Nemea; retrieving the man-eating horses of the Thracian king Diomedes; killing the boar that dwelled on the mountain range of Erymanthus; seizing the bull that ravaged Crete (famous for its hundred cities); carrying off the cattle of the triple-bodied Geryon who lived in far-off Spain; opening up the Straits of Gibraltar (called the Pillars of Hercules: not one of the traditional twelve labors); obtaining the golden apples of the Hesperides, which were guarded by a dragon; defeating the Lyrnaean Hydra by cauterizing its hundred heads so they could not regenerate; shooting down (in this version) the birds that plagued the region of Stymphalus; bringing back the belt of the Amazon queen Hippolyte; and cleaning out the stables of the king Augeas.

26. The reference is to Creon, Megara's father.

27. The original inhabitants of Thebes were imagined as arising from dragon's teeth sown in the earth by Cadmus, who had slain the beast after arriving at Thebes from Phoenicia; one of these sown men was named Ophion. Amphion was said to have constructed the city's walls

by playing the lyre so tunefully that the stones followed him and glided into place (his twin brother Zethus had to carry his).

28. That is, the yoke of slavery, though he rescued mankind from it.

29. Hercules is occasionally credited with opening the gorge of Tempe in Thessaly.

30. Keeping *cecidit* rather than Leo's emendation of *cessit* adopted by Fitch; cf. *dirutis iugis*, 283.

31. Ceres, identified with Demeter, who had her shrine in Eleusis (near Athens).

32. Syrtes was the name of sandy shallows off the coast of Libya, dangerous for ships; the adventure mentioned here is not known from other sources, but for Hercules in Libya, see Apollonius of Rhodes, *Argonautica* 4.1268–80 (this after the Argonauts were similarly stranded).

33. Phocis was the name of a mountainous area bordering Boeotia, the region around Thebes, to the northwest; the river Ismenos and Mount Cithaeron are in Boeotia; the Isthmus that separates the Peloponnese from the rest of Greece is to the south.

34. Scylla represents the Strait of Messina, separating Sicily from the rest of Italy; Euripus is the narrow channel between Boeotia and Euboea, proverbially variable.

35. Agave, daughter of Cadmus (who was turned into a serpent at the end of his life and driven from Thebes), killed her son Pentheus in a bacchic frenzy; Ino, Agave's sister, attempted to kill her stepchildren, Phrixus and Helle. The "mingled name" refers to Oedipus; Niobe was the wife of Amphion.

36. Phlegra was the site (in Thrace) of the battle between the gods and giants, in which Hercules took part.

37. Because of a murder, Apollo was condemned by Jupiter to serve as a shepherd, and he elected to do so in Pherae (Thessaly), where Admetus was king.

38. A reference to Apollo's birth on Delos; Juno hounded his mother, Leto, out of Olympus. Apollo slew the serpent Pytho.

39. The reference is to Dionysus, whose mother, Semele, was incinerated when she beheld Jupiter fully armed; Jupiter rescued the infant.

40. The infant Jupiter was hidden in a cave on Mt. Ida, in Crete, to protect him from his father Cronus (or Saturn), who sought to prevent any of his children from overthrowing him (as Jupiter ultimately did).

41. Because of a murder, Hercules was compelled to serve as a slave to Omphale, queen of Lydia, who made him do women's work; Roman poets represented him as in love with her and voluntarily exchanging clothing (Sidonian suggests bright purple).

42. Eurytus was the father of Iole, with whom Hercules was enamored; to obtain her, he destroyed Eurytus' city, Oechalia (there is a slight anachronism: Hercules introduced Iole into the house of his second wife, Deianira, after Megara's death). The reference to other women is a generalizing, suggesting Hercules' indiscriminate lust.

43. King of the town of Eryx in Sicily, killed by Hercules in a boxing match when he was en route to capture Geryon's cattle. Antaeus of Libya forced passers-by to engage him in wrestling; he was invincible so long as he was in contact with the earth (Earth was his mother), and Hercules defeated him by lifting him up and crushing him. Busiris, a tyrannical king in Egypt, sacrificed strangers at an altar to Zeus till Hercules turned the tables on him. Hercules killed Cycnus, the son of Mars, though he is not described as invulnerable (another Cycnus, slain by Achilles, was impervious to wounds and had to be crushed or strangled). Geryon, unlike the others, was among Hercules' labors and is added as further evidence of his strength and courage.

44. Amphitryo will cede his daughter to Lycus, as he did his wife to Jupiter

45. Grandfather of Oedipus. Of the fifty daughters of Danaus (called Danaids), forty-nine killed their husbands (all sons of the Egyptian king Aegyptus); one spared hers.

46. The Hesperides, tricked out of their golden apples.

47. A people in western Scythia, the scene of Hercules' battle with the Amazons; the waters are those of the Black Sea.

48. Castor and Pollux.

49. During an attack on Pylos, a town in the western Peloponnese, Hercules wounded Hades, who fought in its defense, armed with a trident.

50. Eurydice; Orpheus was given permission to rescue her from the underworld, on condition that he not look back at her till they reached the

light (Taenarus in the southern Peloponnese was imagined as a gateway to Hades).

51. Presumably, as the sun circles below the earth when it is night above.

52. The reference is to Cerberus.

53. That is, of slaughtering so unworthy a foe.

54. Hades; the next phrase alludes to Persephone.

55. Reading *afflicti* with the manuscripts, rather than *affecti* with Fitch following R. Bentley's emendation.

56. A river in Hades, along with Cocytus, Styx, and Acheron; the Maeander is a winding river in what is now southwestern Turkey.

57. Aeacus, the father of Peleus, Thetis' husband.

58. The standard series of punishments in the underworld include Ixion, condemned for attempting to rape Juno; Sisyphus, a cruel and wily king, tricked Persephone into letting him return to the upper world; Tantalus, forever tantalized, cut up his son and served him to the gods to test their omniscience; Tityos' liver was consumed daily by a vulture for attempting to rape Leto; the Danaids were obliged to carry water in leaky urns. Unusual in the list are the Cadmeids, including Cadmus' daughter Agave, who killed her son in a Bacchic fit and is here punished by a perpetual state of frenzy (the plural Cadmeids presumably refers to Theban women generally, and certainly not to Cadmus' daughter Semele, who was the mother of Bacchus); and Phineus, punished for blinding his children by Harpies who befoul his food whenever he attempts to eat. The last two have connections to Thebes (Phineus was Cadmus' brother) and are also associated with the slaughter of their own offspring.

59. The Lapiths, a tribe in Thessaly, fought the Centaurs in a famous battle; Hercules fought both on separate occasions, which explains the reference to them here.

60. The reference is to the lion skin (with jowls and head); Cleonae is near Nemea, where Hercules slew the lion.

61. Retaining *bonos* with inferior manuscripts (taken with *animos*) instead of *novos* (with Ageno's emendation, followed by Fitch).

62. This may be a new chorus of celebrants, its entrance announced in the manner of Menandrean comedy.

63. When Jupiter declared that the next-born descendant of Perseus would rule Mycenae, Hera accelerated Eurystheus' birth; he then imposed the twelve labors on Hercules.

64. To see the Olympic games, presided over by Jupiter (the games were said to have been founded by Hercules); Ceres' rites are the mysteries celebrated at Eleusis in early autumn.

65. The wife of Ocean, here representing the world-encircling stream.

66. Bacchus.

67. Jupiter's children, but not by Juno.

68. Dirce was tied to a bull's horns and killed by her stepsons, Amphion and Zethus, whom she hated (she attempted to kill their mother, Antiope); a stream in Thebes was named for her. Cadmus had immigrated to Thebes from Tyre, in Phoenicia.

69. The word *opima* suggests wealth but also plumpness, as of an animal, and, further, the *spolia opima* or spoils a Roman general received upon defeating an enemy leader in single combat.

70. The Giants Otus and Ephialtes piled Mount Pelion (home to the Centaur Chiron) upon Mount Ossa in an attempt to storm Olympus; Hercules imagines outdoing them by piling on Olympus itself.

71. A mountain near Thebes; Pallene is the westernmost of the headlands of Chalcidice, northeast of Thebes; Mount Pindus is in western Thessaly.

72. One of the rebellious Giants.

73. The walls of Mycenae were imagined as having been constructed by Cyclopses.

74. Reading *clava* with I. H. Withof (a study of metrical cruces from 1749) rather than *valva* with Fitch; the manuscripts have *aula*.

75. This would seem to be the original chorus, if indeed the preceding chorus was different in composition.

76. A son of Amphion and Niobe, for whom a river in Thebes was named.

77. Caspian cliffs are where Prometheus was suspended, exposed to an eagle that tore daily at his liver; Hercules freed Prometheus. The Symplegades or clashing rocks were located at the mouth of the Bosporus and stopped colliding after the Argo passed safely through them; Hercules was originally one of the Argonauts.

78. Now called the Don, the Tanais runs into Lake Maeotis (now the Sea of Azov); the Tagus (Tajo in Spanish, Tejo in Portuguese) is the longest river in the Iberian peninsula.

79. Mars was acquitted of murder in the Athenian Areopagus, "Hill of Mars," the site of the first court.

Hercules on Oeta

Introduction

1. For a recent and thorough survey of the question (arguing against Senecan authorship), see Lucia Degiovanni, *Hercules Oetaeus: una tragedia attribuita a Seneca: Introduzione, testo e commento dei vv. 1–705* (doctoral dissertation, Scuola Normale Superiore, 2010), 2–73.

2. The question of the connection between Seneca's tragedies and his Stoic commitments has been much discussed, and opinions vary. In addition to the works by Zwierlein and Fitch cited in the Introduction to *Hercules Mad*, see King (1971) and Rosenmeyer (1989), the latter with a particular emphasis on Stoic physics. For a literary analysis of *Hercules on Mount Oeta*, see Walde (1992) and Marcucci (1997).

3. An example: Hercules bestows his bow and arrows on Philoctetes, and says (in my translation), "Boy destined to be happy, you'll never fire these / at your foe in vain" (1652–53); but Philoctetes was abandoned by the Greeks on a barren island where he barely managed to survive for ten years before being rescued and brought to Troy—hardly the story of a man destined to a happy life. The reading of the other manuscript tradition, combined with a rather slight emendation, eliminates "destined to live" and leaves simply "O happy lad, these you'll never / fire at foe in vain" (this version is adopted by both Fitch and Zwierlein). If we stay closer to the manuscripts, are we to see dramatic irony at work (though on his deathbed, Hercules misreads the future)? Or are we to understand that from Hercules' perspective, triumph (Phi-

loctetes' arrows are needed to conquer Troy) after long suffering is the pattern of a blessed life?

Hercules Oetaeus

1. That is, in the east and the west; The Latin has *Phoebus* where I have Sun.

2. The Latin has "Nereus" where I have Sea.

3. Punctuating as a statement, not a question.

4. Juno, by her hostility to Hercules.

5. The Nemean lion, slain by Hercules, begins the recital of his labors (Nemea is nearer Argos than Arcadia, and some editors emend to "Argolian"); Hercules shot down the birds that plagued the region around Stymphalus; killed the fierce boar that haunted Mount Maenalus in Arcadia; stole the golden apples of the Hesperides guarded by a serpent; destroyed the hundred-headed Hydra; captured the man-eating horses of Diomedes, a king who ruled in Thrace (where the river Hebrus is located); captured the belt of the queen of the Amazons, who dwelled near the river Thermodon, in Pontus (on the southeast shore of the Black Sea); brought the guard dog Cerberus up from Hades; defeated Antaeus, who was invincible so long as he was in contact with the earth (Earth was his mother), by lifting him from the ground and crushing him; slew the Egyptian king Busiris at the altar where he sacrificed all strangers; killed the triple-bodied Geryon (hence the detail, "by a single hand") and stole his cattle; and conquered the bull that terrorized Crete, famous for its hundred towns.

6. The reference is to the northern constellation of Ursa Major; the Indus river is to the east, near the Sun's rising; the sun enters the constellation of the Crab in summer, hence the association with heat and (here) with Libya.

7. The Sun god (Helius) was one of the Titans.

8. The reference is to the conical markers at either end of a racecourse.

9. In his crib, Hercules strangled two snakes that Juno sent to destroy him.

10. That is, in addition to the labors imposed by Eurystheus; cf. *Hercules Furens* 477–87.

11. Juno sent a crab to distract Hercules while he was battling the Hydra, but he kicked it and sent it flying skyward, where it became a constellation (in other versions, Juno placed it in the heavens); Astraea, a goddess associated with justice, fled the earth because of human vices and became the constellation Virgo, east of the (Nemean) Lion (i.e., the constellation Leo): the Sun is in the Lion in midsummer, then moves to Virgo.

12. The sun passes from the constellation of Leo into that of Virgo.

13. Alcaeus was Hercules grandfather; Alcides (accent on the second syllable, pronounces like the pronoun "I") = "descendant of Alcides." The Styx is a river in Hades.

14. Retaining the manuscript order (Fitch places 79–80 after 91).

15. That is, eliminating the Strait of Messina (cf. *Hercules Furens* 376); the Corinthian Isthmus connects the Peloponnese to the rest of Greece, dividing the Ionian and Aegean seas; the Ister is the ancient name of the Danube; the Tanais (now the Don) runs into what is now the sea of Azov, to the northeast of the Black Sea.

16. Apollo killed the Python at Delphi, where his oracle was then located (Cyrrha is the port of Delphi); Bacchus journeyed as far as India; Perseus slew the Gorgon.

17. Hercules briefly relieved Atlas and supported the heavens.

18. Father of Iole, whose kingdom of Oechalia Hercules sacked to obtain his daughter.

19. Ceneum is a headland of the island Euboea, separated by a narrow strait from Trachis.

20. Composed of maidens from Oechalia, part of the booty Hercules has brought to Trachis.

21. That is, Charon's ferry, that carries the dead to Hades; the float refers to the practice in Roman triumphs of displaying the conquered in chains during the procession.

22. The text is problematic; on another reading, followed by Fitch and Zwierlein, the sense is "we abide, but our nation's place will granted to crops and forests."

23. Dolopians were a people in Thessaly.

24. Inachus is a river in Argus. Dirce was the great-aunt of Amphion and Zethus, who built the walls of Thebes (a stream in Thebes was named for her); Ismenus is a river in Thebes.

25. Mount Rhodope is a mountain range in northern Greece; in myth, a queen of Thrace and wife of Haemus, both turned into mountains for comparing themselves to Zeus and Hera, and hence a symbol of pride, like Hercules.

26. That is, the Caucasus, to the east of the Caspian Sea.

27. Jupiter lengthened the night during which he slept with Alcmene and Hercules was conceived.

28. A people in western Scythia; the Parthians, famous for their bowmanship, occupied a part of what is now Iran; the Nabataeans were a people in northern Arabia; the Cretans too were known for their skill in archery.

29. Briareus was one of the "hundred-handed" giants who helped Jupiter overthrow the Titans; for "Giant," Averna, following Delrius, reads "Gyas," the name of a Giant.

30. Reading *Gigas* with manuscript A rather than *Gyes*.

31. The reference is to Mount Pelion piled on Mount Ossa, so as to storm Olympus.

32. Probably "all" refers to her fellow Thessalians (reading *cunctos* with Peiper rather than *cuncta*, which results in an irregular short syllable at the end of the metron).

33. A mountain in ancient Lydia (west-central Turkey), thought to be the rock into which Niobe was transformed after her children were slain by Apollo and Diana; the Eridanus, identified with the Po in Italy, was imagined as the site where the sisters of Phaethon, who was killed when he attempted to drive the chariot of the Sun (his father), turned into trees that wept amber tears for him; the Sirens were often thought of as inhabiting the coast of Sicily. Tereus, king of Daulis, raped Philomela, upon which she and her sister Procne, Tereus' wife, killed Tereus' son Itys and fed him to his father; subsequently all three were turned into birds: Tereus into the hoopoe, whose cry was imagined as being in mourning for his son, Philomela into a swallow, and Procne into a nightingale (or, in some versions, the reverse). Edonia is a region, Ismarus a mountain in southern Thrace.

34. The bird of Daulis is a reference to Procne.

35. There is a pun: the Greek word *trachys* means "rough."

36. Four examples of metamorphosed sufferers: Myrrha, passionate for her father, was turned into the myrrh tree (her tears are the resin); Ceyx and Alcyone were turned into halcyons for comparing themselves to Zeus and Hera; Tantalus' daughter is Niobe; for Procne and Philomela, see note 33 above.

37. That is, Procne: she and her sister Philomela were Athenians.

38. One of Iole's brothers.

39. Reading *proavos* instead of *casus*.

40. As is Juno, Jupiter's (the Thunderer's) wife, since Hercules' mother was Alcmene.

41. Reading *reperi* with late manuscripts (following Zwierlein) rather than *peperi*, "I have given birth," with manuscript EA following Fitch.

42. Reading *non* with manuscripts E and A rather than *num* with the late manuscripts accepted by Zwierlein and Fitch.

43. That is, Ursa Major, which never dips below the horizon.

44. A river (in Aetolia) and its god, who fought with Hercules for Deianira's hand; it was known for its winding course.

45. Reading *rogos* with manuscript A rather than *Argea* (following Fitch) and *parens* instead of *lares*.

46. Hesione, whom Hercules rescued (in certain versions), he then bestowed on Telamon as a prize; Dardanus was an ancestor of Priam. Auge, daughter of Aleus, king of Tegea, was (according to one version) a priestess of the virgin goddess Athena. Thespius wanted an heir by Hercules, and had his fifty daughters sleep with him on successive nights (in some versions, pretending to be the same woman; in other versions, all on the same night); fifty sons were born. Timolus in one version was the husband of Omphale, queen of Lydia, whom Hercules was obliged (because of an accidental murder) to serve as a slave (in some versions, he was represented as being in love with her); Omphale forced him to do women's work.

47. The Sabaeans were a people in Arabia, where myrrh, a perfume associated with amorousness, was produced.

48. Following the manuscripts; Fitch rather adventurously emends *labat* to *soror*, but I think the *husteron proteron* can stand.

49. Reading *siluit* instead of *novit*.

50. Reading *tenent* with manuscripts A and E rather than *tenet* (accepted by most editors), which would mean "nothing retains its [natural] laws against my incantations."

51. Pondus is a region on the Black Sea; Pindus is a mountain in Thessaly, an area known for magical drugs.

52. The centaur Nessus, born of Ixion, a member of the royal family of the Lapiths in Thessaly, and a cloud (Nephele is the "Cloud") modeled to appear like Juno (whom Ixion had attempted to rape), offered to carry Deianira across the Evenus river (in Aetolia), and then attempted to assault her; Hercules killed him with an arrow dipped in the Hydra's poison, and he gave some of his infected blood to Deianira under the pretense that it was a love potion.

53. A mountain in southern Thessaly.

54. Jupiter, whose Thunderbolts were imagined as being forged in Aetna's volcano.

55. Reading *horridum* with manuscript E rather than *horridus* (referring to Love) with manuscript A.

56. That is, horns emerged on his brow as he metamorphosed into a bull.

57. That is, Europa ("Assyrian" loosely for Oriental, here more precisely Phoenician).

58. A city in Aetolia, near the Evenus river.

59. Lycormas is another name for the river Evenus.

60. The baskets contained items for the celebration of Bacchus' cult in Thebes, celebrated every three years; the mystery rites in Eleusis were dedicated to Ceres.

61. The reference is to the *salutatio*, the morning call Roman clients paid to their patron.

62. A Fury.

63. Reading *convocat* with manuscript A; manuscript E (adopted by Zwierlein and Fitch) has *concitat*, "stirs up."

64. Hister, the modern Danube.

65. The west wind; the reference is to Iberia, location of the gold-rich Tagus river (today, Tajo in Spanish, Tejo in Portuguese). The Hebrus is a river in Thrace; the Hydaspes, modern Jhelum, is a river in India (it runs into the Indus).

66. The moon; Cynthia is another name for Artemis, who was associated with the moon.

67. Following the manuscripts; Zwierlein and Fitch accept Axelson's emendation *texta*, "fabrics."

68. The Bruttii inhabited a region in the southern tip (or toe) of Italy.

69. To escape Crete, Daedalus prepared wings bound with wax for himself and his son Icarus; flying to high, Icarus' wings melted in the sun, and he fell, giving his name to the Icarian Sea.

70. Leo, followed by Zwierlein and Fitch, posits a lacuna between "sort of fear" and "contrived a trick," so that Deianira's fear is that Nessus may have tricked her.

71. Following manuscript E; manuscript A reads *virus*, "poison."

72. A mountain in Ionia, across from the island of Chios; Point Leucas is a promontory on the island of Leucas, in the Ionian Sea.

73. Something is missing in the transmitted text, variously filled in by editors.

74. Roman household gods.

75. Reading *luctu* with manuscript E; Zwierlein and Fitch both accept the emendation *luctum*, "bemoan the grief."

76. One of the three Fates who spin human destinies.

77. A promontory on the south end of the island of Euboea; the Sea of Phrixus: here, the Aegean. Euripus is the narrow channel between Boeotia and Euboea, its waters proverbially shifting.

78. Reading *gravi* with manuscript A rather than *graves* with manuscript E, which would modify "shoulders."

79. The Getae were a tribe to the north of Thrace, known for their skill at archery, as were the Cretans.

80. Zwierlein, followed by Fitch, indicates a lacuna after this verse.

81. Reading *abrogat* with manuscript E; manuscript A (followed by Zwierlein and Fitch) reads *irrogat*, "inflicts a penalty on himself."

82. Hercules' first wife, killed by him, along with her children, when he was possessed by madness; the episode is enacted in Seneca's *Hercules Mad.*

83. "Hydra-poisoned": literally, "Lernaean," in reference to the Hydra of Lerna which Hercules killed as his second labor.

84. A river in Lybia.

85. That is, Hades.

86. The reference is to Tantalus; the Thessalian king is Ixion, who was punished by being bound to a rotating wheel; the vulture gouged daily the liver of Tityos, punished for attempting to rape Leto, mother of Apollo and Diana.

87. That is, Medea, who murdered her children and her brother; the Phasis is the chief river of Colchis, Medea's home city.

88. That is, Procne, who killed her child; Althaea was the mother of Meleager, responsible for his death.

89. Literally, Belias or descendant of Belus (grandfather of the Danaids); all but one of the Danaids murdered their husbands.

90. Reading *armatae . . . valent* instead of the unmetrical *armata . . . valet.*

91. The stag that ravaged Arcadia; capturing this magical beast was one of Hercules' labors.

92. Literally, "with light"; reading *luce* instead of *in luce.*

93. This verse is found in manuscript A but not in manuscript E (which has slight changes in 997 and 999 as well); Fitch follows manuscript E.

94. Furies, among them Tisiphone and Megaera.

95. Reading *diras* following manuscript E; Gronovius, followed by Zwierlein, emends to *laxas*, "loosened"; Fitch prints *apertas*, "open."

96. Reading *neci* instead of *scelus.*

97. One of the Muses.

98. The Bistones (accent on first syllable) were a Thracian tribe.

99. A region in north Africa.

100. A promontory in Laconia where there was believed to be an entrance to the underworld; the Manes are spirits of the dead, sometimes translated here as "ghosts."

101. Charon, ferryman of the dead; reading *aurito quoquo*, the conjecture of Gronovius; Birt (followed by Zwierlein and Fitch, who however move the line to follow 1078 [Fitch] or 1082 [Zwierlein]), emends *audis tu quoque*, "you too are listening."

102. That is, added thread to the destiny the Fates had spun for her.

103. Averna marks a lacuna after this verse.

104. Members of a nomadic tribe dwelling in the Sahara.

105. A Giant who participated in the battle against the Olympian gods.

106. That is, Saturn, imprisoned in Hades after Jupiter overthrew him.

107. The Giants Otus and Ephialtes piled Mount Pelion upon Mount Ossa in an attempt to storm Olympus.

108. Typhoeus is a monster (also called Typho) buried under Mount Aetna; Inarime (accent on the second syllable) is an island off Sicily (now Ischia); "Tuscan," in the Tyrrhenian Sea.

109. That is, the three-headed dog Cerberus.

110. Reading *lapis* instead of *latus*.

111. The allusion is to the spinning fates; I have put "spindle" where the Latin has "distaff."

112. Reading *furebas* instead of *ferebas*.

113. Reading *mortis* instead of *sortis*.

114. That is, the cattle of Geryon; the twins snakes were sent Hera to strangle the infant Hercules in his crib.

115. Reading *miserande* (following by Zwierlein and Fitch); the manuscripts have *miseranda*, modifying "reason."

116. That is, crab—Hercules is thinking of the crab that assisted the Hydra and was made a constellation.

117. Fitch emends *sanguinis* to *aëris* and adopts Bentley's *specus* for *iecur* in 1212, which makes the lungs (formerly able to inhale air) the subject of

the sentence; this makes good sense, and avoids repeating "liver," but the manuscript reading may just be what Seneca wrote.

118. The hind with golden horns, sacred to Diana, which Hercules captured as one of his labors; Calpe is an ancient name for Gibraltar; it was the northern Pillar of Heracles (the southern was modern Ceuta), erected by him to commemorate his deeds.

119. Reading *miser* with manuscript E; Zwierlein and Fitch follow manuscript A's *mihi*, "for myself."

120. Tethys, the sea; Tethys was the wife of Ocean.

121. Clashing rocks at the mouth of the Bosporus; their motion stopped after the Argo passed safely through them.

122. Reading *rictus meos* with the manuscripts; Axelson, followed by Zwierlein and Fitch, emends to *victus minas*, "conquered, has checked its threats."

123. A mountain range in Thrace; "Getic" refers loosely to Thrace.

124. Literally, "the Parrhasian axis"; "Parrhasia" refers to Arcadia, and thence to Callisto, the Arcadian girl who was transformed into Ursa Major. The idea seems to be that this constellation never sets.

125. Reading *audieris* with manuscript E; Zwierlein and Fitch read *audierit*, "it [i.e., the day] will hear."

126. Roman goddess of war; for "Mars," the Latin has Gradivus, one of his Roman titles.

127. Athena was born from the head of Zeus.

128. Reading *quidem* with manuscript A; manuscript E reads *pater*, "father."

129. Reading *alius* with manuscript A, as does Zwierlein; Peiper, followed by Fitch, emends to *ultor*, "avenger."

130. The sites of two volcanoes, home to Vulcan's forges.

131. That is, the area between the ecliptic and the celestial equator.

132. That is, where Prometheus, whom Hercules rescued, was bound, an eagle pecking constantly at his liver; the Argo, on which Hercules sailed, passed through the Symplegades, after which they ceased to move.

133. Reading *excutiens* with manuscript E; manuscript A, followed by Zwierlein and Fitch, has *excipiens*, "receives."

134. Sinis tied his victims to two bent trees, which when they sprang upright tore them apart.

135. Reading *sopore . . . dolor* with the manuscripts instead of *dolore . . . sopor*.

136. Reading *clara* with manuscripts rather than *cara*, "dear."

137. Reading *caecus dolore es! manibus* with Fitch instead of Averna's *recte dolor es<t>; sed manibus*, which introduces an anapest into the second foot.

138. The speaking oaks at the oracular site Dodona; these bring to mind the whispering laurels at Delphi, alluded to in the following verse.

139. Philoctetes.

140. Here equivalent to the Moon.

141. That is, Ursa Major, again (as in line 1524) signifying the far north.

142. The reference is to the man-eating mares of Diomedes, king of the Bistones in Thrace.

143. Averna, following Peiper, marks a lacuna after 1556.

144. Minos, legendary king of Crete, and his brother Rhadamanthus (in some accounts king before Minos) were, along with Aeacus, judges of the fate of souls in the underworld.

145. Chaonia is a region in Epirus, where Dodona and the speaking oaks were located.

146. Reading *et truncum fugit* with manuscript A; Zwierlein and Fitch, following Bothe, read *et rigidum est parum*, "and is not hard enough" (manuscript E has *frigidus*).

147. Reading *domos* instead of *nemus*.

148. Reading *nullum . . . nemus* with the manuscripts; Jortin, followed by Fitch, emends to *priscus . . . metus*, "primeval dread did not safeguard any grove."

149. Reading *augustum* with manuscript A; manuscript E has *anguste*, emended to *angustum* (Zwierlein, Fitch), giving the sense "a narrow pyre for Hercules," too small for his great frame.

150. Reading *summa* instead of *silva.*

151. Reading *frondis Herculeae nemus* with the manuscripts rather than *frontis Herculeae decus.*

152. Reading *aeger* with manuscript A; Leo, followed by Zwierlein and Fitch, emends to *aegro*, modifying "chest."

153. Greedy: eager to receive the blows.

154. Reading *cui . . . quievit* instead of *quem . . . quaesivit.*

155. Line transposed by Fitch (Averna retains the order of the manuscripts).

156. Reading *fieri* instead of *stare.*

157. Reading *minima* instead of *nimia.*

158. Reading *spolium* with manuscript A following Zwierlein; Fitch reads *solitum* with manuscript E, "usual" (sc. spoils).

159. That is, Amphitryon.

160. Like Semele, who bore Dionysus to Jupiter.

161. Cleonae, a town near Nemea, where Hercules' slew the lion.

162. Reading *rex* with the manuscripts; Zwierlein, followed by Fitch, emends to *sus*, "boar."

163. As a river that surrounds the world, the Ocean is both in the east and the west.

164. Reading *quis deus quicquam* with manuscript A; Axelson, followed by Zwierlein and Fitch, emends to *quod deus quisquam*, "which any god."

165. The reference is to Niobe.

166. A people of Crete, who worshipped Zeus by clanging armor; they were imagined as drowning out the cries of the infant Jupiter when Saturn (Greek Cronus) tried to destroy his children, to prevent them from overthrowing him; the Corybants were priests of Cybele, sometimes identified with the Curetes. Legend had it that a grave of Jupiter existed on Crete, and Seneca has evidently adapted the noise made by the Curetes and Corybants to be a sign of mourning. Ida is a mountain on Crete.

167. Reading *Phoebe* instead of *Phoebus*; the Arcadians were called *proseleni*, "prior to the moon."

168. Reading *furata* following Birt (followed by Zwierlein and Fitch) instead of *velata* with the manuscripts.

169. Cocytus is a river in Hades (pronounced Co-SI-tus), along with Styx and Lethe.

Thyestes

Introduction

1. I cannot do justice here to the full complexity of Schiesaro's argument, which explores, besides the passions, the metatheatrical nature of the play and the aesthetic-sadistic pleasure of the audience at the denouement. Also central to Schiesaro's interpretation, and that of many others, is that we admire Atreus against our will and cannot help identifying with so powerful and energetic a character. On metatheatricality in the Thyestes, see also Littlewood (2004, 181ff.).

Thyestes

The first draft of this translation benefited greatly from the reviews of my fellow members on the Chicago Seneca Board and from a painstaking reading by Susanna Braund. Many thanks to all. Quirks, of course, remain entirely my own. Throughout, I have used the edition of Richard Tarrant (1985). A full list of his manuscript readings and emendations may be found on pages 251–53 of his volume.

1. Tantalus was a Greek king and son of Zeus/Jupiter. In the most common version of the myth, Zeus sentenced him to a life of starvation in Tartarus for inviting the gods to a feast and trying to feed them his son Pelops. In the underworld, he stands in a pool of water that recedes when he tries to drink, and under a fruit tree whose fruit spring out of reach whenever he grasps for them.

2. Sisyphus, another occupant of Tartarus, had to roll a boulder up a hill only to see it roll back down, over and over for all eternity.

3. Ixion, king of the Lapiths, violated the custom of *xenia*, guest-friendship, and even tried to rape Hera but was foiled by a Hera-shaped cloud. As his punishment in Tartarus, he was bound to a fiery wheel that was always spinning.

4. One of the Giants, he tried to rape Leto and was killed by Apollo and Artemis. In the underworld he was stretched out over nine acres, and two vultures ate from his constantly regenerating liver.

5. Reading *visceribus* with Tarrant (1985), a sixteenth-century emendation for *vulneribus*. Cf. *Hercules on Otea* 947.

6. That is, Cerberus the three-headed dog who guarded the entrance to Hades.

7. Minos, once king of Crete, was appointed one of the three judges of the underworld after his death. The sense is that he will be too busy judging the members of the family for their crimes.

8. The Furies, or in Greek *Erinyes*, were goddesses of the underworld who presided over retributive justice. There were at least three, most often identified as Alecto, Megaera, and Tisiphone.

9. On the use of terminology such as "sin," "evil," and "soul," see the discussion in the introduction to this play.

10. The Latin admits of two meanings here: the son can fear the father, or the father the son. Both fit the house of Tantalus. See Tarrant 1985, ad loc.

11. A reference to Clytemnestra, part of the long and sorry story of the Atreids.

12. *Facinus* is Bentley's conjecture (adopted by Tarrant) for the manuscript reading *fratris*.

13. Procne killed her son Itys and fed him to her husband, who had raped her sister Philomena and cut out her tongue. Thyestes has three sons, a larger number than Tereus' one.

14. Tarrant (1985, ad loc.) believes line 58 to be spurious.

15. One of the five rivers of the underworld; it flows with fire.

16. Zeus actually was Tantalus' father. Here Seneca seems to refer to another offence of his against the gods, telling their secrets.

17. The narrow Isthmus of Corinth.

18. In other words, the waters on either side of the Isthmus of Corinth have receded, with the result that the Isthmus itself is wider.

19. Lerna was a marshy region near the Argolic Gulf known for being the Hydra's lair. Phoroneus was a primordial king of the Peloponnese; Alpheus was a river and river-god; and Cithaeron a mountain range in central Greece.

20. Seneca's drama uses iambic trimester for dialogue and different meters for the lyric passages (that is, the four choral passages and Thyestes' monody at 920ff.) In this translation, all the passages of dialogue are in iambs, and all the lyrics except for the first chorus in loose anapestic form, usually with three to four stresses per line. The first chorus, with its slightly longer line lengths, has also been translated into iambs.

21. Taygetus was a mountain with five peaks near Sparta. "Winter winds" translates *Sarmeticus Boreas*, the north wind that was thought to come from Sarmatia, a region reaching from the Caspian Sea in the east to the Vistula River in the west. The "boat-propelling breezes" are the dry Etesian (annual) winds that blow over the Aegean in the summer.

22. Myrtilus was the charioteer of King Oenomaus of Pisa. When his king tried to win the hand of Hippodameia through victory in a chariot-race, Myrtilus took a bribe from Oenomaus' rival Pelops, and sabotaged the chariot by substituting waxen axle pins for the original ones (cf. 661). Oenomaus died in the resulting accident; later Pelops himself would throw Myrtilus into the sea, for which Myrtilus cursed him and his line.

23. Pelops as a child.

24. Before he was exiled, Thyestes seduced Atreus' wife Aerope. As a result, Atreus worries that his children might not be his, a recurrent theme in his remarks in this play.

25. The Latin has "the Odrysian house," a reference to Thrace and to the crime of Procne.

26. For the double meaning of this line, see Tarrant 1985, ad loc.

27. The Syrtes, famous for causing shipwrecks.

28. In his Loeb edition and translation, Fitch gives 309 to the *satelles*, but I would argue that Tarrant's arrangement makes more sense.

29. The founding king of Argos.

30. The longest river in the Iberian peninsula, believed to carry gold and precious stones.

31. The kings of this region allowed the Sarmatians (Slavs) to travel south through the mountain passes in the Caucasus.

32. When the river is frozen.

33. That is, the Chinese.

34. This line is missing in the A manuscripts. Lines 388–89 were bracketed by Leo, as they are by Tarrant.

35. I have unwittingly reproduced F.J. Miller's Loeb translation word for word in line 406.

36. Following Tarrant (1985, ad loc.), who suggests the presence of volition here.

37. A very Stoic sentiment. Roman Stoicism—especially as voiced by Seneca—emphasized a man's freedom to die if his life should ever become unbearable. To kill oneself represented the ultimate in control over the self (even if it was to escape, say, an imperial death-sentence), and so represented a sort of "kingship" over oneself.

38. The Getans were a Thracian tribe living around the lower Danube.

39. More precisely, "when Corus pounds the Bruttian sea." Corus was the northwest wind; the Brutti were an ancient Oscan-speaking people who inhabited what is modern Calabria.

40. Odysseus' father; he ruled over the island of Ithaca.

41. The translation reproduces that of Miller. The Cyclades are an island group in the southern Aegean; originally nymphs, they were turned into rocky outposts by an angry Poseidon.

42. Clotho, the youngest of the three fates, who spins the thread of each man's life span on her distaff.

43. An Asiatic people sometimes conflated with the Scythians.

44. A soft cap that bent forward, worn by the Phrygians of Asia Minor; Pelops, before he emigrated to the Peloponnese, was himself Phrygian.

45. An act of divination carried out by interpreting the entrails of sacrificed sheep and chicken.

46. Typhoeus (or Typhon) was the son of Gaia and Tartarus; he had a serpentine body and a hundred heads. One of the giants, he attacked Zeus (or Jupiter) and was confined by him under Mt. Etna.

47. The Giants, so called because they battled the Olympian gods at Phlegra, in the Chalcidice.

48. The dawn-goddess, poetically called "rosy-fingered" by Homer.

49. That is, the rays of the Sun.

50. The following are all constellations, mostly in the Zodiac. The Ram is Aries; he is here equated with the golden-fleeced ram that rescued Phrixus and Helle from their stepmother, and whose fleece was later sought by Jason.

51. The Bull is Taurus, in whose head is set the star cluster of the Hyades, originally daughters of Atlas.

52. Gemini and Cancer.

53. The constellation Leo was identified with the Nemean lion killed by Hercules.

54. The Virgin is another name for Astraea, a goddess who personified justice. When humans deteriorated after the Golden Age, she left the earth to become the constellation Virgo.

55. Chiron is here the name given to the constellation Sagittarius. Chiron was the centaur who tutored Achilles; his bow is called Haemonian, a poetic reference to Thessaly.

56. The "Goat" is Aegoceros, properly "Goat's horn," a reference to Capricorn; there seems to have been some confusion about the identity of Aquarius.

57. "Stars" translates the Latin *monstra*, so called in Latin because of the bestial size and shape of the Bear and the Snake (see Tarrant, ad loc.).

58. The Snake and the Serpent are one and the same, the constellation Draco.

59. A nymph placed in the heavens by Zeus as Ursa Minor.

60. Another constellation, the Serpent.

61. Arctophylax, the Bear-Keeper, a constellation usually called Boötes.

62. Tarrant 1985, ad loc., notes: "Atreus' last play on words is especially brilliant. The ostensible meaning is 'a cup that belongs to our family' . . . but also present is the sense 'a drink consisting of your *gens*, with wine poured on it.'"

63. Literally, "Heniochan thief." Apparently a people in the area of modern-day Iran.

64. Procrustes was an Attic ("Cecropian") bandit who offered lodging to travelers but then either truncated them or stretched them out to fit the exact size of the iron bed he offered.

65. It's hard to render the dyspeptic pun here. Tarrant (1985) notes at 403 that the Stoic idea of death weighing heavily on the nonphilosopher is picked up here in a rather gruesome way.

66. Pelion, Ossa, and Olympus were piled up in one heap by the Giants, who threatened to ascend to the home of the Olympian gods in this way.

67. He means that because his sons helped him trap Thyestes, he need no longer worry that they were actually fathered by Thyestes in his adulterous relationship with Atreus' wife. (The logic of course is dubious.)

Agamemnon

Introduction

1. The play is probably among Seneca's earliest; see Fitch (1981).

Agamemnon

For my translation I have used the following editions: J. G. Fitch, ed. and trans, *Seneca: Tragedies*. 2 vols. (Cambridge, MA, 2002–4); R. J. Tarrant, *Seneca's* Agamemnon (Cambridge, 1976); and O. Zwierlein, *L. Annaei Senecae Tragoediae* (Oxford, 1986).

1. Dis was the ruler of the underworld.

2. Pelops, the son of Tantalus, was father of Atreus and Thyestes. The house of Pelops was cursed.

3. The Pelasgians is another name for the Argives.

4. At the feast of Thyestes his brother Atreus served up Thyestes' sons and Thyestes ate them unwittingly.

5. There is a problem with the text: the transmitted verb *incolere* does not properly govern "the guardian"; one must either read *uidere* or else posit a lacuna after line 14. See Tarrant's edition.

6. Cerberus, the three-headed dog that guarded the entrance to the underworld.

7. Ixion, punished for trying to rape Juno by being tied to a whirling wheel. Thyestes catalogues four famous punishments of criminals in the underworld.

8. Sisyphus was punished by having to roll uphill a huge rock which constantly rolled to the bottom again.

9. Tityus was punished by vultures continually tearing at his liver which constantly regrew.

10. Tantalus was punished for offering his son to the gods to eat by suffering eternal hunger and thirst while fruit and water was offered in front of his mouth.

11. Thyestes compares himself with Tantalus, who served up one son (Pelops) to the gods to eat; by contrast, Thyestes consumed three of his own sons.

12. Literally, "whom the Cnossian judge turns out of his urn as defendants"; Minos, king of Crete, became a judge in the underworld after his death. Cnossos was the major city on Crete.

13. Thyestes was commanded by the Delphic oracle to impregnate his daughter Pelopia in order to produce an avenger (Aegisthus).

14. Adopting Koetschau's emendation of *sed cepi* to *suscepi*. See Tarrant for discussion.

15. Adopting Zwierlein's emendation of *uterum grauem* to *utero graui*.

16. At the feast of Thyestes, the sun turned back in its course to avoid the sight of the father eating his sons, hence day became night.

17. The Syrtes are dangerous shallow waters off the north African coast.

18. Euxine is a euphemistic name ("Hospitable") for the Black Sea, which is stormy.

19. The constellation of the Bear-keeper, Arctophylax in Greek, which Seneca imagines as never dropping below the horizon so far north.

20. The Roman goddess of war.

21. The Latin word *viduus*, which gives us the English word "widow," generally denotes widows, hence Clytemnestra's usage to denote her husband's empty throne is unusual.

22. Medea, who ran away from her father's kingdom of Phasis with the Thessalian hero Jason.

23. Aegisthus. I have translated the Latin word *socius* as "partner" to indicate that this is unusual language to use of a lover.

24. Helen.

25. Clytemnestra's daughter Iphigeneia was taken to Aulis on the pretext of marriage with Achilles but was there sacrificed by her father Agamemnon so that the Greek fleet could sail for Troy.

26. The house of Pelops had a history of killing children.

27. Literally "Phoebus' old man," the priest Chryses, whose daughter Chryseis was taken as his war prize by Agamemnon. "Zminthean" is an epithet of Phoebus Apollo.

28. Later he conceives a similar passion for Cassandra, another sacred virgin.

29. Briseis, the woman from Mysia assigned as war prize to Achilles.

30. The word *melior* could be taken with Ajax meaning "the better Ajax" or, better, as governing the ablative phrase, as translated here, meaning that he was a better man once he had decided to die. The reference is to Ajax son of Telamon, who, in a frenzy after the arms of Achilles were awarded to Ulysses, killed cattle thinking they were Agamemnon and the other leaders; once clarity returned he decided to commit suicide.

31. Reading *ultrix*, as transmitted by manuscript A; manuscript E has *uictrix*, "victorious." Both have good justifications.

32. That is, Trojan, named from Dardanus, a son of Jupiter and ancestor of Priam.

33. Aegisthus was born from the incestuous rape of Pelopia by her father Thyestes.

34. Literally, "for a private bed," meaning the bed of an ordinary citizen.

35. The missing text probably would have said: "But my husband's brother, himself a monarch, [forgave Helen]." See Tarrant.

36. Atrides is the patronymic, meaning "son of Atreus," here Menelaus; reading *hunc*, following Damsté, for *sed* of the manuscripts.

37. The main river of Laconia in the Peloponnese.

38. Literally, "If that's too little, add 'grandson' too."

39. Clearly this is the moment when Clytemnestra agrees to side with Aegisthus against her husband. However, it is hard to make any sense of the text as transmitted and the appearance of *siquidem* here is unparalleled in Seneca's tragedies. My translation assumes that *cruentum*, not *cruenta*, is the correct reading—that is, "bloody deed" not "bloody daughter of Tyndareus." Another emendation worth consideration reads *equidem haud*, "For my part, even though I am a bloody daughter of Tyndareus, I wouldn't allow it to happen."

40. The manuscripts have "Theban" (*Thebais*) here, which makes poor sense; I accept Richter's emendation *Thespias*, "inhabitant of Thespiae," a town in Boeotia.

41. The female visitors are identified by their local rivers: Erasinus denotes those from the southern Argolid, Eurotas those from Sparta, and Ismenos those from Thebes.

42. A song celebrating the defeat of the Titans when they attempted to dethrone Jupiter by piling up mountains; the order of the mountains varies from source to source. Seneca has Olympus on Ossa on Pelion, as at Virgil, *Georgics* 1.281–82.

43. Seneca appears to retroject the Roman custom of giving the conqueror's laurels to Jupiter Optimus Maximus.

44. Trivia and Lucina are two manifestations of Diana.

45. Niobe, descendant of Tantalus, who vaunted her fertility (she had seven sons and seven daughters) over Latona's and was punished by Latona's daughter, Diana.

46. Literally "as great-great-grandfather look with kindness on your progeny." The line of descent is Jupiter-Tantalus-Pelops-Atreus-Agamemnon.

47. The manuscript reading translates "please reveal if my husband's brother lives," but since Clytemnestra knows that Menelaus is alive, this must be wrong; given her question in the next line, she must be asking where Menelaus is.

48. Atrides is the patronymic, meaning "son of Atreus," here Agamemnon.

49. Manuscript E has *meas*, "my" ships; although Seneca masculinizes Clytemnestra, for her to claim the fleet belonged to her would be excessive here.

50. Sigeum was a promontory in the Troad.

51. Priam, king of Troy, was killed at the altar of Zeus Herkeios.

52. Dolphins, here called Tyrrhenian as a nod to Ovid's story of the metamorphosis of the Tyrrhenian sailors at *Metamorphoses* 3.670–86.

53. Spots seen on the setting sun were regarded as a sign of a storm.

54. Zephyr is the west wind, Eurus the east wind, Notus the south wind, Boreas the north wind, and Aquilo the northeastern wind. Auster is a southern wind associated with North Africa; the Syrtes were sandbars off the coast of Libya.

55. The Nabataeans were an Arab people.

56. The transmitted text has *est malae* at the end of the line, which makes very poor sense; I have translated *et malae*, assuming a comma before the phrase.

57. Reading *alio* for *alto*: see Tarrant for discussion.

58. Pyrrhus was the son of Achilles. In each case, the survivor envies someone who died at Troy. "Atrides" below refers to Menelaus.

59. The transmitted text does not make sense: one minute the Greeks say they are dying because of the Trojans traveling with them, the next they appeal to the gods to stand off because there are Trojans on the boat. In addition the plural *sistite* is strange. I propose that line 525 ("for whom we are dying . . . Calm this hostile sea") is an intrusive gloss.

60. Reading *haut* in 529 not *aut*.

61. The shield is Athena's famous aegis, which incorporated the head of the Gorgon Medusa.

62. Seneca's narrative is so elliptical here that I posit a lacuna of a few lines, in which Athena's hostility toward Ajax would have been narrated.

63. Ajax, son of Oileus, called "the lesser" to distinguish him from Ajax, son of Telamon.

64. I have removed these lines, which seem to be full of textual problems and where the mention of Pallas in the middle of this list, makes no sense: "It's a joy that I have overcome the savage sea and fires | and conquered heaven, Pallas, lightning , ocean." See Tarrant for the textual problems.

65. Caphereus was a rocky promontory at the southeast end of the island of Euboea.

66. The Ionian Sea is to the west of Greece; the sea of Phrixus refers to the Hellespont.

67. The women of Lemnos were punished for an offense against Venus by being made to smell, which sent their husbands into the arms of slaves; the women then murdered their husbands. For geographical reasons, I have substituted Chalcis for Calchedon.

68. Nauplius, who took revenge for the death of his son Palamedes at Troy by lighting beacons along the treacherous coast of Euboea to lure the Greek fleet onto the rocks.

69. Cassandra, daughter of Priam. Apollo gave her the gift of prophecy but the curse of never being believed. Her prophetic trances are typically described as frenzies.

70. Hercules sacked Troy after Laomedon's treachery.

71. Patroclus, beloved by Achilles, who donned Achilles' armor to drive back the Trojan attack, but was killed by Hector.

72. Astyanax is the son of Hector and Andromache. Seneca treats the deaths of Polyxena and Astyanax in *Trojan Women*. The "virgin" is Polyxena, the daughter of Priam and Hecuba, who was later sacrificed on Achilles' tomb, who was from Thessaly.

73. The nightingale was formerly Philomela and the swallow ("the Bistonian bird") was her sister Procne. Procne was wife of the Thracian (Bistonian is equivalent to Thracian) king Tereus who raped Philomela. As revenge the sisters killed the son of Tereus and Procne, who was called Itys, hence the song called "Itys." Tereus' crime is here referred to his "secret depravity"; the Latin is literally "wicked thefts."

74. Turned into a swan when mourning the death of Phaethon.

75. The Danube and the Don rivers.

76. Cybele, the Great Mother (Magna Mater), whose ecstatic cult originated in Phrygia (Asia Minor), typically depicted wearing a crown with turrets. Attis was her lover who died. The male devotees of Cybele (the Galli) castrated themselves and slashed their arms in their religious frenzy.

77. I translate Bentley's emendation *immoti* instead of the manuscript reading *immites* ("harsh" or "unblinking").

78. The shepherd is Paris, whose choice of Venus over Juno and Minerva, at the judgment of Paris on Mount Ida near Troy, sealed the destruction of Troy (hence "deadly").

79. The phrase "covert breed" links Paris and Aegisthus, both of them adulterers, as well as designating Aegisthus as the product of an incestuous union. Both Paris and Aegisthus were raised in the countryside, hence "rustic."

80. Cassandra foresees the murder of Agamemnon (the lion) by the lioness (Clytemnestra) assisted by the "base-born" Aegisthus. Seneca adapts the imagery used by Aeschylus at *Agamemnon* 1258ff.

81. Achilles fastened Hector's body to his chariot and dragged it around Troy to disfigure it. Seneca adapts Virgil, *Aeneid* 2.270–9 here.

82. Troilus and Deiphobus are also brothers of Helen. Deiphobus married Helen after the death of Paris but was betrayed by her and disfigured after his death. See Virgil, *Aeneid* 6.494–97.

83. The filthy sisters are the Furies.

84. Tantalus, the great-grandfather of Agamemnon, here forgetting the eternal torment of his thirst to grieve for Agamemnon's imminent death.

85. Dardanus was the ancestor of the Trojan race.

86. Adopting manuscript A's *incisa* over manuscript E's *incertum*, a reminiscence of Virgil, *Aeneid* 2.224.

87. Or perhaps "the fact that he is not afraid."

88. Seneca imagines the ritual presentation of spoils in Roman terms: weapons captured in war were presented to Jupiter Feretrius.

89. Juno, who was angry at Jupiter's affairs that produced children including Hercules, who will be the subject of this choral ode. This ode must

come from the Argive chorus, as the chorus of Trojan captives would not choose to glorify Hercules or Argos.

90. Jupiter doubled the length of the night of Hercules' conception while he had sex with Alcmena.

91. The "star" that we know as Venus was called both the evening star (Hesperus) and the morning star (Lucifer). Here, Venus arrives in the morning expecting to be called Lucifer but is instead hailed as Hesperus.

92. The first of Hercules' twelve labors.

93. Hercules was sent to capture the Arcadian hind (here called "Parrhasian," a more obscure word), a special deer sacred to Diana. Traditionally the third labor.

94. The Erymanthian boar, which terrorized the countryside round Mount Erymanthos. Traditionally the fourth labor.

95. The Cretan bull, which Hercules captured alive. Traditionally the seventh labor.

96. The hydra of Lerna, a snake with nine heads, which produced two new heads every time one was cut off. Traditionally Hercules' second labor.

97. His capture of the cattle of Geryon, a three-headed ogre, from the far west. Traditionally the tenth labor.

98. The Thracian Diomedes, who fed his mares upon human blood. Traditionally the eighth labor. Hercules fed Diomedes to his horses and they then became tame.

99. Hippolyte was the queen of the Amazons and wore a belt given her by Mars, which Hercules seized as his ninth labor.

100. Man-eating birds from Stymphalus in Arcadia which Hercules shot and drove away. Traditionally the fifth labor.

101. The golden apples of the Hesperides were kept in a garden in the far west and guarded by a never-sleeping dragon. Traditionally the eleventh labor.

102. The Trojan War was brought to an end by Philoctetes using Hercules' bow and arrows.

103. I translate Bentley's emendation *popa* ("attendant" or "priest") for the manuscripts' *prius*, redundant with *antequam* (899).

104. I translate Tarrant's emendation *e medio* instead of the manuscript reading *emerito*. The Sun turned backward on his path to try to avert his eyes from the sight of Thyestes feasting on his own children.

105. Seneca imagines Strophius as an Olympic victor. Phocis was an area in central Greece. Elis was the state in the Peloponnese in which the Olympic games were held. Seneca's depiction of the palm of victory is an anachronism.

106. Omitted: "Good fortune calls for loyalty but adversity demands it."

107. Pisa was the area in the state of Elis where the Olympic games were held.

108. Literally, "let me be joined with your chaplets," the chaplets (*vittae*) being the emblems of a suppliant.

109. Adopting manuscript A's *obsita* rather than manuscript E's *obruta* ("overwhelmed").

110. The "craziness" that's coming to Clytemnestra and Aegisthus will take the form of Orestes avenging his father's murder.